HARVESTING
SHADOWS

HARVESTING SHADOWS

Untold Tales from the Fur Trade

H. D. Smiley

Sunflower University Press®

1531 Yuma (Box 1009), Manhattan, Kansas 66502-4228 USA

Cover painting, "Setting Traps for Beaver," by Alfred Jacob Miller, courtesy of the Joslyn Art Museum, Omaha, NE.

ISBN 0-89745-126-0

Edited by Sonie Liebler

Indexed by Terry G. Colbert

Layout by Lori L. Daniel

For
Evelyn

"Wonders of the New World" — One of the earliest depictions of the European conception of the North American continent.

Contents

List of Illustrations

Introduction

Dr. H. D. Smiley has chosen an effective method of enlightening both the history buff and the professional historian about the many aspects of the fur trade that have long been in need of clarification. As he states in his *A Word to the Reader* the book consists of a series of essays or chapters with no closely linked theme except that all pertain to the fur trade in some respect.

The author has a long-standing interest in and knowledge of fur-trade history. This knowledge has been gained through extensive reading combined with personal knowledge of much of the area about which he writes. Dr. Smiley's enlightened interest in the subject is combined with a clear writing style and the result is a series of very readable, informative articles.

The 13 essays provide a broad coverage of complex aspects of the fur trade. The author examines some perplexing questions and gives his informed opinion as to probable or possible answers. In all the essays Smiley has established a fine balance of objectiveness that goes a long way in making it clear that it was not the American sodbuster or the Selkirk colonist who pioneered the western United States and Canada but rather the fur trader *cum* explorer.

The opening chapter expounds the view that the fur trade was really a worldwide business comparable to today's multinational corporations. It is evident that the fur trade developed ramifications much beyond the usual concept of lone trappers bringing in pelts or some illiterate trader conning the Indian out of his winter's catch in return for a few tawdry trinkets.

The first chapter, *Global Aspects of the Fur Trade*, along with *Principles of Indian Trade, The Ripple Effect of the Horse and Gun, The Sleep by the Frozen Sea, In Defense of the Indian,* and *Topography's Influence on Colonial Mores,* contribute significantly to a better understanding of the whole topic. The chapter *Tobacco in Indian Trade* is particularly well researched as Dr. Smiley's ranch is in the heart of one of the Indian tobacco-raising areas, and the subject has been of long-standing interest to him. *The Jeremy Pinch Enigma* is a fascinating exploration of an historical puzzle. The remaining chapters, *The Rendezvous, A Reappraisal of the Blackfeet Hostility to the American Trader, On the Dalliance of David Thompson, Spy and Counterspy?*, and *Blue-Eyed Indians*, all deal with specific subject matter that should be better known and is here brought clearly into public view.

Chapter notes and the appendix provide additional information for readers who want to pursue certain topics in greater depth. Dr. Smiley's book demonstrates effectively how secondary sources can be used.

Hugh McMillan
Liaison Officer
Archives of Ontario

(Ed. note: Mr. McMillan is in charge of searching out manuscripts, diaries, journals, and memorabilia, many relating to the fur trade, for the Public Archives of Ontario Province. He is well versed in the fur trade, not only from his work but also from his family's background. He is a collateral descendant of James McMillan, who founded Fort Langley at present-day Vancouver, British Columbia.)

A Word to the Reader

This book was not written for the professional historian. I have turned up no dusty journals long buried in some archive, nor have I rooted in dusty attics for diaries and sought their verification in governmental files and old records. Rather, I have relied upon the immense number of secondary studies dealing with the era.

Many eminent scholars have delved and probed into this period of our history, but, in the main, their seed has fallen on stony ground. The period has been so condensed, ignored, or treated in such an inconsequental manner that we do not realize the impact it had in the development of our continent. The politics of the eastern "establishment," economic phases, the cattle drives, the homesteader, the railroads have received acclaim as the determinate forces in our development. Yet the forerunner of all these, the fur trader and his relations with the Indians, laid the groundwork and set the pattern for the latecoming shopkeeper, banker, farmer, and cattle baron.

In too many cases the latecomer, whether in the Ohio Valley or on the Great Plains, chose to dismiss the lessons learned and the practices followed by the fur traders. They bulled their way into the new country and tried to impose the ways of the "old country," the common law, or the agricultural or business concepts of their previous habitat. The fur trader was dismissed as an uncouth hillbilly. Eventually, the newcomers had to adjust to the country and hark back to his experiences.

All this background has been so overlooked in our preoccupation with the drive and ingenuity of the "early settlers" that we are just beginning to realize that some of the age-old Indian ways were the best — ecology, conservation, environment — the balance imposed by the Laws of Nature.

This collection of essays has no common thread running through it intimately linking one chapter to the next. The purpose of this book is to cover intriguing episodes that, although generally unknown, had a bearing on the formation of our present society. These episodes illustrate the many problems imposed by the "New World" upon the European intruders and how those people had to accommodate to them by abandoning the concepts they brought over here.

I am indebted to Thane White, Mrs. Tex Kauer, and Mrs. Coralee Paull for helping me over some rough spots. My special thanks go to David Swanberg for his help with my grammar and syntax.

H. D. Smiley
Eureka, Montana

Chapter 1

Global Aspects of the Fur Trade

The fur trade was not a small-time, hand-to-mouth individual effort engaged in by a few ne'er-do-wells hanging around the edges of white settlements. Nor was it a sideline activity of frontier storekeepers who plied the Indians with whiskey and then cheated them with tawdry goods. Such were latter-day developments.

The true fur trade was Big Business. In its day it was comparable to today's IBM Corporation or General Motors. Its tentacles encompassed the northern world from Siberia westward through Europe and North America to Alaska, engaging the attention of princes and paupers, merchants and laborers, bankers, and housewives. Its effects were diffused through all strata of society. In later years it was outmoded and receded in importance, existing today on a much reduced scale.

In today's context the fur trade is considered synonymous with "the Indian trade," and this is the aspect that receives the most attention. The political shenanigans employed by shameless, crooked politicians in dealing with reservation Indians who were captive customers; the derogatory and contemptuous referral to "the Indian Trade" as if it were something engaged in by dissolute and amoral characters; the foisting of cheap and shoddy goods on Indians — all form part of the common viewpoint that is in the public mind today.

The true fur trade was bigger than this worm's eye view. A bird's eye view puts it in proper perspective and relegates the above concept to its proper place as a remnant of the once worldwide, truly major business. It is the Big Business phase with which we are concerned. It was not exotic; it was a basic industry. The fur trade existed because it filled a need of the world, and people of all levels benefited from it.

Fur has filled a need from prehistoric times. When modern man arrived in

FUR TRIBUTE (IASAK) PAID AT A SIBERIAN OSTROG

Early Russian woodcut demonstrating Siberian fur trade. (Courtesy of University of California Press)

this world, hairless except for his head and face, he coveted something to shield his body from the elements. Not only could he eat the flesh of his prey, he could use its pelt for clothing and bedding.

The demand for fur was constant as man's culture developed slowly. Early housing was crude and elemental; four walls and a roof that leaked, holes in the walls for windows, doors to bar entry, not to keep out the weather, floors of bare dirt, heat supplied by an open fire. Manufacturing was done at home — handcrafts. Knit and woven wool was the mainstay; cotton being a scarce commodity. To obtain woolen cloth sheep had to be raised and sheared, the fleece carded, then spun into thread before cloth could be woven. It is no wonder that people wanted pelts; they were ready-made.

Under these conditions fur filled a need and was much in demand as Europe progressed from the Middle Ages to the Renaissance. As this development occurred labor was delegated to the common man, the ruling classes eschewing such ties. To formalize this distinction the ruling classes issued various rules and edicts regulating who could wear what in the way of fur; ermine was reserved for royalty, sable authorized for bishops, with the common man limited to sheepskin and rabbit fur.

As the Renaissance progressed the economy changed. Individual, self-supporting families began to collect in hamlets for various purposes; one hamlet tanned sheepskins, another ground wheat into flour. The hamlets grew into villages as men saw an opportunity to deal in fleeces to be sold to weavers. Then someone bought a loom and began using this supply of wool. Then tailors moved in. Hamlets grew into villages which became towns, then towns into cities. Thus, the merchant class emerged.

The merchants, setting at the hub of commerce, extracted a profit from their dealings as they were no longer producers or consumers. As the wheel of commerce gathered momentum, the profits increased and more men were attracted to the system. The wealth of this class soon rivaled or surpassed the wealth of the ruling class. As this new economy grew, means had to be found to employ the new wealth. Thus, the Industrial Age was born. It meant more jobs and put more money into more peoples' pockets. Uncomfortable under the restricted use of fur, they began agitating for relaxation of the edicts. The edicts finally broke down and the common man, with money in his pocket, became a buyer of fur for his comfort in his crude house and on his person.

This yearning of people for status is the basis of the story of Cinderella and the glass slipper. Originally the story concerned a *vair* (an expensive fur) slipper, but through a printer's error or changing values it became a *verre* (glass) slipper.

This new, widespread demand for fur soon exhausted the indigenous European furbearers, especially after Columbus's voyages initiated a tremendous flood of Inca gold into the European economy. The vast hinterlands of Russia were the only known remaining source of fur. Russian entrepreneurs, responding to this focus of interest, began a systematic, short-sighted depletion of their furbearing animals. They organized fur-gathering expeditions which would move into a river system close to Moscow and browbeat the natives into becoming fur trappers. This ploy didn't satisfy the greed of the entrepreneurs, as it didn't supply enough fur to soak up all the pelt money that was flowing into Moscow and Novgorod. So, they revised their operations.

Their employees were converted into a private standing army which would move into a river system and enslave the natives, who were ordered to garner fur. This mode of operation entailed supporting those natives with food and clothing, which was a drain on profits.

They revised their operation again. If any subjugated natives demurred, the

Russians executed them until there were only enough left to efficiently exhaust that river system of fur. As soon as one river was raped, these avaricious Russians would move to the next eastward river and repeat the process. This hop-scotch, martial method was very expensive as the standing army had to be paid and supplied, and the natives had to be supervised and supported with necessities. The Russian market absorbed these expenses for a time because the demand was strong enough to withstand a continually increasing price. However, the system finally passed the point-of-no-return; the source finally became so far away that the costs made the fur prohibitive.[1]

This transport problem became acute when the Russians established settlements on the Aleutian Islands and the Alaskan Coast. Those outposts had to become more or less self-reliant, and there was no way for the fur to be taken back to Moscow profitably. They had to settle for trading at Kyakhta, which was the only point on the Chinese-Russian border that the Chinese emperor would open for trade.

The American and British ships engaged in the "China Trade" soon learned about the fur traffic with China. They would load their ships with Indian trade goods, go to the North Pacific waters, trade with the Indians for fur, take it to Canton (another port the Chinese emperor opened for trade), sell the fur and buy tea, spices, porcelain, chinaware, and nankeen, returning to their home ports to report a double profit from the voyage.

While this trade with China was developing, the fur shortage in Europe became serious. Into this impasse stepped the fishermen of France, Britain, and Portugal. These men had been routinely fishing the Grand Banks off Newfoundland from about the time of the Norse settlements in Greenland. They, thoughtlessly and haphazardly, took a little fur back to their home ports from time to time, but fur was incidental to them; their minds were occupied with fish. They acquired the fur in their occasional meetings with the inhabitants of the shores of this codfish bonanza when the sailors put in to shore for fresh water, or wood, or to cure their catch.

Then Columbus initiated the mad scramble by European powers for a sea route to the wonders of Cathay. Denied by Spain the use of the southern waters, England and France deduced that the Strait of Anian lay northward of Spain's domain and eagerly embarked on a search for it, using the fishermen's route to the Grand Banks. In their probing of our northeastern shores they came into contact with the same natives as had the fishermen. A little fur trading ensued, and then the English and French (mainly the French) suddenly awoke to the trade possibilities.

This new enterprise was truly a bonanza. The European market was crying for more and cheaper fur than the Russians were providing.

To tap this virgin supply the Europeans needed only to bring the incredibly marvelous products of the Industrial Age to the Indian, who gladly harvested the fur and brought it to the sailors. The initial cost of the goods was minimal as the majority of the items were of the trinket class and sea transport was cheap. The trader "had it made." His stock of goods consisted of beads, awls, cheap muskets, gunpowder, lead, gun flints, knives, fishhooks, hatchets, cording for fishlines and seines, coarse woolen yardage, copper kettles, "brazil" tobacco (meaning a special curing process), woolen sheeting, and vermilion, to name a fair sample. Alcohol was added later. All these cheap items nevertheless provided jobs in Europe and they were priceless to the Indian who had no other source of supply. The Indian had no standards of exchange as the goods were unique to him while the furs that the crazy white men so avidly desired were free — the woods were full of it. The trader swapped these cheap European goods to the Indian for "cheap," readily accessible fur, took the fur back to Europe, and sold it. This new activity posed no problems for the Indian. He had trapped for countless years and had preserved the pelts for his own use. It meant merely that his desire for European goods determined the extent and scope of his labor.

All this trade was done on a double seller's market. Europe wanted the fur and the Indians wanted the trade goods. No wonder it became Big Business with bizarre and fantastic fortunes made and lost.

The same era that saw this new source of fur trapped by the Russians and the China Trade saw the opportunistic European financiers grasp the advantage of organizing the fur trade, just as 50 years ago the Chevrolet, Buick, Oldsmobile, and Cadillac companies amalgamated to form General Motors. Instead of a multitude of individual traders competing against each other for their supplies and then engaging in cutthroat competition in the field for pelts, the idea dawned that the business was big enough to reward large-scale organization.

Thus, the Hudson's Bay Company, the North West Company, and John Jacob Astor, merchant, came into being. The Astor enterprise was not a closed company like the other two major competitors which were composed of stockholders, elected officials, and employees. Rather Astor was an independent, directing and controlling many ventures. He was the American Fur Company, but he also would buy from or sell fur to the other big companies, as well as on the open market. He would organize or buy out other small companies such as the Southwest Company, the Pacific Fur Company, or the Upper Missouri Outfit. He would act as broker for smaller concerns, either supplying them with trade goods or marketing their furs, or he would enter into a partnership with other men for a specific trading venture or a specific time. These three entities, Astor, the North West Company, and the Hudson's Bay Company, were financial and political powers in the world. When they spoke presidents, prime ministers, senators, select committees, lords, treasury officials, bankers, and stock market speculators listened. Their decisions caused world economy to fluctuate. This attention was generated not only by the size of the business itself, but also because of the clout wielded by it in the manufacturing and merchandising community and their bankers.

As Big Business, the industry was built upon the effort of many men from several social strata. Some were astute and of good education, others were day laborers without a care in the world or a thought of the morrow as long as they were on a payroll. They were scattered over the world in various niches. Some were ensconced behind desks in cities, concerned with matters of policy, others were warehousemen. Still others were employed in the transportation of trade goods in one direction and pelts in the other, and some were the actual traders dependent upon the efficiency of all the others. The trader, regardless of his dedication and ability, could not be successful if he could not obtain trade goods or dispose of the furs he acquired. His trading was a full-time job, and he could not take time off to attend to all the other details.

Thus, we come to the role of the traders who, in the usual conception, *were* the fur trade. These men lived their lives far from the amenities of their contemporaries. Most of them enjoyed the life as they followed it for years. If they were not adaptable or did not have the ability to be a success at trading, they disappeared from the scene after a year or two. They were businessmen merchandising wares, but instead of accepting cash, checks, or bank credits, they had to barter.

Their customers, the Indians, had no conception of money; a bank note was just a piece of paper, and a coin wasn't any good even for a button because it had no holes in it, but bartering was a different story. The Indian was adept at that as it was the method of the age-old intertribal trade.

The trader went into Indian country and picked a location he knew was central to and convenient for Indian activity. There he established a headquarters or depot from which he conducted business in one of three ways, or a combination of these ways as circumstances might dictate. He traded directly out of the depot with Indians who brought their fur to him; he sent employees out with a small stock of goods to find bands of Indians to trade with on the spot; or an employee was detailed to live with a band of Indians for a period of time to barter for fur as it was obtained.

The later American traders employed still another maneuver. Employees were sent out from the depot in small parties to trap, the pelts either belonging to the trader if the employee was on salary, or the fur thus obtained was delivered to the trader at fixed prices if the trapper were a "free man" who was merely attached to the trader's organization and obtained his supplies from the trader. In the early part of the summer, after all the winter fur had been collected, the trader took his accumulation of fur to some central point such as York Factory if he were a Hudson's Bay Company man; Fort William if he were a Nor'Wester; Fort Union if he were an American Fur Company employee; or the rendezvous if he were a more or less footloose, independent trader operating in the American area. He obtained his next year's supply of trading goods at this time, made his plans for the following winter, and returned to the Indian country. The fur now started on its trek into world commerce, giving employment and profit to all the canoemen, pack trains, warehousemen, merchants, sailors, bankers, tailors, and storekeepers to the ultimate user of the pelt in Europe.

The size of this business is shown by the number of skins brought into Europe. In 1626, when the trade was in its infancy, there was 45,000 livres of beaver imported into France from Canada. By 1667 France received 550,000 livres worth of fur.[2] By 1800, when the trade was in full stride, England imported 138,000 marten, 45,000 otter, 25,000 wolf, 42,000 fox, 23,000 mink, 248,000 raccoon, 50,000 bear, and 245,000 beaver skins, supplemented by thousands of moose, elk, and deer hides to be used for leather, with an aggregate value of around five million dollars.[3] This listing does not take into account the fur that was absorbed by other markets which were of minor importance by 1800: Amsterdam, Hamburg, Paris, New York, Canton, Novgorod, and Moscow.

Of course, the value of the dollar then was worth many times what it is today. In 1681 beaver pelts were selling for £14/6 in London.[4] To translate that figure into an understandable amount poses difficulties. In 1681 there were no American or Canadian dollars, but 100 years later, we find that the English pound sterling was worth about five American dollars. That would make £14/6 worth about $3.65, but in those days a dollar would buy many times what it does today. So, to put those figures into a contemporary bracket, beaver in 1681 was bringing the equivalent of 40 or 50 1988 dollars per pelt, and a trapper could average several beaver a day.

To bring monetary values into sharper focus for the heyday of the fur trade, an old account book of a storekeeper in Lenox, Massachusetts, gives the following information (converted into dollars from the pound, shilling, and pence of the accounts); in 1775 he bought 8½ pounds of cheese for 75 cents, in 1776 he bought dressed beef for 5 cents a pound, and in 1777 he paid $2.50 for weaving 17 yards of cloth and 50 cents for one day's labor. And these prices were during the inflationary period of the Revolutionary War.[5]

This influx of raw material, pelts, into the European economy gave the hatters and furriers all the business they could handle. Frequently it resulted in a glutted market, but the continually increasing tempo of the economy always overcame the glut until the Industrial Age began to economically produce woolen and cotton goods — rugs, mittens, socks, coats, and other things — that had been served by fur, but now were cheaper than fur.

While Europe prospered from this supply of North American fur, the Indian also prospered. He could abandon his Stone Age tools and the commitment to that way of life. The sad part is that the jump from the Stone Age to the Industrial Age was more than any race could accomplish in one, two, or three generations. His back-breaking toil and marginal existence were alleviated, but his ability to comprehend and efficiently employ the new tools could not develop apace. As the dominant race on this continent the Indian was doomed by the tidal wave of the white man and his superior utilization of the products of the Industrial Age.

Chapter 2

Principles of Indian Trade

Contrary to popular impression, the white man did not initiate the Indian into the mysteries of trade. He did not foist, through his sharpness and experience, a new feature of life upon the Indian to the Indian's detriment.

Indians had engaged in trade among themselves from prehistoric time. The advent of the white man only enhanced a practice with which the Indian was familiar and in which he was an expert.

The Indian, at the time of Columbus, had trading centers, trade routes, trade practices, and trade customs that were interlocking and intracontinental. Even inveterate enemies observed truces for trading, and certain sites, such as the pipestone quarries in the *Song of Hiawatha*, were inviolate as they were connected with the trade practices. Indian mores and tradition dictated that people were privileged to obtain their supplies or dispense their wares there.

Within this trade framework objects traveled tremendous distances. Turquoise and silver work out of the Southwest and Mexico was conveyed to the Great Lakes region; obsidian for arrow points and knives traveled from the Columbian Plateau to the Mississippi Valley; seashells from the Atlantic and Pacific Oceans ended up on the High Plains. But such dispersion was not haphazard. It followed developed routes to known trading centers and thence to other centers until it had hopped, skipped, and jumped across the continent.

The Indian was sharp, knew values, and being cognizant of the function of profit, knew that some items in his territory or manufactured by his tribe were desired by other Indians not so favored; and by astute handling of his affairs he could obtain another horse, or some corn which his tribe did not raise, or some specially dressed and tanned antelope hides which he needed for a new ceremonial shirt. He was an experienced trader and merchant when the white man arrived on the scene.

Most of the Indian trading centers, the tribes which frequented them, and the routes connecting them have been identified.[1] Rather than a detailed

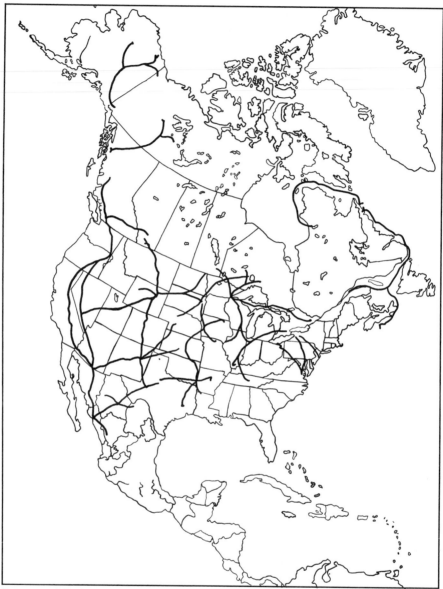

Patterns of Prehistoric trade. (Sources: *Smithsonian Handbook of North American Indians*, vol. 4; *Traders of the Western Morning* (Southwest Museum); *Smithsonian Book of North American Indians; Historical Atlas of Canada)*

discussion of individual tribes we will take a look at the overall activity. Neighboring tribes, even though enemies, traded almost constantly, and the far-ranging trade was planned and programmed on a constant basis. Some trading was catch-as-catch-can, as the opportunity occurred, but planned and organized trade was carried on in an established, interlocking network. It was a feature of Indian life.

The merchandise involved was as varied as the stock in an old-time general store. The list is almost endless — not only eagle feathers for "war bonnets," but oriole, woodpecker, duck, and other feathers for all sorts of religious and personal purposes; corn, squash, beans, and tobacco; bows of special material or construction; blankets and head and arm bands of buffalo or mountain goat hair; porcupine quills, bear claws, silver and copper necklaces, and other ornamentations; seashells ranging from the wampum of the New England area to the dentalia shells of the Pacific; dried meat, pemmican, dressed hides; moccasins of special design or manufacture; household articles such as clay jars, bone spoons, bone and stone knives, native dyes and paints; and especially horses in the trans-Mississippi West after Indian acquisition of the horse in numbers, which occurred in the late 1600s and early 1700s.[2] Reflection upon the list will make it clear that the Indian was well-versed in the practice of trade and that it was no mystery to him. The white man, when he came along, did not capitalize on the ignorance of a Stone Age people.

We do not know when European man first stepped ashore on this continent. That act certainly took place long before Columbus. The earliest known adventurers were the Norsemen who created colonies in Greenland in A.D. 1000, give or take a few years. After founding the new settlements, the Norse began to fish in the Greenland-Newfoundland region and maintained contact with Iceland and Norway. There is evidence that Breton, Briton, Basque, and Portuguese fishermen followed the Norse to this new fishing site. From time to time they had to put into shore for fresh water, to dry their catch, obtain wood for their cooking, or to make repairs. In 1534 when Jacques Cartier, one of the early white men to seek gold, the short route to Cathay, or a quick fortune from any windfall, first encountered Indians they approached him holding furs aloft, indicating to him that they were peaceful, and that they wanted to trade.[3] These Indians had learned sometime, someplace, about bartering for European goods, probably from the early fishermen.

Although the Indian had survived for countless centuries under the limitations imposed by the crudity of his culture, he found the European items a godsend. Steel fishhooks, steel knives, even old nails or scraps of iron that could be beaten into arrow or harpoon points were fantastic additions to his arsenal. We can only imagine the impact such articles had on the Indians' daily life. Think of what a copper pot, a butcher knife, a steel awl, and a hatchet meant to an Indian woman in her household chores. And there was only one place these incredible items could be obtained; they had to come from bearded men in the big, white winged canoes from the land of the rising sun. Since this was the only source, the bartering could be done only with the bearded men. Their items were priceless.

The white man rapidly capitalized on this trade. He began to increase his inventory of knickknacks since they were the most profitable and also added to his competitive edge over other traders.

The trade rapidly involved the trading pattern of the Indians. A case in point: the Hudson's Bay Company founded their posts on the shores of that bay in 1670. The western shore is low and swampy, with muskrats as the major furbearer. Indians frequented the area only temporarily to hunt ducks and geese during the seasonal migrations. The traders, before long, managed to persuade some of the Cree Indians to move into permanent proximity to the posts and become hunters as, until then, the traders' food had to be largely imported from England.[4]

These transplanted Cree soon began to act as middlemen in the trade, making contact with their brethren to the west, either leading those brethren, with their fur, down to the posts, or trading with the inland Cree, and bringing the resultant fur down to bayside. Later the inland Cree, who were within a 400 or 500 mile radius, began to take over the trade. These Cree, in turn, acted as middlemen by trading with more distant Indians during the spring. In early summer they took all these furs to trade for more goods. They could be home again before the rivers froze, stopping canoe traffic. The goods were held until early the next spring when the whole process was repeated. The farther Indians welcomed this supply of goods since either they were not "canoe" Indians or the distance to the trading post was too great for them to make the journey between breakup and freezeup. This Indian-to-Indian trade involved a middleman's markup.[5]

Such Indian activity occurred not only in the Hudson's Bay area but in all the early trading centers — Montreal, Albany, Boston, Harrisburg.

The pragmatic white trader would then try to establish another post near the trading Indians' homeland. He wanted the profit of the Indian middleman. But each time the astute Indians contrived every ruse to prevent contact with farther tribes. The Indian understood trade and the advantages that accrued from it.[6]

These trade goods, when they entered the Indian trade network, had to comply with the standards and rules of that economy and were based on more or less fixed scales and values (e.g., one horse was worth two bushels of corn or three buffalo robes). Of course, that had to vary to some extent as a crippled horse was worth nothing and an old or worn-out horse was worth less than a young, well-broken, perky one. In the main, though, there were set schedules of values. When the Indian first started bartering for European goods, he fixed in his mind that a gun was worth, say 12 beaver pelts, or he could get a hatchet for a beaver, or 20 fishhooks for a beaver skin. To him that became the standard and he resisted any change in the price by another trader or a year later by the same trader. He had no conception of fluctuation in European prices. That the

July 14th. 1703.
Prices of Goods

Supplyed to the

Eastern Indians,

By the several Truckmasters ; and of the Peltry received by the Truckmasters of the said *Indians.*

ONe yard Broad Cloth,*three* Beaver skins,*in season*.
One yard & halfGingerline,*one* Beaver skin,*in season*
One yard Red or Blew Kersey,*two* Beaver skins,*in season.*
One yard good Duffels, *one* Beaver skin, *in season.*
One yard& half broad fineCotton,*one*Beaver skin,*in season*
Two yards of Cotton, *one* Beaver skin, *in season.*
One yard & half of half thicks, *one* Beaver skin, *in season.*
Five Pecks Indian Corn, *one* Beaver skin, *in season*
Five Pecks Indian Meal, *one* Beaver Skin, *in season.*
Four Pecks Pease, *one* Beaver skin, *in season.*
Two Pints of Powder, *one* Beaver skin, *in season.*
One Pint of Shot, *one* Beaver skin, *in season.*
Six Fathom of Tobacco, *one* Beaver skin, *in season.*
Forty Biskets, *one* Beaver skin, *in season.*
Ten Pound of Pork, *one* Beaver skin, *in season.*
Six Knives, *one* Beaver skin, *in season.*
Six Combes, *one* Beaver skin, *in season.*
Twenty Scaines Thread, *one* Beaver skin, *in season.*
One Hat, *two* Beaver skins, *in season.*
One Hat with Hatband, *three* Beaver skins, *in season.*
Two Pound of large Kettles, *one* Beaver skin, *in season.*
OnePound& half of smallKettles,*one*Beaver skin,*in season*
One Shirt, *one* Beaver skin, *in season.*
One Shirt with Ruffels, *two* Beaver skins, *in season.*
Two Small Axes, *one* Beaver skin, *in season.*
Two Small Hoes, *one* Beaver skin, *in season.*
Three Dozen middling Hooks, *one* Beaver skin, *in season.*
One Sword Blade, *one & half* Beaver skin, *in season.*

What shall be accounted in Value equal
One Beaver in season : Vit.

ONe Otter skin in season, is one Beaver
One Bear skin in season, is one Beaver,
Two Half skins in season, is one Beaver
Four Pappcote skins in season, is one Beaver
Two Foxes in season, is one Beaver.
Two Woodchocks in season, is one Beaver.
Four Martins in season, is one Beaver.
Eight Muncks in season, is one Beaver.
Five Pounds of Feathers, is one Beaver.
Four Raccoones in season, is one Beaver.
Four Seil skins large, is one Beaver.
One Moose Hide, is two Beavers.
One Pound of Castorum, is one Beaver.

A notice to English colonists of the "Standard of Trade" in effect on 14 July 1703. (From Don Taxay's *Money of the American Indians*)

price of beaver might fall in London or steel prices go up, increasing the cost of guns or traps, was beyond his comprehension. It was doubly necessary for the Indian to insist on the "Standard of Trade," as this set price structure was known, because when he entered the goods into his trade network he had to conform to the accepted Indian bartering level.

A sense of quality, custom, and value was so ingrained in the Indian that he not only demanded rigid adherence to the Standard of Trade but looked askance at familiar articles if they had an unusual form or size or were from an unfamiliar manufacturer. When the English conquered New Netherland and took over the Dutch settlements, the merchants at Albany were allowed to continue their trade with Holland. It was feared, however, if the merchants were forced to switch to English manufactured goods, the Indians would reject those goods.

One of the interesting features of the Standard of Trade was that the trader could not increase his volume of business by offering bargains. Such aroused the Indian's skepticism — perhaps the goods were inferior — perhaps the trader was trying to softsoap the customer to take advantage of him later. Also, the Indian could use only one gun at a time, another would be only a burden; his wife had need for only two copper pots which nestled inside one another, one butcher knife, and one hatchet. He didn't want to be bothered with more. Those considerations dictated how much merchandise he wanted. If, some year, he actually needed none of the necessities, no amount of price cutting would tempt him.

Another consideration entered into the Standard of Trade. If, say, a gun was listed as worth 12 beaver skins, what was a trader to do if an Indian showed up to trade for a gun but had a conglomeration of fur — six beaver, one wolf, twenty muskrat, three otter, and four deer skins? The trader solved this problem by transposing this miscellany into "Made Beaver," which was another schedule based on the price of various pelts in London, and which gave the equivalent value of other furs as related to beaver: ten muskrat, or two wolf, or four deer equalled one beaver, and so on. The Indian understood this system, and usually knew just what he had in Made Beaver and how much it would buy under the Standard of Trade. This seemingly complicated procedure bypassed the Indian's ignorance of pounds, shilling, and pence. Even as late as the Oregon Trail days, there were several incidents in which emigrant wagon trains were destroyed by Indians who, in their looting of the wagons, disdainfully discarded chests of gold and silver coins. On opening the boxes and seeing these shiny bits of metal, the Indians were contemptuous. They could imagine no use for them.

The Indian was a practical person and couldn't comprehend the abstract forms of the white man's economy. He did have an understanding of credit, though. He knew that he could draw some basic supplies prior to a hunting trip, but that he would have to bring back some peltry if he wanted to remain on good terms with the trader. After a couple hundred years the Hudson's Bay Company did succeed in getting the Indians to accept the company's special tokens in the denomination of 1 MB and 2 MB (Made Beaver).

After the first furious onslaught on the beaver by American trappers in the Upper Missouri River region, with a consequent depletion of that animal, and the inauguration of steamboat travel up that river, the Made Beaver standard became less applicable in the Missouri River area. A market had developed for buffalo robes, and the traders had cheap transportation for those heavy, bulky hides. They were shipped to Saint Louis, then to New York, London, or wherever. Buffalo robes soon had their own Standard of Trade — one horse, ten robes; a yard of woolen goods, one robe.[7]

The rigid codes, the Standard of Trade and Made Beaver, left the trader with little leeway, especially since the Indian-trading custom dictated the exchange of gifts prior to trading. The gifts were a formality to indicate goodwill and openhandedness, but the avarice of the white man for fur and his desire to build up a devoted clientele to the detriment of his competition, soon led to a great expansion of the gift giving on his part. The Indian had no qualms about accepting this new development. Needless to say, this practice soon became an additional burden on the profitability of any trading, since the Indian didn't reciprocate in the increase of gifts. If anything, the Indian tended to cut back on the value and amount of his gift tendered to the trader. Under this pressure the trader began to rely more and more on alcohol as the major part of his gift. The alcohol could be in the form of French brandy, English rum, whiskey, or "High Wine," which was nothing more than straight alcohol diluted on the spot. As there was less bulk and weight in the straight alcohol than in the other forms, and in transporting it, the trader had an advantage. When trading was imminent, all the trader had to do was add some water, a handful of tobacco so that the juice would give the solution some color, and some pepper to give it flavor. The drunker the customer became, the more water the trader could add. Eventually the practice got out of hand and led to much of the disrepute that became attached to Indian trading. The white trader, under pressure to make a profit, would make a liberal gift of the beverage and then, after the Indian was under the influence of it, offer more. The Indian, with his low tolerance for alcohol, gladly accepted the offer. The drunker the Indian became, the more water the trader would add, until the Indian was getting pure water and had traded all his fur. This chicanery was a later development which came into existence long after the principles of the trade were set.

To offset the strictures imposed on the trader by the Standard of Trade and Made Beaver, little peccadillos came into being. They were known as the Overplus. Overplus was accomplished in several ways. Since it was hard for the trader to blatantly advance the price of well-known standard items such as guns, hatchets, or blankets, the trader would resort to subterfuge. He would object to the quality of the pelts — some were immature, some damaged, other improperly cured — and anything else he could quibble about. Another tactic was to give short measure on those items traded by yard, pound, or gallon. Spirits could be watered if the deal was for a keg or two. By the drink, a short measure could be used with the added short measure accomplished by placing the thumb inside the cup. This last trick could be used only if the customer had become befuddled.

For the yard and pound measurements the goal was reached by such deception as giving two feet instead of three for a yard, rigging scales so that 12 ounces of beads would show as one pound, insisting that a two-quart kettle was actually a three-quart size. Sometimes, in a new territory in which the Indians had not had direct contact with white traders, the traders would start business by raising the Standard of Trade. Instead of asking ten Made Beaver for a gun they would ask 12 or 15, and raise other prices accordingly. The new Indian customers didn't know the difference, and, if they suspected it, didn't care as they were only too glad to have direct trade for new, unused items and were accustomed to the markup imposed by other Indians in the Indian trade network. These fudgings were not entirely unrecognized by steady customers who remonstrated if the trader became too flagrant in his use, or abuse, of it. But it had its points; it gave a basis for a little haggling and bargaining to both sides.

While the Indians demanded that these standard measures be employed, the scale was not uniform or strictly adhered to by all traders at all times. That led to much comparison-shopping by the Indian. The French-Canadians operating out of Montreal had a long canoe haul to their trading posts in the interior, causing them to concentrate on the more valuable fur, offering a little more for it and less for coarser, less valuable pelts. The Hudson's Bay Company, before founding their inland posts, insisted that their employees adhere to the Standard of Trade and Made Beaver schedules as much as possible. This insistence usually ended up with the French, who had penetrated into the interior before the Hudson's Bay Company and were in constant contact with the trapping Indians, getting more of the fine fur, leaving the rough, coarse fur to find its way to Hudson's Bay. The early colonial Dutch and British traders, having direct access to sea transport, could offer better trade terms than the French. These three differences in the trade economy led to sharp competition.

Traditionally, the Standard of Trade and Made Beaver schedules were set by some authority in a trading organization to give each trader an idea of what was expected of him and a common basis for all. The schedules were based on prime, top-quality fur. In actuality, it was little more than a computation of the necessary rate of exchange that would give a fair profit when the fur was sold in Europe.

Everyone concerned realized that rigid adherence to the standards was not feasible. One post might have a larger overhead than other posts due to local circumstances. The location of another post might be dictated by Indian traffic patterns, but the location was in a poor hunting area so the post had to buy more than the average amount of food from the Indians and thus expend trading goods with no fur to show for it. Provision had to be made for poor-quality furs, as an Indian expected a trader to trade even if some of the fur was from young animals, summer trapped, torn, poorly skinned or cared for pelts.

The trader had to make allowance for these conditions if he wanted the continued patronage of the Indians.

These considerations led to the Overplus. A trader soon learned whether the Indians in his area were excellent fur-gatherers or indolent, careless trappers. The trader would adjust to reflect those prevailing conditions. If he were astute and had a good season, his return of fur would often be more than the standards called for. But this Overplus had to be a matter of each trader's judgement or he would alienate his customers.

The Indian soon woke up to the avid desire of the white man for fur and took advantage of the traders if more than one happened to be in the vicinity. The Indian would visit one trader, accept the gifts offered; then repeat the process with the other traders. This shopping technique put an added burden on trading. Each trader, as soon as he realized what was going on, would increase his gift and adjust his Overplus, hoping to secure the Indian's trade then and there.

There was another problem, though, that the traders never did succeed in solving — fickle fashion. Some woman would make her husband a new ceremonial shirt decorated with round blue and long white beads. As soon as other Indians saw it they wanted one just like it. The trader's stock of round blue and long white beads became exhausted in a matter of days. The next year he brought more of those two items and they soon sold out. The next year he tripled his order, but by then the demand was for red and green beads. Or, solid-colored blankets were standard until some trader introduced striped blankets. Then everyone wanted striped blankets. Of course, certain basic items weren't subject to these whims of fancy.

After the Revolutionary War and the opening of the trans-Mississippi West, the trader, now American, refused to adhere to this long-established trading pattern. It was every-man-for-himself-and-the-devil-take-the-hindmost. Every one of them had a vision of a quick fortune and was determined to get it by hook or crook. This was the cornerstone of much of the Indian troubles that plagued the American West.

No apology can be offered for this last phase of Indian trade in the United States, but the beginnings of the trade in the earliest days of North American settlement were beneficial to both the Indians and the white men. The usual textbook statement that the Indians were cheated at every turn is simply not true. Denys, an early French writer on America observes,

> They have abandoned all their own utensils, whether because of the trouble they had as well as to make as to use them or because of the facility of obtaining from us, in exchange for skins which cost them almost nothing, the things which seemed to them invaluable, not so much for their novelty as for the convenience they derived therefrom.[8]

The old myth about the Dutch obtaining the whole of Manhattan Island for a mere 24 dollars worth of beads as proof of the white man's rascality is a distortion. The Indian valued the beads or whatever other trade goods he got far above that little dab of land. The Indian had land galore, but no beads, no copper pots, no steel knives, no awls, no metal fishhooks, and no place to get them except through the Dutch traders. In addition, the Indian believed that he was only permitting the Dutch to utilize the land in common with the Indians. In history, it is always necessary to "separate the description of action from the interpretation of that action."9

Another misconception has developed from an incomplete understanding of the Indian-white trading practices. It is the statement that the white man derived an unconscionable profit from each transaction; that a butcher knife, for instance, costing one shilling at the factory in England was marked up to a value of ten shillings to an Indian. While that bare statement is true on the surface, all the factors entering into the markup are not accounted for.

Let us follow the route of a butcher knife, as an example of trade items, from its manufacture to its final home in the hands of an Indian.

Some firm, functioning in New York or Saint Louis as a wholesaler, places an order with an agent in London for a shipment of knives of a certain quality and size. The agent obtains the knives from a factory for one shilling apiece and adds his commission. Shipment to the colonies accrues a freight charge. The wholesaler pays the drayage from the dock to his warehouse and adds a warehousing charge. When a trader comes in to obtain a supply of goods the wholesaler adds his markup, which has to include interest on the money invested, and passes the knives on to the trader, maybe on credit.

The trader assembles all his goods and help and leaves with his packhorse train, if he is going overland, or his canoe fleet, if he is going by a river route. He has to add on to the cost of the knives their proportionate share of the transportation cost to his destination. This charge is not trivial, when the cost of the horses or canoes and their trappings and the wages and subsistence of the men are considered. On this final leg of the knives' journey, the trader is assuming the risk of a canoe capsizing, which often occurred, or striking a snag and sinking, or encountering a band of Indians who were in a bad humor over some incident, thus losing his whole stock of goods and maybe his life. At his destination he had to make presents to each Indian to initiate the trading session, and this had to be added his costs.

When the knife was finally traded to an Indian for ten shillings worth of fur, it represented the value of the fur on the London market. But the trader had it in his hands out in the hinterland. It was a perishable commodity that had to be protected, and he ran the same risks getting it back to his base as he did in getting the knife out to the Indian. When he finally got back to his wholesaler, the fur was credited to his account but at less than its full London value. The wholesaler had to pack it and ship it to London, where he had to pay a commission to have it sold.

The receipt of ten shillings worth of fur for a one-shilling knife was not all gravy for the trader. Few traders became rich, most merely eked out a living, if they managed to survive. Starvation, freezing, Indian fights, drowning, thirst, and disease took a terrible toll among them.

The lure of this trade was its potential. At its best, if everything went according to plan, these one-shilling knives, and the other goods, returned more than a good profit for the time and expense involved. One canoe load of goods would return to civilization as two canoe loads of fur. With each canoe carrying 40 packs of 90 pounds each simple arithmetic gives 7,200 pounds of fur. If the trader sold it at three dollars a pound (an average price of the time) and allowed the merchant his profits, the trader got a return of several hundred percent for his one or two years' effort.

But, if everything did not go according to plan, the trader — with his investment of two or three thousand dollars in goods, wages, provisions, and material — came back with only a few paltry packs of fur, or nothing.

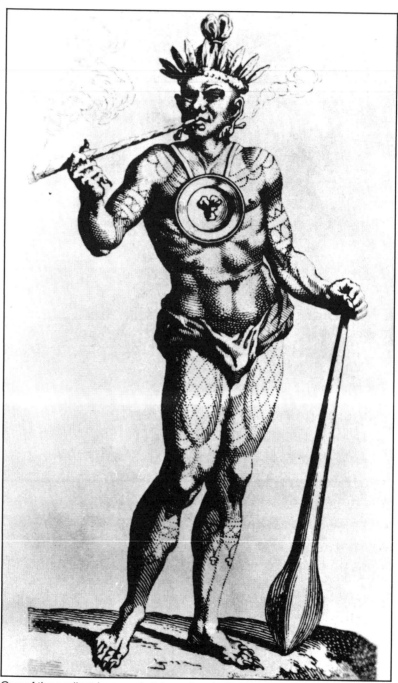

One of the earliest known sketches of an Indian smoking tobacco. (Courtesy of American Tobacco Company)

Chapter 3

Tobacco in Indian Trade

So ancient is the Indian use of tobacco that they have only legends concerning its origin. It was part of their sacred rituals and became an object of veneration, much the same as the Christian use of bread and wine.

Very seldom did an Indian smoke for pleasure as the use of tobacco was a sacrament, homage paid to the supernatural. Many Indians showed their veneration of it by smoking at sunrise, asking the gods for a favorable day, and again at sunset to ask that evil be warded from them during the night. They used it at funerals, at puberty rites, in ceremonies to placate foes, and in harvest festivals. It had a place in peace ceremonies, in organizing war parties, to influence weather, to cement alliances, and was used by ambassadors as a passport. Tobacco was used by medicine men in the treatment of sickness and occupied an important place in many medicine bundles. The Ojibwa placed a packet of tobacco in one hand of a corpse to pay its passage across the River of Death.

There are 60 varieties of tobacco in the world, of which 36 are native to North and South America, Meso-America, and the Caribbean Islands. The rest are found in Australia and some South Pacific islands. The plant belongs to the nightshade family, which includes the Irish potato, egg plant, tomato, belladonna or foxglove, henbane, jimson weed, some peppers, bittersweet, and matrimony vine.

The western hemisphere varieties ranged through the two continents. Some of them were adopted and cultivated by the aborigines. They harvested the plant either from a cultivated plot or from the wild. After gathering the flowers and leaves, sometimes one or the other or both depending on the tribe, they exposed the harvest to the action of the sun and air. When thoroughly dry, they would store it in rawhide pouches or caves. This crude curing left much to be desired since the product, in that form and with no packaging, was strong tasting and acrid. As time went on, the tobacco became more bitter as it continued to dry, leaching the volatile oils.

To make this tobacco palatable the Indians mixed other substances with it, calling the mixture *kinnikinik*. *Kinnikinik* is an Algonkian word meaning a mixture and refers to any substance used to mix with the tobacco. It was not a standard mixture throughout all the tribes, but varied from region to region as tastes and available adulterants changed. The most common additives were sumac, bearberry bark and leaves, roots and bark of two kinds of willow, manzanita leaves, jimson weed, touchwood, dogwood bark, arrowwood, laurel leaves, maple bush, and the bark of cherry, poplar, and birch trees. One tribe, the Haida of the Queen Charlotte Islands, mixed lime with it and chewed the mixture. Some tribes steeped tobacco in water and drank the brew. The Aztecs and, later, other Central American tribes sniffed it.

Contrary to the impression implanted in our minds by novels, movies, and television, not all Indians were Plains Indians and "Horse" Indians. By far the heaviest concentration of pre-white Indian population was along the Gulf of Mexico, the East Coast, the Mississippi Valley, and around the Great Lakes. The reason is obvious: those areas offered a soil and climate best suited for intensive food gathering and, thus, could support more people per square mile. The same conditions fostered the development of agriculture, and corn became their main crop; meat was not their main food. Considering the continent as a whole, agricultural products comprised 75 percent of their diet, and corn provided more than all the other crops combined. The non-food-crop tobacco came next after corn in the amount of planting by these peoples.

While tobacco was native to all of North America, except the Arctic and sub-Arctic regions, it was cultivated mainly in the agricultural areas. In the remainder of the continent, that part outside the maize area, tobacco was indigenous and commonly was gathered from the wild state. Only a few of the other tribes learned to plant the wild tobacco seed of their region to insure a better supply of the plant. Some of those tribes who cultivated tobacco grew more than they needed, using the surplus as a commodity in the Indian trade network. The Petuns, one of the tribes of the Iroquois family, are a striking example of this, acquiring the pseudonym Tobacco Indians from their constant surplus of tobacco.

The properties of the several varieties ranged from a mild, pleasing, slightly stimulative effect to others which were hallucinogenic or narcotic. The Indians used these many attributes in different ways — tobacco could be used for sacred rites with little side effect, another for its hallucinogenic property in prognosticating, treating sickness, divining, or visions concerning war, hunting, or harvesting. Others which had a narcotic effect were used by some tribes for religious purification rites or the alleviation of hunger, thirst, or fatigue. South American Indians often ate tobacco mixed with coca leaves

Modern-day "twist" tobacco. Still available in southeastern states in limited quantities. (Photo by Winton Weydemeyer. Sample furnished by Mrs. Jack Parrish)

or peyote for the narcotic effect. (Coca leaves are the source of cocaine and should not be confused with cacao, from which chocolate is obtained.)

The tobacco role in Indian trade grew out of this background. When the white man arrived in the New World the Indians of the Caribbean area and the northern part of South America were using the mildest, best-tasting variety, *Nicotiana tobacum*. The Gulf and Atlantic Coast Indians, not having access to that variety, had settled on the next best, *N. rustica*. There were two other stronger, more bitter tobaccos, *N. attenuata* and *N. bigelovii quadravalvis* and *mutivalvis*, in general use in the western part of the continent because they were the best native tobaccos available to those western Indians. Some of this tobacco was harvested in the wild, but in many cases, especially in the East, the Indians cultivated them in their crops of corn, pumpkins, squash, and beans, using any surplus in the Indian trade network which spanned the continent.

When Columbus returned to Spain he took some of this curious plant with him, calling it *tobago*, which is an Arawak Indian word signifying the tube through which the Arawaks sniffed tobacco. The use of this import found widespread acceptance in Europe, quickly becoming a fad.

In 1559 Jean Nicot, the French ambassador to the King of Portugal, sent some tobacco seeds to Catherine de Medici as a present to serve as a source of tobacco for the royal family. Hence the deriviation of the word nicotine and the naming of the plant as *Nicotiana*.

Tobacco use in Europe met with resistance as well as acceptance. King James I of England, in *A Counterblaste to Tobacco* published in 1604, proclaimed that its use was "a custom loathesome to the Eye, hatefull to the Nose, dangerous to the Lungs, harmefull to the Braine, and in the blacke striking fume thereof neerest resembling the horrible Stygian smoke of the pit that is bottomelesse." The Sultan of Turkey went so far as to decree beheading for anyone smoking or dealing in tobacco. The Sultan lost his battle. Today, Turkish tobacco is one of the staples of the world tobacco trade.

The European demand for tobacco became so great that the early American colonists, desperate for a way to make a living, searching frantically for credit or cash, turned to tobacco raising as a possible solution. Tobacco was a native plant; it was adapted to the climate and soil and a market existed for it in Europe.

In 1612 John Rolfe, who achieved lasting fame by marrying Pocahontas, planted the first commercial crop in America (other than the Indian plantings for the intra-Indian trade). His experiment was successful and tobacco soon became a major export of the colonies and a source of much of the colonists' livelihood. It became such an item of commerce that it was often substituted for money. In one case, a shipload of "spinsters carefully selected and matronized [chaperoned] were sent to the colony. They had no difficulty finding suitors, but no accepted suitor could claim his bride until he should pay the London company 120 pounds of tobacco to defray the expenses of her voyage."

In meeting the demands of the European marketplace the colonist found that he had to abandon the tobacco native to our eastern shore, *N. rustica*, and grow the milder, more aromatic tobacco of the Carribbean area, *N. tobacum*, and, also, that he had to make changes in the Indian curing method. Air-dried tobacco became too powdery and acrid to survive the lapse of several months between its production in the colonies, shipment to Europe — whenever a ship became available — and the distribution lag to the consumer. When this became apparent the colonist started tinkering with other curing ideas such as hanging the harvested leaves in a shed and building a smudge fire so that the heat and smoke would stabilize the chemicals in the leaf; packing partially air-dried leaves in hogsheads so that fermentation would take place, which would also "set" the characteristics; controlling the temperature and humidity of the process; the addition of herbs, spices, molasses, rum, licorice, and even chocolate to modify the taste and aroma of the final product.

Out of this melange of experimentation the Portuguese, who were settling Brazil, evolved a form of cured tobacco which became known as "brazil" or "twist." Twist was whole, cured, moist tobacco leaves rolled into a rope three-quarters of an inch in diameter. It was then formed into several sized packages: carrots of one or two pounds, bundles of 25 pounds, or rolls of 45 or 90 pounds. These parcels were then wrapped in various materials to protect them from the hazards of handling and to preserve the moisture.

Twist was ideally suited for the Indian trade. It was a great improvement over the tobacco to which the Indian was accustomed because of its uniform mildness and compactness. The trader could cut off an inch, a foot, or a yard as the occasion required, and it left little room for argument over the amount or quality. The Indian welcomed this new addition to the traders' stock, soon becoming as much a devotee of the social use of tobacco as the white man.

This new twist tobacco did not replace the Indians' traditional native tobacco in the religious ceremonies but was universally adopted by them for social and diplomatic use. The trader soon learned that the product had to be of standard quality as the Indian was a shrewd customer. Traders' journals and letters carry references to the receipt of unsatisfactory tobacco that hindered profitable trading efforts. The Indian, naturally, wanted a quality product when he was greeting ambassadors from another tribe or trying to create a good atmosphere during an intertribal trading session.

Indian customs grounded in centuries, which the flow of years have obscured, demanded that a social or political event proceed with an exchange of gifts to show goodwill and openhandedness. Since Brazil produced the most acceptable form of tobacco and entered it into world trade, it was readily available to the European merchants who furnished the trader with his stock of goods. These two factors, availability and Indian preference, soon made it a standard item in traders' inventories. The Indian expected the trader to employ generous amounts of it as his gift while the Indian would contribute a packet of prime fur, some pemmican, or a fancy leather shirt. Without an acceptable supply of twist the trader could not comply with Indian custom. In that case, the Indian would trade only under necessity and for a minimum of articles that he had to have at that moment.

In the later years of the trade, alcohol became a substitute for tobacco in the gift-giving formalities, but it never supplanted tobacco as an article of trade.

If the trader ran out of tobacco or had only a poor quality, the Indian traded for a few necessities but looked down his nose at the remainder of the trader's goods; beads, vermilion, mirrors, small hawk bells, fishhooks, cording for fishnets and fishlines, ribbon, bracelets, rings, brooches, earrings, buttons, pendants, jew's harps, firesteels, hats, fancy jackets, sugar, coffee, tea, combs, thimbles, awls, and lace. Guns, gunpowder, lead, blankets, axes, kettles, and knives were in great demand and were the main items of trade, but the profit was in the geegaws and trinkets.

Without twist tobacco the trader had a hard row to hoe.[1]

Chapter 4

The Ripple Effect of the Horse and Gun

Whenever we think of an Indian we have a mental image of a man decked out in an ornate "war bonnet," a breechclout, a mass of beaded personal ornaments, mounted on a spotted horse, carrying a repeating rifle, and gazing off into the sunset.

There are many things wrong with that image; it is merely a latter-day, romantic flight of fancy. The horse culture of the Plains Indians arose a mere 250 years ago. It was not a prehistoric or universal part of Indian life. The Indian, in his everyday life, was a practical person. He wore ceremonial dress only during the appropriate ceremony, just as Masons wear their regalia only during their meetings, or as college professors wear the academic robes that signify their school, degrees, and honors only during a graduation ceremony. The Indian's gun ranged from a short-barrelled, smoothbore musket to a sophisticated repeating rifle (in the later days of Indian potency). And, while he like spotted horses — they appealed to him the same as red neckties appeal to some white men — his horses actually came in all sizes, shapes, and colors. Often he carried this preference for "paint" horses to an extreme. If he didn't have a spotted horse or one spotted enough to suit him he would paint spots on it. And he rode a horse only if he was a Horse Indian. All Indians did not adopt the High Plains horse culture. Some remained pedestrian Indians, horticultural Indians, canoe Indians, or fish Indians.

The rise of the horse culture among the Plains Indians was occasioned by two things — the gun and the horse. To understand the interaction of the two and why they gave rise to such a dramatic change in some Indians' lives, they must be considered separately. The forces unleashed by the gun and horse came from two directions, and it was the meeting of these potent harbingers of the future in the Missouri River area about 1700 that caused the new Horse Indian culture to be born. Each of these new white-man additions to Indian life created its own whirlwind, destructive in their own locale but thousands of miles apart. They didn't reach hurricane force until the two met.

It is the purpose of this essay to chart the development of each of these factors and show the upheaval that occurred when they joined.

The eastern Indian had a woodland environment and lived a horticultural, sedentary life. He used more or less permanent towns and cultivated corn, beans, squash, pumpkins, and tobacco. He fished in the neighboring streams and hunted in the surrounding forest. His needs were great, but his wants were simple. He led a precarious life threatened by famine, weather, and assaults by his neighbors because of some incident. But it was a stable existence.

Then along came the white trader with a wondrous assortment of goods, including the gun. The Dutch at Albany traded with the Iroquois Confederacy who lived on the headwaters of the Hudson River. The Indian desire and need for trade items and the white man's greedy desire for furs soon combined to deplete the number of fur-bearing animals in these tribal territories. To satisfy themselves and the traders, those Indians then started to raid their neighbors — they put their firepower to use. By driving a neighbor out of all or part of its recognized territory the invader would have more territory to trap or hunt and thus have more pelts to trade for desirable European goods. Or, if he did not displace a neighbor from the desired land, demand that that neighbor, under penalty of military reprisal, trade all its fur only through the gun-possessing tribe. This gambit assured the gun-toting Indians a middleman's profit without the expenditure of any time, labor, or bother. Of course, those exploited Indians didn't like the situation and resisted to the best of their ability. If they continued to resist they were invariably forced to retreat, give ground, in the face of this firepower.

It may come as a surprise to some readers that what they think of as modern developments existed in pre- and protohistoric societies — but they did. Alliances between tribes to promote war or peace in an area, truces made between enemies for trading, a numerical superiority, a strategic location, a possession of a good supply of a much desired item — all these could and did influence intertribal relations. When one tribe, by the possession of guns, could alter any of these balances that tribe could dictate a new alignment of compacts.

The Iroquois Confederacy made a major application of this power in the early days of the fur trade. Greedy for the profit to be made by acting as middlemen, they saw the advantage of using the guns they obtained at Albany to expand their fur-gathering. They moved against their kin, the Eries and Wenros, subjugating them. Next, they tried raiding the Ottawa fur convoys on their way to Montreal. Since the Ottawas were supplied with guns by the French, the Iroquois were unable to overcome them, so they moved against the Hurons on the north side of Lake Erie who were a major source of the Ottawa's fur supply. The Hurons were also kin to the tribes of the Iroquois Confederacy, but they were destroyed as a tribe; one remnant moving to the protection of the French at Montreal and the remainder crossing Lake Huron to become known as Wyandots.

The Iroquois tribes who were doing all this marauding were known as the Five Nations, being an alliance of Senecas, Oneidas, Cayugas, Onandagas, and Mohawks. While they were exerting their might against the Iroquois tribes to the north and west, another Iroquois tribe, the Tuscaroras, ran into trouble. The Tuscaroras were living in the Virginia-Carolina area and became involved in disputes with the white colonists. Unable to withstand the white man's gun, they fled to northern Pennsylvania and petitioned for admittance to the Iroquois Confederacy. When it was granted the confederation became known as the Six Nations.

Here are two examples of gun ripples. One tribe fled from the gun to the protection of its brethren who had guns while those same brethren were using their guns against other brethren.

The French traders were also the cause of gun ripples. As they carried the fur trade up the Saint Lawrence Valley and into the Great Lakes region they came into contact with the Cree and Ojibwa. Those tribes lost no time in trading for some guns and bringing them to bear upon their hereditary enemies, the Sioux. At this time the Sioux were canoe Indians living to the south and west of Lake Superior. The gun in the hands of the Cree and Ojibwa soon forced the Sioux farther west. They couldn't go south because the same trickle of guns was coming across the Allegheny Mountains from the Pennsylvania traders and up the Mississippi River from the Spaniards. That left only the West.

Some of the Sioux eventually reached and crossed the Missouri River, but they maintained links to the East. While the French traders established posts at Green Bay and Prairie du Chien, and the Spanish extended their efforts up the Missouri River, the Sioux gained a source of guns. With guns in hand, they became entrenched and able to resist further dislocation.

While the Sioux were being forced westward, they had run into the Cheyennes who, at the time, were living on the headwaters of the Mississippi River. This pressure, maybe bolstered by a few guns the Sioux had managed to obtain, forced the Cheyennes into the area claimed by the Mandans and Hidatsas on the Missouri River. These last-named tribes were far from happy over this trespassing and applied their own pressure on the Cheyennes.

The unremitting Sioux pressure behind them and the lateral pressures from the Missouri River tribes forced the Cheyennes across the Missouri River and up into the valley of the river now known as the Cheyenne.

The Mandan and Hidatsa, having to contend with other people similarly dislocated, continued to harass them. They roamed on west to the Black Hills

A Chief and his staff. (Courtesy of Kamt-Mann & Co)

of South Dakota with some of them continuing south down the Front Range of the Rockies.

By the time the United States government started writing treaties with the Plains Indians, there was enough separation between the Black Hills and Platte River bands that the treaties specifically referred to them as Northern and Southern Cheyenne.

The principal advantage of the gun to the Indian was its man-to-man potency. The gun increased the Indian's hunting prowess very little as it was noisy and, after one shot, scared all the game for a mile or so. Several quiet arrows could be shot while a musket was being slowly reloaded. Also, it was cumbersome to carry in underbrush and hard to reload on horseback.

The possession of guns by one tribe put pressure on the neighboring tribes and, as they recoiled, that act applied pressure to a farther neighbor. As the French went on to Lake Winnipeg and on up the Assiniboine and Saskatchewan Rivers and the English came over the Allegheny Mountains into the Ohio Valley, it was like a man walking along the shore of a pond throwing in pebbles every 50 paces. As ripples from successive pebbles spread, they soon meet and clash. By the time the man reaches the end of the pond the center of the lake is severely agitated. The ripple effect produced by the gun was even more pronounced than the interaction of the concentric circles in the pond as the water circles could spread backwards toward the preceding pebble point, but the Indian couldn't. If he tried to go backwards, he ran into other angry Indians who had also suffered from this imposition and who were close to a priorly established supply of guns which made them dangerous.

This pattern of gun ripples can be followed west from the East Coast to the Mississippi Valley. It explains many of the fragmentations of tribal families. Of course, there were other factors which entered into this drift. Things such as population pressures finally dictating either an enlargement of tribal territory or migration to new lands, family feuds that developed into schisms, fleeing from a contagion, famine, or drought — all figured into these shifts. But the gun caused some and accentuated others.

While the literature frequently mentions the ascendancy of particular tribes as an ongoing process in the early days of the fur trade — before the white traders had spread their posts over a large extent of the continent — that literature usually does not make explicit that the gun furnished the means by which these shifts were accomplished. A cursory reading of the accounts leaves the impression that the availability of trade goods to one tribe and the desire of further tribes for those goods led to the penetration of a tribe into another tribe's domain. The displaced or subjugated tribe, relying on the established, age-old balance of power, would have foiled such a displacement if it hadn't been for the gun in the hands of the encroaching tribe.

The rate at which a tribe was armed by the traders added to the disarray of intertribal relations. The Siksika and Kainah, of the Blackfeet Confederacy, complained that the Cree were accumulating guns faster than they. They failed to take into account that the Cree were to the east of the Siksika and Kainah (closer to the trading posts at that time), had had longer contact with white traders, and that the Cree lived in a country in which fine fur was plentiful, while the Siksika country provided mostly wolf, buffalo, and coyote skins. This didn't lessen the Blackfeet vexation; the number of guns in the hands of the Cree was the problem. The balance of power was imperiled.

Only a few trader journals and accounts specifically state that the "abc" tribe used their guns to drive the "xyz" tribe farther away or had made vassals of the "xyzs" and were now occupying or dominating the "xyz" territory and that the gun was the decisive factor. Perhaps the tribal shifts were so frequent in the turmoil created by the Indians' pursuit of fur that the trader accepted all of it as a routine measure of Indian life. Or the trader may have been so busy trying to forge ahead to new sites to expand his trade that these ripples did not attract his attention; he was keeping abreast of them.

Later writers apparently assumed that everyone understands the gun would cause such friction. Glossing over the role of the gun and the turbulence that it caused, has to be extrapolated from the history of the fur trade or the ensuing ferment may be misunderstood or even missed.

The white man had imposed his society upon the eastern Indians by the time the worst turmoil was affecting the Indians in the Lake Winnipeg-Missouri River-Mississippi River areas. (The English land acquisition policies had also contributed to these ripples now appearing in the mid-Continent area.) These new, uprooted Midwest Indians had been woodland canoe Indians with a corresponding culture while the "regular" ones had been longtime residents with an established economy and culture. The influx of the new Indians upset the equilibrium. The westward surge was the compounded wave of frustrations and disruptions in the East. New accommodations had to be worked out among the tribes. The possession and availability of guns counted for more than the supply of pelts in this jockeying for living room. All this contention and unsettled conditions were fermenting when the horse arrived on the scene.

The horse was a Spanish contribution to the western hemisphere. As Spanish colonization expanded from the Caribbean Islands to the mainland, the ranches followed. As expansion of mainland activity continued, so did the size of their herds and establishments. Since the Spanish *caballero* believed that he should hold himself above menial tasks to maintain his status, Indians were either hired or pressed into service for those chores.

Although this strange beast, the horse, caused much wonderment and awe among the Indians when first seen, they soon accepted it. Their friends and relatives who were serving as herders and stablemen, of course, became accustomed to the horse and its use. The Indians saw that usage and, undoubtedly, talked about it. They realized that the horse would provide mobility; it would release them from their foot-slogging way of life. As a pedestrian, the Indian in the American West led a circumscribed existence. He was limited to the waterholes and food-gathering areas he could reach on foot, packing his possessions either on his own back or on dogs. His mobility was sorely limited. A horse to ride and another to pack his belongings enlarged his range and food-gathering beyond belief. He could go where the game was, not wait for it to come to him; if a local drought made life miserable in one area he could drift until he found better conditions. He could expand his war and trade to distant regions. He saw all these potentials in the horse.

It was only a small step to obtain a few of the numerous Spanish horses. The Indians could capture strays without much risk as the Spaniards had so many, and they ranged so far on the unfenced plains that often they were not missed, or, if they were, they weren't worth wasting time and effort to find. Then there were the wild horses, descendants of the strays, but these were difficult to capture, gentle, and train. By far the best source was stealing from the Spanish herds. No doubt the stealing often was with the connivance of the Indian herdsman. It would take no legerdemain or ingenuity to engineer such a theft. When the overseeing Spaniard made a routine count of the herd and found a few head missing, who knew when, where, or how they disappeared? And, anyway, those few horses weren't worth the trouble and effort it would take to recover them. Added to these means were deliberate Indian raids on Spanish herds. After the Indians had a few horses they could use them to make quick, lightning strikes against about any herd they chose.

In these ways, the Indians of the Southwest began to obtain a few horses. The horse began to occupy a special place in the Indians' lifestyle and became a valuable possession. All Indians wanted some once they saw what their neighbors were accomplishing with them. The horse gradually spread throughout the Southwest, then up the Mississippi Valley and north along the eastern slope of the Rocky Mountains.

It is noteworthy that the Gulf Coast Indians, such as the Cherokees and Choctaws, never became Horse Indians and, also, that the Woodland Indians of the Northeast and Pacific Coast never abandoned the canoe in favor of the horse. The reasons are simple; the horse offered those Indians few advantages since they did not need the mobility and its use was impractical in the woods. Those Indians were sedentary and well-favored in their food-gathering. The horse gave them nothing except ease in their jaunts, so it wasn't worth bothering with.

An example of the exposure of the southeastern Indians to the horse is afforded by De Soto's meanderings in search of gold, pearls, and the Strait of Anian. The Indians of that region, no doubt, observed the horse and its use, and may have obtained a few of them from that ill-fated, vagabond tour. In the literature there are several inconclusive references to herds of wild horses on the borders of the English colonies in about 1670. This only reveals that horses were known at an early date to the Cherokee, Creek, Choctaw, and other neighboring tribes. But, unlike the Plains Indians, they utilized the horse only to a small extent.

As the Plains Indians became conversant with the horse and saw that it added no burdens to their scramble for existence, they enthusiastically accepted it. The western Indians didn't have to provide for it, as on the plains the horse was self-sustaining. The grass of the Great Plains is different from the grass of the eastern part of the continent. The eastern grasses lose their nutritional value as soon as they are frosted, while the western grasses, commonly lumped together as buffalo grass or short grass, are high in protein and retain that protein all winter, even though frozen. A horse, thus, can forage for itself the year around by pawing through the snow. Its single digit, solid hoof makes an efficient scoop, as contrasted to the cloven hooves of ruminants. This holds true even though there seems to be an exception in that the buffalo is a cloven-hoofed ruminant and had lived in countless numbers on the plains and prairies for millennia, subsisting on grass rather than browse as other ruminants do. The common plains buffalo (differentiated from the woods buffalo variety) also had another characteristic which enhanced their viability on the plains. During winter storms they would resort to wooded areas or well-sheltered valleys until the storm abated, then would venture up to the ridges where the storm had blown away the snow and, using their well-furred muzzle, sweep away what snow remained to get at the grass. During severe storms suffering horses could subsist on cottonwood saplings or branches from which they would peel the bark. Sometimes, during prolonged storms, the Indians would cut such nourishment for them. Also, horses have no quibbles about eating snow as a source of water.

To go back to the Horse Indian culture and how it developed, we will pick up the story again with the Pueblo Indian Revolt of 1680. The horse had become valuable by that time to the Indians, but in short supply considering what they could steal or raise.

The Indian finally became fed up with Spanish policy and rose in revolt in 1680. He drove the Spaniards out of their farthest outlying, scattered posts and holdings in the American Southwest back to the better organized, more settled regions of Mexico. The Indian thus fell heir to vast, unknown numbers of livestock. The only important legacy was the horse since the buffalo already was there as a meat supply. The cattle and sheep of the Spaniards were of little moment to him.

This tremendous herd of horses caused an explosion of Indian-to-Indian trade. The Indians of the Southwest now had a glut of horses. The neighboring tribes could acquire all they wanted and trade them to their neighbors farther removed. This is the reason the early-day literature remarks, wonderingly, about the absence of horses among the tribes on the edge of the Great Plains until around 1700, when chroniclers began to mention the presence of the horse in the Crow, Shoshoni, Pawnee, and Sioux tribes. Those observations speculated in amazement on Spanish brands, bits, and bridles among the horses.

When each tribe obtained enough horses that tribe had the means to move from an area of limited resources, hemmed in by forbidding land and pressure from neighbors similarly situated. Many tribes on the periphery of the Great Plains were thus hemmed in. Now they had the means to escape, opening virgin lands that could be utilized because of the mobility provided by the horse.

Upon that release, the Indians saw a whole new vista, a way of life radically different from their previously accepted limitations. The self-sustaining horse let them follow the buffalo, and they learned to use that animal's meat, hide, and bones to provide an abundance of life's necessities. The laborious, and often unrewarding, chore of raising agricultural products on the fringe of the Great Plains was eliminated: they learned to live off the buffalo exclusively. If they wanted a little corn or a few squash they could always trade with some horticultural tribe still following the age-old way of life.

Wood and water became their only problems. The horse transported them to those needs and kept them in touch with the drifting buffalo herds. A whole new culture, the Horse Indian culture, rapidly came into being. Its basis and practices were so different from the horticultural and canoe Indian life, with aspects so exciting and romantic, that it captured the imagination of the white man and has never become obsolete.

Here was the ripple effect of the horse among the Indians. For example, the Hidatsa were a sedentary tribe living on the upper Missouri River, depending mainly upon horticultural products for a livelihood. Sometime in the past something occurred which caused a disruptive dispute to arise in the tribe. A portion of the tribe split off and moved to the Yellowstone River Valley. This new location was not as good horticulturally as the area they had left, but provided superb buffalo and elk hunting.

These pedestrian Indians, though, were hard put to avail themselves of this alternative source of food. They could kill a buffalo now and then when they had an opportunity to slip up on a herd, or once in a while they would find a herd so positioned that they could get behind it and stampede it over a cliff. Such action would kill or maim some of the buffalo. Another hard, time-consuming recourse was to build a strong corral out of logs and then extend camouflaged wings out from the gate. When a herd of buffalo got in the right position the Indians could then maneuver it into those wings. As soon as the herd was within the wings they would spook it into a crazed run which ended with some of the animals confined in the corral where they could be dispatched with arrows and lances.

None of these three methods was efficient. Buffalo meat was hard to obtain and was only a supplemental food. But when the horse became available the situation was reversed. The Indian, at any time, could search out a herd, ride into it, and kill as many as he needed.

This new mobility changed the Yellowstone River Indians' whole conception of life. They became a roving, nomadic people with a buffalo-oriented way of life. They ranged the Yellowstone Valley and became known as the Absoroka or Crow tribe. The horse and gun were responsible. The mobility provided by the horse to search out the buffalo herds and provide transportation to distant wood and water supplies, and the security assured by the gun, were irresistible to this element of the tribe. The original portion of the tribe, the Hidatsas, were fuddy-duddies who couldn't abandon their age-old way of life.

Again, the portion of the Sioux who were forced into the Missouri Valley also acquired the horse. Since the canoe way of life, in which they had been raised, wasn't practical in this new location, they eagerly seized upon the horse and developed into a far-ranging, nomadic people living off the buffalo.

The already related forced migration of the Cheyenne into the High Plains of South Dakota, Colorado, and Wyoming was made possible by the horse. It had become available in the upper Missouri Valley about the time the Cheyenne had been forced into the Cheyenne River Valley where their ancestral horticultural mode of living was not too profitable. But the horse allowed them to utilize the bounty of the area, to become buffalo hunters rather than corn farmers.

The horse and gun provided the relief valve by which some of the people could escape from this Mississippi-Missouri Valley area of conflict caused by the influx of eastern Indians who had been forced west by gun ripples. The arrival of the horse, coupled with the gun's presence, lightened the pressures building up in this farthest west region in which canoe or pedestrian Indians could prosper.

When these two new influences entered into Indian life, they caused a shuffling and reshuffling of Indian affairs. Shifts in locales and affairs had always occurred in the Indian community, but those shifts were gradual. This new shift was abrupt and dramatic. An apt illustration is provided by the Blackfeet. That tribe had drifted into an area of Canada on the eastern slope of the Rockies and were at a standoff with the Shoshonis, Flatheads, and Kutenais immediately to the south of them. When they began to acquire guns in the early 1700s, they started putting pressure on those neighbors, apparently forcing the Kutenais westward across the Rockies into the Kootenai River

Valley. But about this time the Flatheads and Shoshonis obtained horses and could resist the onslaught of the Blackfeet. It was a balance of power. Then the Blackfeet acquired some horses, probably through trade with the Shoshonis, before the Shoshonis and Flatheads obtained guns. With this preponderance of military might, the Blackfeet then drove the Shoshonis and Flatheads westward into the mountains where the white man found them when he began to penetrate that region.

When the potentiality of the horse was combined with the gun's known potency, we can begin to understand why the fragmentations and dislocations in Indian life were so manifest in the trans-Mississippi West, why the Atsina were peripheral adherents to the Blackfeet Confederacy on the eastern slope of the Rockies, while their blood brothers, the Northern Arapaho, lived on the western edge of those plains. Similarly, the Comanches were a southern Horse Indian of the Great Plains while their relatives, the Shoshonis, were a mountain tribe of the Pacific Northwest.

Of all the white man's impacts upon the Indians, four things stand out as decisive — whiskey, the destruction of the primeval ecosystem, the horse, and the gun. No one of them alone would have led to the rapid destruction of the Indians as a people, but each had an effect, and when their combined effects hit the Indian, he did not have a chance. While white men's diseases took a tremendous toll among the Indians, they probably would have survived and recovered if it hadn't been for these other factors. Perhaps some people will question the inclusion of the horse in this summary, but one must realize that the horse made the Indian independent (tied to no habitat or fixed source of food), able to roam at will and live off the buffalo. The eastern Indian, the first to fall under the white man's dominance, did not have the mobility afforded by the horse, the widespread, constant food source provided by the buffalo, and the security of the gun. He was fated to suffer the agonies imposed on him by the white man. The Plains Indian would have quickly succumbed in the same way except for the horse and gun. Without them, he could not have stood up to the white man. He would have been ground down quickly and relentlessly. As it was, he could tenaciously defend his way of life, prolonging the pain and distress of the transition to the white man's lifestyle. He managed to do so until the white man destroyed the Indian's environment.

Thus, the Horse Indian culture was born on the Great Plains. It was not an age-old, universal culture but had its beginnings about 1700. By the time of the arrival of white people in the trans-Mississippi West in the first decades of the 1800s, it had reached a stage of development that made it unique, differing in all its aspects, from the canoe and woodland Indian cultures. For any people to seize such new opportunities and readily incorporate such a radical change in a culture speaks volumes for the innate intelligence of those people. Very few, if any, parallels can be cited for other peoples in other times.[1]

Bartering. (Courtesy of the National Archives of Canada)

Chapter 5

The Sleep by the Frozen Sea

Sir Arthur Dobbs tauntingly derided the Hudson's Bay Company's actions in its first years as "the sleep by the Frozen Sea." He coined the phrase as an expression of his disgust with the Hudson's Bay Company's failure to find the Northwest Passage.

Dobbs was an Irishman who became interested in expanding imperial trade and conceived the idea that the Northwest Passage provided the only means for accomplishing it. In 1733, 63 years after the formation of the Hudson's Bay Company, he started agitating the British public and officialdom with this idea. He soon found that the charter rights of the Company excluded other people from prowling around Hudson's Bay. In spite of this ban he was so committed to the idea that this denial of exploration rights aroused his Irish temper, and he devoted himself to forcing either the Company or the government into an active search for the passage.

The Company knew there was no passage in the southern reaches of the bay since they had thoroughly traversed the region in establishing their several posts and conducting trade with local Indians. As to the northern portion of the bay, they had, from time to time, over the years, sent several ships to the northward from Fort Churchill to trade with the Inuits (Eskimos), and the crews had been told to keep an eye peeled for any minerals or a northwest passage. After several such trips, the Company had come to the conclusion that no such practical passage existed. Dobbs, though, insisted that they were either hiding the truth or didn't care.

While this bull-baiting was going on in England, the actual trading activity of the Company was suffering from French infiltration around the bay. The Company had its hands full with that problem. La Vérendrye was pushing west from Montreal into the Lake Winnipeg area, causing a drain of the interior Indian trade down into French hands. Other Frenchmen were busy exploring and establishing posts along the rivers that emptied into James Bay, thus cutting into the trade of the Company's Moose and Albany posts. These matters were of immediate and pressing concern as they were causing a falling off of the Company's trade.

For these reasons, the Company resisted Dobbs's efforts to force it into making a major effort to locate the Passage. In addition, the Company was apprehensive that such exploratory efforts would entice interlopers into the fur trade. By 1737, Dobbs was so far estranged from the Company by its refusals to cooperate with him that he obtained legal opinion that, regardless of the charter, every British merchant had a right to trade in the bay. This jockeying between Dobbs and the Company went on until 1745 when Dobbs petitioned for parliamentary help in the search for the passage and for a declaration of open trade in the area. The action wound up in 1749 with a parliamentary inquiry into the whole mess, resulting in the upholding of the Company's position and a refusal to open the trade in the bay.[1] During all this imbroglio Dobbs wrote many pamphlets, broadsides, and statements. To emphasize his position, he stressed the belief that the Company was guilty of being asleep by the Frozen Sea.

Even though his efforts were futile, there is much to be said for his charge. The English, for many, many years, have been called a nation of shopkeepers and, in developing their merchandizing customs, certain tenets became firmly implanted in their conception of trade. The proper way for an Englishman to establish a business was to build or rent a shop, stock it with goods, open the doors, and wait for customers. Any other course was undignified. Flamboyant advertising, crying his wares in the streets, or slyly creating an atmosphere to attract customers was considered a breach of business ethics and was just not done by gentlemen.

Coupled with this business attitude was the English concept of distance. A Londoner who had been to Paris or Edinburgh was well traveled; he had been two or three hundred miles from home. The majority of English never ventured farther than 20 or 30 miles from their fireside. To go farther meant that he would be among strange people with different customs and, maybe, a strange language. Joseph Robson, a one-time laborer and part-time stonemason employed by the Company and later a Dobbs partisan, saw fit to publish an indictment of the Company. In his spiteful diatribe to discredit the Company's claims to the vast extent of territory that it claimed, he wrote of a jaunt of 20 miles or so that he had taken with a companion. In his conclusion he stated, ". . . will easily account for the length of time the [Indians] mention [about their trips to Fort Churchill], without supposing that they come from places at several hundred miles distance, and that the continent is of such prodigious extent to the westward."[2] These principles of merchandising and provincialism were firmly established in eighteenth-century England, even though their mariners had begun to cruise the far reaches of the seas.

Thus, when the Company sent its ships into the bay, unloaded their cargoes and men, and built trading posts, there was no thought but that these were stores after the British manner. The duty and responsibility of the storekeepers were to keep the shop open and serve the customers when they arrived. The activity of the employees was limited to securing firewood, hunting for the larder, packing the traded fur, and similar household chores. For its customers, the Company depended upon chance and Indian inclination. If only a few Indians came to trade, the storekeepers were exhorted by the London Committee to offer better terms of trade, find out if trade items other than those in stock were more desired by the Indians, and to temper the store's attitude in whatever manner necessary to appeal to the Indian. It never occurred to the London Committee or the storekeepers to go out and drum up trade. It was beyond their conception of trade and travel to undertake journeys of several hundred miles in search of Indians and to trade on the spot.

The justly celebrated journeys of Henry Kelsey (1690-1692), Anthony Henday (1754-1755), and Matthew Cocking (1772-1773) out into the High Plains of Canada were instigated by the Company, not as trading ventures, but to solicit the Indians to bring their peltry to Fort Churchill and York Factory for trading. While these men had been sent out into the hinterland to entice the Indians, the official reaction to their journeys was displeasure. The men had been overzealous and had made a lark out of a prosaic business trip by going so far and staying so long. This attitude is shown by a remark in the *Churchill Journal*, concerning Kelsey's trip to the prairies. He was accompanied by a Thomas Savage, apparently an Indian youth attached to Fort Churchill. About a month out from Fort Churchill, Kelsey recorded that he was admonished by Savage for continuing: "I was a fool & yt he would go no further [*sic*] for I was not sensable [*sic*] of the dangers." And when he returned to York Factory he was received by the governor merely with the statement "that I had my labour for my travell since yt ye Govr Never did Require any further acco^t . . . of me."[3]

Bayly, Company governor in 1674,

> saw the remedy to the French outposts [to the south of James Bay] in sending men inland to draw the Indians down to the trade by the Bay. It proved the right and inevitable solution; but it took the Company the best part of a century to carry it out effectively and Bayly, like so many of his successors, was prevented by lack of men and goods from pursuing this course.[4]

This unawareness of the London Committee of the facts of life in Canada was not the only thing that kept the Company's efforts confined to their posts. The post masters were also Englishmen whose minds were colored by the same dye as the Committee's regarding the function of shopkeepers. And their subordinates were men who had been hired on the basis of availability rather than initiative, education, or experience. Few were skilled men — carpenters, blacksmiths, stonemasons, and such — but their employment was for a specific purpose and their abilities ran no further than competency in their craft. The majority of the employees were day-laborers who could be obtained for a yearly stipend of five, six, eight pounds plus their board and lodging. Men of this caliber had no impetus. They were satisfied to draw their grog and rations and to perform no tasks other than the minimum required of them.

Indicative of British storekeepers' conventions and proprieties was the manner in which the Hudson's Bay Company employees reacted to the French-Canadian traders. These Montreal-based traders, with their totally different concept of the proper way to conduct the business, were contemptuously referred to as "pedlars"; they didn't conduct themselves as responsible, circumspect businessmen, but as itinerant gypsies. Such conduct was reprehensible and unbecoming to staid, well-mannered storekeepers. The two ideologies were poles apart. The French, raised in the Saint Lawrence Valley, were familiar with Indians from childhood and having adopted much of the Indian way of life and language, realized that to further trade it was more profitable to take the trade to the Indians, instead of waiting for the Indians to bring in their furs. This venturesomeness by the French forced the Company, against its will, inclination, and judgment to expand into the interior.

As early as 1750, the Company, prodded by the Dobbs incident and the French inroads into its business, began to bestir itself and consider the problem of expansion to inland posts. Such wasn't simple. The bayside people, unfamiliar with canoes, believed them to be totally unsuitable. Boats made on the English pattern for English waters proved unsatisfactory. Finally, as a last resort, the Company tried the costly method of hiring Indians to haul traders with their goods to inland locations. Such transport turned out to be far from desirable. Often the Indians would change their minds and leave the traders stranded halfway to their destination, or abscond with pilfered goods.

Despite its drawbacks Indian transport proved the only way into the interior. Then the problem of manning the new posts had to be solved. English manpower was at a premium. The 13 colonies in America were fomenting a rebellion. France, Spain, and Holland were preparing to even their score with England, and Prussia was eagerly eyeing the opportunity to join those three countries. India, too, was showing signs of unrest.

Nevertheless, the Company sent the necessary goods and men to York Factory. Soon, a whole new set of issues arose. The men had to become accustomed to canoes, be weaned away from the amenities of the bayside posts, and engage in more and different labor than in their previous employment. All these things plus strange Indians who had not developed a response to the white man and his ways proved baffling. The men were up against a mode of existence for which neither their upbringing nor background offered any help. They were timid and made a point of applying British civility to the new customers even though its implications were not grasped by those customers. The Britishers groped their way.

On the other hand, the French-Canadians became embroiled in Indian affairs because they were thoroughly conversant with Indian mores and entered completely into Indian life. They became involved in band or tribal affairs (both internal and external), to the amazement of the English.

There are many short, but telling, remarks unconsciously made in the journals kept by the British inland traders that bring out that frustration.

Samuel Hearne was sent out from York Factory in 1774 to establish an inland post. He selected a site on the Saskatchewan River about 150 miles west of the north end of Lake Winnipeg, calling the post Cumberland House. The Company transferred him to another job the next year, and Matthew Cocking assumed charge of the post. Cocking had traveled through the area previously but had not operated a trading post. But he learned fast. He arrived at Cumberland House on 4 October 1775. On 21 January 1776 his experiences led him to understand that his artifice of sending one or two men at a time with a band of Indians, not to conduct trade but to relieve the pressing food problem at the post, and to have those men invariably return in a short time, was not working. He wrote in his journal, "The Pedlers [*sic*] method it seems is to divide their men into Companies of Six each whom they supply with two Nets and Hooks to provide for themselves. . . ."5 He had the demands of the trade, the country, and the competition boring in on him.

In July he had perceived the mercurial temperament of the inland Indians and found that he could not rely on an understanding that an Indian would trade at his post ". . . as there is no dependence to be had in their Promises this way. . . ."6 He had learned that he needed to employ new tactics such as circulating men with goods through the country to take advantage of the trading whims of the Indians, as the French-Canadians were doing. To implement it was another matter.

Cocking took a cargo of fur to York Factory and conferred with Humphrey Marten, the master of that place, leaving William Tomison in charge of Cumberland House. On 13 September 1776 a new contingent of men arrived from York Factory with a consignment of trade goods. They bore a letter from Marten to Tomison which mentioned the "ill-usage" reportedly practiced by the French-Canadians. The letter instructed Tomison to make every effort to send out trading parties of "not less than Six men (but more if they can be spared) to intercept parties of Indians and trade on the spot." He was admonished, however, that, "the Men you send should be advised to be careful not to say or do anything that could be construed into personal abuse or insult

. . . ."[7] While this instruction referred particularly to dealings with French-Canadians, it indicates the timid approach to the strange situation. Marten went on to write that the Hudson's Bay Company would take "all lawful Means" to protect the men and property.

Cocking returned to take charge of the post, and its affairs continued in the same tenor as before. Cocking, apparently in a despondent mood, remarks in the journal on 24 January 1777:

> I believe the chief reason of our Men not being well with the Natives; Is their not being affable and otherwise endeavoring to make themselves agreable [sic] seemingly frequently displeased and unwilling to render little Assistances in their way. Our Men some of them like very well to go off at first with the Indians, as they are removed from under the Eye of a Master and expect to have nothing to do; There are none of the Indians who are exempted from endeavoring to obviate the necessities of themselves and families, the appelation [sic] of a Gentleman being unknown among them; Therefore no wonder that they require our men also to render some help, which they are unwilling to do; by this means they become dissatisfied with each other and our Men the first opportunity they get of coming in, will make some complaint Such as Ill Usage, want of Provisions &c.[8]

The British still had not learned to be salesmen as indicated by this passage, and Cocking's further remark of 10 December 1779 reinforces his above complaint by stating, "I do assure Your Honour's its dangerous to send men with the Natives at present, as several of them is of a very savage nature."[9]

Professor Rich, in his introduction to the Second Series of the above-mentioned journals, offers an apology for this constant British difficulty in developing a steady trade with a dependable clientele. He wrote, referring to the attempts to send men out among the Indians to trade or stimulate trade: "This all too intimate relationship is notoriously less easy than the mere intermittent contacts of good business acquaintance."[10] Yet, the French-Canadians made it work because they were aggressive and met the Indians on their own ground and within the Indians' periphery of reference.

The British reliance on English law and English ways is reflected in their growing antagonism to the "Pedlars." The English were not gaining on those "Pedlars" in the competition, and their growing resentment found expression in calling for the application of English law to the trade. In one instance, some Indians came to Cumberland House with the story that the French-Canadians had kidnapped some Indian men on suspicion that the Indians, maybe, had killed a Frenchman. The journal records the story and continues: ". . . it is a pitty [sic] that Government should allow such a parcel [sic] of villians to spoil the Natives. . . ."[11] Previously, the same whining was recorded on 11 May 1780:

> I find by those [Indians] that arrived yesterday, Your Honor's have lost two Bea[ver] Coats, which I sent an Indian man and his Wife in the Winter marked with your Honour's mark and at the same time informed the Canadian trader thereof not to trade the said coats, as they belonged to your Honor': This I think is not consistent with the English Law's, as I can deem it nothing but plain robbery. . . .[12]

The Britishers were whistling in the dark as the Montrealers ignored British law in the far reaches of Upper Canada. Who was there to administer it? And the Indian was completely ignorant of its existence.

On the other hand, the French-Canadians had grown up along the Saint Lawrence River and had been intimate with Indians since childhood, and, as they grew up, had spent time living with Indians for short periods. They understood Indian philosophy, custom, tradition, language, and mores. As they matured they absorbed fur-trading lore from their fathers, uncles, and the patriarchs of the community. When they entered the trade they met the Indian as an equal and could live with the Indian as an Indian.

The new, novice British trader at the English posts could not understand this familiarity. To the Britisher it was gross, crass, and entirely unbecoming. Nor did this beginning of routine traffic between Hudson's Bay Company posts and distant Indians result in an overwhelming desire by Company personnel to probe and develop their own trade extension. The Company directed its expansion efforts against the French-Canadians rather than trying to bypass the Indian middlemen. The Company still did not comprehend that certain favorably situated Indians in their application of age-old Indian trade principles were availing themselves of a middleman's effortless existence. The Company could undermine that drain on profit by adopting an aggressive salesman's "door-to-door" approach. The London, bayside, and inland personnel were intimidated by the problems inherent in such an expansion. And, besides, that was not the way to conduct a proper store, nor were the men hired for such duty. The Britishers constantly berated the French-Canadians as mere "Pedlars" who employed underhanded practices and engaged in squabbles and vulgar arguments with the Indians.

These frictions originated from the basic differences between the Hudson's Bay Company and the early French-Canadian trader, before the ultimate development of the North West Company. The London Committee of the Hudson's Bay Company was concerned with a long-range mercantile program, anticipating steady dividends on their capital stock year after year, while the first stirrings of the embryonic North West Company were made by individuals trying to turn a yearly profit. These given conditions generated different impulses. The Hudson's Bay Company demanded a steady, plodding, methodical development of a stable trade base. The French-Canadians, with an uppercrust of Scot and Yankee supervisors, were individual entrepreneurs struggling for enough annual profit to pay their way and leave enough surplus to enable them to enlarge their operations the next year. In the back of their minds were visions of being able to retire within a few years.

The prior French government had compounded the problems of the French traders by constantly vacillating from one policy to another. This experience with government had set the pattern and ideology of the Canadian traders even though they were now under British political control — the fall of Quebec having preceded the Hudson's Bay Company's penetration of the interior. The Canadian traders, through the years, had developed a contempt for edicts, laws, and directives issuing from a government.

To a possible charge that I'm making a mountain out of a molehill, let us look at other early English endeavors in the English colonies to the south. We will find they all fit the same pattern.

Since Albany became the foremost fur-trading center of the English colonies, we will start by considering the development of the trade at that point. The Dutch were the first people to settle there. They began trading with the Indians at Manhattan and then pushed the trade progressively up the Hudson River as far as navigation permitted. At this farthest reach they established a settlement which they named Fort Nassau (not to be confused with the later Fort Nassau on the Delaware River). The sole purpose of this outpost was to engross the fur trade for the Dutch New Netherland Company. No other consideration entered into its founding. Due to its strategic location Fort Nassau achieved immediate success, and, since the parent company was interested only in immediate profit, the Company limited the outpost's activity to the fur trade and forbade any person going outside the fort to trade directly with the Indians. Any such activity would cut into the Company's profits and, most likely, would lead to smuggling of fur out of the country with a complete loss to the Company.[13] The Dutch had matured in the same mercantile tradition that the English had and operated in the same manner and for the same reasons.

Due to Dutch financial maneuverings, the New Netherland Company was reorganized into the Dutch West Indies Company, which continued the policies and purposes of its parent company. About this time, the name of the post was changed to Fort Orange, and grants of land were made to proprietors of the Company. These grantees, interested in stuffing their pockets (their reason for owning stock in the Company), began to encourage trade with the Indians by the settlers on the granted tracts. By this hocus-pocus, contrary to standing orders of the Company, the stockholders would realize more profit than if the trading went through regular Company channels.

Finally, the whole New York area passed into English hands in 1664, and the little town was rechristened Albany. In accordance with the requirements of the new government, land had to be purchased from the Indians, the deed had to be approved by the governor and recorded, and any new settlements had to be compact and close together. The English could not envision a viable society developing from dispersed, nonstable communities.

All this change did not alter the basic characteristics of Albany. The Dutch continued to live there and dominate the economy, reiterating their position that all trading must be done within the town. They maintained this stance in the face of the English inclination to make land grants in the Hudson River Valley. They would not "suffer others to goe [*sic*] beyond them [the walls of Albany] to intercept the trade." They tried all kinds of ordinances and prohibitions to insure adherence to this policy. At times, they designated certain stores as the only places where trading could be conducted, no liquor was to be given or traded to the Indians, no enticement of Indians into stores or homes, no meetings with Indians outside the town hall. They even went so far as to build cabins outside the town for Indians to sleep in and allowed Indians in the town only during certain hours of the day. But to no avail. Ambitious and energetic men continued to violate the bans, slipping off into the woods to trade with the Indians and then, by subterfuge or in cahoots with Albany merchants, getting the peltry into the Albany economy or taking it to New York.[14] The Albany merchants pressured officials, from the governor and Indian agents down to local magistrates, to inveigh against this practice on the grounds that it was "considered dangerous in principle for colonists to mix in Indian affairs."[15]

By the end of the seventeenth century, the demands of the trade and the widespread disregard of these self-assumed prerogatives of the Albany merchants forced a relaxation of the adamant attitude. The merchants recognized the inevitable and expanded their activity to include Indian country trading either by means of outpost sites or by emissaries traveling through the Indian country with a stock of goods. Prolonged contact with the conditions in the New World forced a new concept on their old ideas.

When this new trading policy went into effect, the Dutch immediately came into contact with the Iroquois Confederacy. The Five Nations had long seen the advantage of being middlemen in the trade. They had depleted their stock of fur-bearing animals by this time, but had become addicted, often to their detriment, to the new mode of life ushered in by the trade goods. They were now serving as middlemen between the Dutch and farther tribes and between Albany and Montreal. The French colony was, for several reasons, leading a precarious existence. Its sole support was the fur trade, and the French officials were determined that all revenue produced by the colony would be enjoyed solely by France, Therefore, there was a strict embargo against any trade outside except with Mother France.

The English also looked askance at any trade with Montreal or Quebec, because it would strengthen their neighbor to the north and they didn't want that. But there was money to be made in such exchange, and the French and Dutch traders couldn't overlook it. So the Five Nations, chiefly the Caughnawaga Mohawks, entered into a smuggling pact — French fur into Albany and English goods into Montreal. While the Albany merchants stood in their front doors mouthing imprecations against the knavish French, they made sure the back door was unlatched for the Mohawks. At the same time, they began sending Dutch, English, and Indian emissaries into the Great Lakes region to actively trade in the Indian country. These acts parallel the Hudson's Bay Company's decision to enter into the inland trade.[16]

Having made this comparison, let's look at the Massachusetts area. While that area had two groups, the Puritans and the Pilgrims, they were both founded at about the same time and by men who were contemporaries. They were financially tied into the British mercantile system. It was their backing, their only means of securing a foothold. The English at this time were operating strictly on the mercantile theory of economics. A good summary of that theory was expressed in 1721 by a resolution in the English House of Commons, which stated: "to make exportation of our own manufactures and the importation of the commodities used in the manufacturing of them as practical and easy as may be."[17]

The well-being of the "tight little Isle" was paramount and all portions of the economy — industry, agriculture, sea traffic, and commerce of all kinds — had as its main function the observance of regulations on trade to produce the greatest profit for England. An example was the English perception that the export of raw wool to Holland, where it was processed into woolen goods, eliminated profit for England. The English immediately promoted the manufacture of woolen goods within England, converting unemployed English hands to furthering national goals. The success of this maneuver prompted other innovations. Instead of selling any product to any buyer, England stimulated the processing of material into finished products and promoted trading companies to distribute the goods in the world markets, returning with raw material to be processed by English hands.

This policy was shortsighted in that all eyes were focused on immediate profit rather than long-range goals. The immediate profit goals were set by politicians and leading trading companies on the basis of the broad spectrum of trade in the empire and caused vitriolic differences between the powers that were and the small businessman in any colony, be it Massachusetts or Jamaica.

While the purse strings of colonial trade were being pulled and relaxed by considerations of world trade, such considerations were of no moment to colonial merchants in their struggle for existence. The colonist was understandingly concerned with only pennies of profit in his daily transactions within the compass of his small community.[18] The American colonies shipped cargoes of butter, flour, meat, timber, and lumber to the West Indies under this price control and received in return sugar, molasses, rum, indigo, mahogany, and ready money.

At the same time, these merchants were shipping surplus commodities, as they could be scraped together, to England. These products, except for fur, were basic items more or less in good supply to the British wholesalers who had no crying need for them, and demurred paying more than the bottom price in a volatile market. The products included corn, wheat, flour, linseed, walnut and oak lumber, medium-quality iron, hides, fish, fur, and tar. The colonies needed, in return, articles of more value, such as fine and coarse cloth, linen, wrought metals, and manufactured goods of all kinds.[19]

Class distinctions further complicated relations between England and the colonial merchants. Imperial policy was set by the upper stratum of society. The large wholesaler group belonged to the upper middle class, while the retailer was traditionally from a socially inferior group whose wants and desires were subservient to the other groups. These points affected the colonial methods and manner of trade.

The explorer Gosnold, coming out of England in 1602, traded with the Indians for some fur during his search for a cargo of sassafras. In 1603 Martin Pring, also searching for sassafras, remarked on the possibility of a profitable trade in furs, saying that he had been informed that the French, in one year, had taken to France fur valued at "Thirty thousand Crownes." George Weymouth, in 1604, traded "knives, glasses, combs, and other trifles to the value of four or five shillings" for "forty good Beaver skins, Otter skins, Sables, and other small skins."

Captain John Smith, in 1614, came over here to kill whales for their oil or to find a gold or silver mine. Failing in that, he resorted to fishing. While most of the crew fished, Smith, with a few crew members, ranged the immediate coastline and traded with the Indians. They successfully acquired "for trifles near 1100 Beaver skins, 100 Martins, [*sic*] and near as many Otters."[20]

These results and other reports were the major inducement for English merchants to finance the Pilgrims' and Puritans' venture to these shores.

Immediately upon the founding of the Massachusetts colonies, the fur trade was recognized as a ready-made source of income to satisfy the colonies' backers and creditors in England. Setting up the trade, though, was a matter of much concern. The colonists, knowing their predicament in this new land, decided that it should be a communal project. They wanted it under control so they could channel the proceeds to their backers and so no man could become rich to the exclusion of other colonists or become a disruptive influence in their dream of a new life.[21] Initially, they decreed that Indian trade could be carried on in only one designated house and under set terms. Adventurous and unscrupulous characters soon made a mockery of this program. The method was then changed to the licensing of "persons of good character" (meaning men who met the criteria of the colony's leaders) to conduct the Indian trade. This change entailed the payment of either a flat tax per skin or a fee to be paid to the colony, and was part of an attempt to regulate the colony's affairs by prescribing rules for the fishing industry, the operation of sawmills, and prohibiting trade outside the colony.

As happened so frequently in these first attempts to formulate a new lifestyle by edict, this concept didn't endure. The fishing fleets caused a breakdown because the fishermen couldn't resist the opportunity to trade for fur with the Indians along the coast. As accommodation of this stituation was forced upon the colony, it relaxed its rules and established fur-trading posts on the Kennebec and Penobscot Rivers. The needs of the growing colony dictated land-based expansion into other settlements. These new villages could be, by new rules, founded only by the consent of the General Court which mandated that all such new settlements must be compact and planned. Needless to say, the General Court was particular in approving these expansions. The settlers had to be members of a team, not lone scouts or intrepid pioneers, and the Court was exceedingly reluctant to approve any expansion beyond a few miles as it was fearful of losing contact with and supervision over the new entity.

This new policy led to an expansion of the fur trade and excited some individuals with the trade's prospects. Eventually, the controls on the trade broke down and the trade alternated from *laissez-faire* to a complete cessation and on to prohibition. The desperate financial straits of the colonies finally caused a resumption of the trade.[22] During this vacillating time, the colonies settled up with the London creditors and received full right to the fur trade. This step was taken for the welfare of the colonies, as the bickering and accounting methods of the London brokers caused much dissatisfaction.[23] The colonies now began to expand because the "hive of the Commonwealth is so full that Tradesmen cannot live one by another."[24] Thomas Weston, in defiance of the authorities, set up a trading post in the vicinity of Boston. He was driven out after a short time by Thomas Morton who continued to thumb his nose at all attempts to bring him into line. Morton was finally seized by Miles Standish and sent to England. William Pynchon went through the proper channels for permission to found a trading post in the "interior." He called it Agawan, and it soon became a thriving community. Today it is called Springfield. As part of this new burst of mercantilism, the Laconia Company was formed. It was authorized to organize a headquarters at the mouth of the

Piscataqua River and exploit the trade in the interior toward Lake Champlain in hopes that the French monopoly of the trade in the area could be broken. It has been called "one of the first deliberate attempts by one of the rival fur trading nations to outflank its opponent."[25]

We have seen that the colonists of New York and Massachusetts followed the same course for which Dobbs ridiculed the Hudson's Bay Company. Now, let us turn our attention to the situation in the Middle Colonies.

The Allegheny Mountains were a forbidding barrier to the Middle Colonies. By the middle 1700s, men — Conrad Weiser, Christopher Gist, and George Croghan being the most prominent — began to wander into the Ohio Valley. However, this was enough later than the period covered by the New York and Massachusetts trade efforts that the same conditions didn't apply. The colonies were no longer feeling out their economy and were not totally dependent upon England.

When the first traders entered the Ohio Valley they found several unexpected conditions confronting them. The French had been trading there for many years, the Indians were accustomed to white men and their goods, the French constantly reminded the Indians of the English proclivity of seizing Indian lands, and the French had secured the Indians' loyalty.

The merchants eagerly backed the traders when they heard of this new territory. They had visions of a gold mine. The Ohio Valley was vast and full of fur and prosperous Indians.

But the gold mine failed to yield any gold. The Indians were suspicious of the English and the French were their good friends. The trade languished while the Indians mulled over their resentment of the English land policy and realized that they could play the French and English traders against each other to the Indians' advantage. In desperation the English traders began to use threats and force which, in turn, further antagonized the Indians.[26]

The profits turned out to be minimal, and the merchants became increasingly reluctant to underwrite trading ventures, demanding that prior debts be settled and future requirements be kept current and on a cash basis. This turn of events put an economic pressure on traders in the Pennsylvania-Ohio region that was not present in the earlier, northern trade. Even after the defeat of France by Great Britain at Quebec and the treaty of 1763, which extinguished all French claims to the area east of the Mississippi River, the English traders continued their mode of operation. The new political situation gave them a free hand in their dealings and they took advantage of the opportunity. Men with dreams of large-scale land speculation and visions of lucrative Indian trade to finance it flocked into the area. The traders were "rash and unprincipled men who did not scuple [*sic*] to cheat and insult their Indian clients at every opportunity."[27] An observation by a contemporary writer reinforces this assessment. John Sergeant, in 1741, reported that the Shawnee

Indians "had a prejudice against Christians, at least Protestants, 'derived it seems from the French, and confirmed by their own observation of the behavior of that vile sort of men, the Traders, that go among them; for they said (which I believe an unhappy and reproachful truth) that they would lie, cheat; and debauch their women, and even their wives, if their husbands were not at home.[28]

The Indian trade and traders with whom the average American is familiar got that way because the Ohio Valley trade produced the future pattern of American-Indian trading relations that expanded from the Cumberland Gap through the Old Northwest, up the Missouri River from Saint Louis, and on out into the Santa Fe Trail and Oregon Trail areas.

To return to the early phases of the colonial trade and make a comparison between it and the Hudson's Bay Company's attitude, we can see that the Hudson's Bay Company did not have a strange, illogical, benighted, or parochial attitude toward the Indians and their trade. Rather, it was the customary and accepted method of the times and in conformity with the English mores of the period. By using later standards, the term "sleep by the Frozen Sea" seems apt, but using the customs and ideology of the time and place, it was the normal English practice.

Chapter 6

The Rendezvous

The rendezvous was a unique American innovation that developed in the waning years of the fur-trade era. It was a flamboyant, exciting, romantic institution ideally suited to the needs of fiction and the movies, but it needs to be placed in its proper perspective — a minor, last gasp flowering that served its purpose in the hectic days of an economic expansion period and which, combined with industrialization, made inroads into the base of the fur needs of the populace.

After the Louisiana Purchase, a westward expansion mood seized the American people. As part of that, Americans rushed into the new country to make their fortune since there was money to be made in fur. The dream was to make a fortune *now* and then retire to a life of leisure and the fruits of the fortune.

In the pell-mell course to cash in on the fur trade, trappers soon exhausted the quick profits to be had in the easily accessible sites. The Missouri and Mississippi River areas, with their tributaries, were soon overrun. Frantically, the men sought new sources of beaver. They found it on the High Plains and in the Rocky Mountains.

This drive for quick wealth led them to discard the Indian as the sole collector. They did not completely abandon the Indian trade but relied on their own efforts more.

In so doing the trapper assumed a burden that was to his disadvantage. He had to spend valuable days and much effort traveling between his supply point and the Rockies — time he could spend to better advantage in searching out new trapping grounds.

A man with vision and drive, William Ashley, conceived the idea of forsaking the accepted formula and substituting the carrying of trade goods by pack horses onto the High Plains and into the Rocky Mountains to temporary, floating trading posts.

"The Rendezvous." The rendezvous was always held in a wide mountain valley accessible to both trappers and Indians. It was held during the summer and afforded the trappers a release from a year's hard work. They caroused, drank, gambled, raced horses, and fought. The collected Indians enthusiastically entered into the fun and frolic. (Sketch by Debie Doble)

Ashley didn't dream this up out of a fertile mind but was pushed into it by the cutthroat competition, the treacherous Missouri, and the troublesome Indians.

The Indian troubles had developed along with the trade. As merchandise became increasingly available along the river, the river Indians saw an opportunity. By blocking farther penetration of the upriver country, the upriver Indians would be denied an opportunity to obtain goods firsthand. Further, by seizing the goods or levying a heavy tribute, the river Indians could obtain a supply of trade items for nothing, and when those items were entered into the Indian trade channels, the result would be all profit. And, importantly, by exerting their force of arms, they often could count coup, which was a very important part of life.[1]

Ashley, with Andrew Henry, an experienced mountain man, as his second in command, first ventured up the Missouri River in April 1822, having organized and outfitted in Saint Louis, Missouri. The party numbered about 100 men and had one boatload of merchandise.[2] Ashley's plan was to send Henry with part of the men as far as the three forks of the river (the river, by this late date, had become well known), build a more or less permanent post, and stay three years. He intended to explore and trap the various rivers "under the Mountains," and even envisioned going as far as the mouth of the Columbia River.[3] Ashley remained in Saint Louis outfitting another boat with merchandise. On 8 May that boat was dispatched upriver, but on 1 June word filtered back to Saint Louis that the boat had struck a snag and sunk several hundred miles upstream, losing all the cargo but no men. Ashley immediately set about getting another boat and cargo ready. About 20 June he, with 46 men, set out upriver.[4]

Meanwhile, the advance party under Henry continued its way upriver, beset by no more than the normal vexations and troubles. The harassing Indians, and principal offenders, the Sioux and the Arikaras, either were dispersed on buffalo hunts or were in an amiable mood. Henry's only major problem was that the Assiniboines had stolen the horses that he had bought for the hunters of the party. He arrived at the mouth of the Yellowstone River about 1 September and immediately set about building some permanent quarters.

The Ashley party, following along as fast as it could, also seemed to be singularly blessed that year as they had no trouble with the Indians either. In fact, when Ashley reached the Arikaras he immediately purchased some horses from them and with a few men proceeded overland to Henry's building site, leaving the boat to follow as fast as it could. The boat arrived at the post about the middle of October. As soon as it arrived, Ashley stored its cargo of goods, made final arrangements with Henry for the conduct of the business during the winter, loaded the boat with what fur they had obtained, and skedaddled back down the river for Saint Louis. Once there, he began making plans and purchasing goods for the resupply of the post for the summer of 1823.

Henry spent the fall getting his living quarters in livable condition and then dispatched detachments of men in various directions up and down the river and its tributaries to trap. Of course, he also traded for any skins the Indians brought into the post.[5]

The men who were trapping started out using boats which they soon found to be impractical. The keelboats they had used on the lower river were large, unwieldy contraptions that had to be poled upstream or dragged by means of ropes manned by men walking along the bank. Even pirogues made of hollowed-out tree trunks were heavy and clumsy. And there were no birch-bark canoes in the area. The birch tree grew only around and north of the Great Lakes, while the elm, the bark of which was used for canoes by the eastern Indians south of the Great Lakes, did not grow in this area to a size suitable for canoes. Thus, these trappers soon found themselves sorely limited as these High Plains streams were shallow and ran rapidly. The trappers soon learned that horses provided the best transport needs in this new locale.

While all this was going on in the upper reaches of the Missouri River, Ashley was busy down in Saint Louis buying a new supply of trade goods and arranging for more boats and a crew to resupply Henry's post for the forthcoming year. On 10 March 1823 all was ready, and he left Saint Louis with a new crew and two keelboats full of supplies.[6] But this trip upriver turned out to be far from the uneventful, prosaic journey of the preceding year. For some reason, the Arikaras had become belligerent during the winter. Perhaps they regretted letting the previous year's merchandise get up to their erstwhile customers, the Crows. Whatever the reason, when Ashley's party arrived at the Arikara villages he found those Indians prepared to oppose any further progress. Since his keelboats were clumsy to maneuver and the Arikara villages were in a position to dispute Ashley's passage, he anchored out in midstream and went ashore in a skiff to parley. The upshot was that the Arikaras agreed to be peaceful and to trade for the horses that Ashley wanted to reinforce the few that Henry had at his post.

The next day, trading for the horses got under way, but in the afternoon the negotiations hit a snag when the Arikaras began demanding guns and ammunition. Trading was suspended for the day to let tempers cool and to reappraise the situation.

The next morning brought a severe wind and rainstorm that effectively stymied all efforts to move the horses to safer ground or to start the boats on upriver. Parleys were held during the day, but the Arikaras were in an ugly mood and nothing was accomplished. During the night an uproar broke out in the Arikara town. At dawn, they opened fire on both the boats and the men on shore who were guarding the horses. The attack was severe and with the

Ashley party split, no concerted resistance could be made. Finally, the men ashore took to the river and tried to swim to the boats. At the same time, the boats were cast adrift to float out of range.

Thirteen of Ashley's men were killed outright and eleven wounded, two of them mortally. Ashley had to withdraw as the casualties amounted to about one-sixth of his force with most of the fit men being greenhorns who were bug-eyed over any thought of reengaging the Arikaras. He dropped on down the river to an island far enough from the "Rees" to be safe and asked for volunteers to carry a message to Henry at the mouth of the Yellowstone. Jedediah Smith and another man stepped forward. When they left on their mission Ashley continued on downriver with the two boats. One boat stopped at the Cheyenne River and the other, carrying the wounded, went on down to Fort Atkinson for medical assistance.

Colonel Leavenworth, commanding this army outpost, and Benjamin O'Fallon, the Indian agent stationed there, decided that punitive action against the Arikaras was decidedly in order. As a whole, the Indians along the river had become more and more bold, and a good chastisement of the Arikaras should have a salutary effect upon all the Indians.

Leavenworth started upriver with six companies of infantry. En route, he persuaded some Sioux to join, by luring them with the prospect of loot and counting coup. He joined forces with Ashley on 30 July. Ashley had been reinforced during this time. When Jed Smith reached Henry's post, Henry had immediately loaded his furs and men and started down the river at express speed.

When he got to the Arikaras, he boomed right by them, even though they, by means of signals, professed friendship. On 9 August Leavenworth and Ashley had reached the Ree villages and went into action. The Sioux, however, in their impetuosity, fouled up the effectiveness of the white forces. The attack, while leaving much to be desired, forced the Rees to withdraw into their palisaded villages. Leavenworth then decided to wait for his artillery to come up. The artillery arrived late in the evening. The bombardment started the next morning, but by noon had achieved no results. Leavenworth then vacillated between storming the villages or withdrawing from this fortified position of the Rees. The Sioux became disgusted and went home.

Late in the afternoon a parley was arranged, and Leavenworth, mindful of the fact that he had entered into this fracas without sanction of higher authority, agreed to a settlement. The Arikaras agreed to restore Ashley's property, behave in the future, and send five hostages to Fort Atkinson. The negotiations continued the next day since the Rees were making no effort to return Ashley's goods and horses. That night the Rees decamped, leaving Leavenworth in possession of the battlefield — but nothing else.[7]

This fiasco dampened Ashley's and Henry's vision of the river as a broad highway to the riches of the mountains and plains. The other traders who were thronging the area took alarm from this incompetent foray and pulled back from their farthest outposts, retrenching in what they thought were secure positions. Thus, the High Plains and Rocky Mountains with their untouched wealth in fur were up for grabs. A determined, maybe bullheaded, Ashley resolved to tap their reservoir come hell-or-high-water. To this end, he started buying horses from the Indians, mostly the Sioux, and as soon as he had the minimum number Henry started overland with the goods he dug up from the cache at the Cheyenne River. After more borrowing and buying of horses along his route, Henry sent Jed Smith with a few men toward the Black Hills of South Dakota, where the Sioux told him there were other Sioux bands who had a surplus of horses.

After some straying around and other vicissitudes, Jed's party finally went into winter quarters on the Wind River alongside some Crows. As soon as winter began to wane, the party set out, after receiving directions from the Crows, up the Popo Agie River and down to the Sweetwater. There they turned west and went through South Pass, crossing the continental divide, to Green River. Here they found a plentitude of beaver and spent the remainder of the spring trapping.[8]

The various small detachments of this party were to gather again on the Sweetwater River about the middle of June. By the time they had all gathered, the river was so much in flood from the spring runoff of the mountain snows that Smith decided to build a boat of buffalo hides stretched over a willow framework (a bull boat) and float the fur down the Platte to Ashley at Fort Kiowa on the Missouri River. Three men were assigned this job, the remainder of the party returning westward for another winter's trapping.

* * *

We must now go back to Henry's party where we left them on the Missouri River just beginning their trek overland for the mouth of the Yellowstone River. Henry followed the banks of the river upstream only a short way when, apprehensive of more Indian trouble, he veered off to the west. Upon reaching the fort, he found that it had been vandalized by Indians. This was not a serious blow to his plans since he wanted to move closer to the untouched beaver territory anyway. Such a move would put him farther into Crow territory and afford some protection as the Crows were friendly to the traders, even though they would and did steal the traders blind at every opportunity, and bragged about it. They also bragged that they had never harmed a white man because, if they did, they knew they would alienate the white man and he would forsake them. Then they would have no trade goods brought to them, nor would they have anything to steal. Henry went as far as the Powder River, where rapids put an end to boat travel. Obtaining some horses from the Crows, he went on up to the mouth of the Big Horn River where he built a new post.

Henry had managed to penetrate well into the High Plains so that his trapping parties, which he immediately sent out, would have their travel distances to and from their base considerably shortened.

For some reason Henry decided to send a message to Ashley, who had gone back to Missouri, where he was running for governor, and making no effort to obtain a supply of goods for the upcoming year. This "express" to Ashley resulted in a momentous decision. Knowing that the Missouri River was frozen over this time of the year, the group went up the Big Horn River from Henry's post, crossed over to the North Platte River, and down it to the Missouri River. After they had delivered their message to Ashley, Fitzpatrick's fur-bearing party dispatched by Jedediah Smith also showed up. Then Henry came down from the Big Horn post, abandoning it as he had had nothing but trials and losses trying to maintain and supply it.

But that summer of 1824 had been all bad news. Two different parties, Fitzpatrick and the "express," had found their way down the Platte River. Discussion and reflection soon revealed that this route offered a direct way into the heart of the High Plains and Rocky Mountains. Jed Smith had found an easy pass (South Pass) through those mountains to the Columbia River drainage. Smith had also found a country rich in fur. By using the Platte Valley all the Indian troubles of the upper Missouri River could be avoided. The distance from Saint Louis to this rich fur country was cut in half. It didn't take long for Ashley to comprehend these points. Without delay he got a license to trade "with a band of Snake Indians, West of the Rocky Mountains."[9] For some reason, Henry declined to participate any further in this trapping business. Ashley hoped he would change his mind, but he didn't and resumed the operation of his lead mine at Potosi, Missouri.

Ashley was in such a hurry to try to tap this new mother lode of fur that he started out from Saint Louis on 3 November 1824 with a packtrain of supplies, abandoning the time-honored Missouri River mode of travel. This date of departure is strange. Ashley should have known, and his men undoubtedly knew, of the severity of the winters on the plains, especially when all they had for protection was a few blankets and what shelter they could find under bluffs or in thickets. The journey was slow and far from pleasant. Ashley finally made it over to the Pacific Slope by the way of today's Bridger's Pass, arriving on the Green River on 19 April 1825. He immediately sent out two parties to trap and took the remainder on down the river 40 or 50 miles to a suitable place for a "rendavouse." This group then split up to trap. All these parties had instructions to meet "on or before 10th July next."[10] By the first of July all his detachments, even Jed Smith, who had gotten the word somehow, were gathered on the Green River. This first rendezvous numbered 120 men including 29 stragglers who had deserted the "Snake Country Brigade" of the Hudson's Bay Company.

Ashley, having picked up the fur brought in by the trappers and made distribution of fresh supplies, left the rendezvous on 2 July 1825 and proceeded to the Big Horn River where he embarked his crew and cargo in bullboats for a return to Saint Louis by way of the Big Horn, Yellowstone, and Missouri Rivers. This route was time consuming. He did not reach Saint Louis unil 4 October, but his cargo of fur was reported to be worth $50,000, a tremendous sum for those days, and a remarkable return on his investment in trade goods, which was said to have been $10,000.[11]

Just 26 days after reaching Saint Louis, Jedediah Smith, who had accompanied Ashley on the return trip, left Saint Louis with 70 men, 160 horses and mules, and an assortment of goods worth $20,000. He went overland again by way of the Missouri, Big Blue, and Platte Rivers to Cache Valley, the place designated at the 1825 rendezvous for the next year's rendezvous. Jed immediately sent out parties from there for the winter and spring trapping seasons.

On 8 March 1826 Ashley also left Saint Louis with a consignment of goods. The information on his route and experience has been lost, but he arrived at the rendezvous and traded for 125 packs of beaver worth $60,000. Tired of this strenuous life, and satisfied with the profits he had made, he sold his interest in this merchandising business to Jedediah Smith, David Jackson, and William Sublette. He returned to Saint Louis by the land route down the Platte River and saved several weeks of travel. This was the end of his active participation as a trapper. From this time on he lived in Saint Louis and acted as purchasing agent for the actual trappers.

The feasibility and practicality of this new method of conducting the fur trade was apparent to everyone concerned. The trappers could stay in the fur country the year round, trapping in the spring and fall, spending the winters in a choice location, and then moseying from the location of their spring "hunt" a short distance to the rendezvous where they turned in their catch, resupplied themselves for the forthcoming year, turned in orders for supplies to be furnished at the next year's rendezvous, and went back to trapping. This method was much better than the old way of spending weeks traipsing to and from a base many hundreds of miles away with the attendant weather and Indian troubles. For the supply train, it meant a shorter journey on a broad highway of land rather than water, and quicker turnover on the investment. Also, the supply train was in a better military position. It could maneuver its force on land to avoid confrontations or more quickly assume a better defensive position than if it were confined to a river and burdened with clumsy boats.

It didn't take the Indians and independent trappers long to find out about the rendezvous and that trading could be done there. Each year saw increasingly larger numbers come in to barter.

By 1827, the rendezvous attracted some Shoshoni Indians who brought in their fur and other trade items and a party of Blackfeet who attacked the Shoshoni, but were driven off by the camp. Accounts mention that there were 300 white trappers in attendance that year. If that figure is correct, there were many more trappers there than those belonging to the Smith, Jackson, Sublette entourage.[12]

The 1828 rendezvous was held at the south end of Bear Lake. The supplies had arrived at the site early and some early trading ensued, but most trading was held off for the regular rendezvous. There were about 60 or 70 white men and several hundred Indians who participated in the fun and games. Since the supplies had arrived in November 1827, there would be no pack train available to take the collected fur to Saint Louis, so William Sublette took the fur back and spent the winter in Saint Louis getting together trade goods for the next spring.[13]

Before breaking up the 1828 rendezvous the partners of the trapping company had selected Pierre's Hole, on the border of Idaho and Wyoming, as the place for the 1829 meeting. But Sublette and Campbell had a rump rendezvous on the Popo Agie River, and Campbell immediately left for Saint Louis with the fur. Sublette went on to Pierre's Hole for the regular meeting. Supposedly, there were 175 whites at this meeting, which means that there were a lot of free trappers in attendance. There must also have been some Indians present but there is no record of them. The next rendezvous was scheduled for the junction of the Popo Agie and Wind Rivers.

The rendezvous of 1830 was unique. Sublette had 81 mounted men, ten wagons, two Dearborn carriages, 12 head of cattle, and one milk cow. This was the first time anyone had attempted to take wagons across the Continental Divide. The inclusion of a milk cow can be understood, but why the cattle when buffalo were so plentiful? At this rendezvous Smith, Jackson, and Sublette sold out to another group of trappers who called the new organization the Rocky Mountain Fur Company. Why this sale occurred has never been solved. It seems likely that the partners saw the depletion of fur in the central region and realized the operations would have to be transferred northward into Blackfeet country. Such a move would meet serious competition from traders operating on the upper Missouri River and from the Hudson's Bay Company, which was firmly established in the area. Smith may have been a prime mover in the sale. The Santa Fe trade was going full blast at this time and, considering all the factors, he may have had visions of less risk and more profit in that trade. All we know for sure is that he embarked the next year on such a venture to Santa Fe and, while searching for a waterhole on the Cimarron River, was killed by Indians.

Jackson and Sublette immediately formed a new partnership to purchase and transport goods to the rendezvous for this new Rocky Mountain Fur Company. Jackson dropped out of the new business after a couple of years, leaving Sublette the sole continuing man of that old crew of Ashley, Smith, Jackson, and Sublette.

The 1831 rendezvous was a mess. There was confusion among the trappers as to whether it would be held on Green River or in Willow Valley. Some trappers gathered at each place and waited in vain for supplies. Fitzpatrick, in accordance with the deal of the year before between the Rocky Mountain Fur Company and Smith, Jackson, and Sublette, was to notify the latter firm, by the spring of 1831 at their headquarters in Saint Louis, of the new firm's requirements for goods. He made it to Saint Louis, but arrived too late to find the old partners, who had left for Santa Fe. Fitzpatrick hotfooted to Santa Fe, obtained the supplies, and started for the rendezvous by way of the Front Range of the Rocky Mountains. He met Fraeb, who was searching for him, turned the supplies over to Fraeb, and started back to Saint Louis determined that the 1832 supplies would arrive on time. Fraeb had his job cut out for him. The trappers had dispersed by this time, and he had to hunt them up in the various places to which they had scattered.

Pierre's Hole was again the site for the rendezvous of 1832. This year saw the seeds of tremendous change in the fur trade and the rendezvous principle; it was the beginning of the end. The westward compulsion of Americans was enticing more and more people into the Far West.

The attendance was augmented this year by a pronounced presence of other fur companies and small traders who were attracted by the convenience of garnering furs here and by the depletion of fur-bearing animals in the traditional upper Mississippi-Missouri River Valleys. This year saw in attendance the Hudson's Bay Company, the American Fur Company, Captain Bonneville's party, Nathaniel Wyeth with his scheme of settling Oregon and paying for it by participation in the fur trade, and several small, independent traders. There were in the neighborhood of 1,000 people, white and Indian, who made it to the gathering. Robert Newell stated that it was "the largest party of Whites ever seen together northwest or west of the Yellowstone mouth." He placed the total white attendance at 600.[14]

In addition to this abundance of trade offered at the rendezvous, Fontenelle and Provost were in camp down on the Green River with a supply of goods. Ashley's principle of placing some employees in the mountains, letting them trap and reside there the year round, then collecting all the fur himself was breaking down. Competition was again rearing its ugly head and led to inflated prices being offered for fur in the hope that some of the competitors would sink in a financial morass. This strife led Sublette and Campbell back into competition on the upper Missouri River, thus forcing their new mountain competitors to pull back to protect their established positions on the river. The 1833 rendezvous was again held on the Green River with 300 whites and a small village of Shoshonis as customers. The American Fur Company, the Rocky Mountain Fur Company, Nathaniel Wyeth, and Captain Bonneville were all there with blood in their eyes vying for the fur. The Rocky Mountain people managed to purchase the supplies brought out by the Saint Louis Fur Company under Robert Campbell, Sublette having taken trade goods up the Missouri River to challenge the old-time traders there. This competition began to foster the excessive granting of credit to the trappers and Indians, as well as promoting a spirit of saturnalia which was to become the common conception and trademark of the rendezvous. All this tempo caused Nathaniel Wyeth to refer to the Mountain Men as "a great majority of scoundrels." An indication of the troubles generated by this flooding of the rendezvous was that the Rocky Mountain Fur Company, the successor to the business founded by Ashley, who retired from it wealthy, was steadily going into debt.

The 1834 rendezvous was held on Ham's Fork of the Snake River. Its main feature was discord and confusion. Wyeth tried to undercut Sublette and Campbell by underpricing his supply of trade goods to the Rocky Mountain Fur Company, but Sublette, by frantic effort, outwitted him, leaving Wyeth holding a stock of goods with no ready market. John Jacob Astor sold out his controlling interest in the American Fur Company's western department to the Saint Louis firm of Pratte, Chouteau and Company, which was a power in the fur trade as ruthless as Astor and was represented at the rendezvous by Dripps and Fontenelle. Bonneville was again present, poking around as a bona fide trader.

In addition, there was an infusion of strange blood, a harbinger of the future. Jason Lee and four companions, who were going to the Oregon Country as Methodist missionaries, and two naturalists, Nuttall and Townsend, who wanted to study the flora and fauna of western North America, made their appearance.

This year also marked the final gasp of the debt-ridden Rocky Mountain Fur Company. From its original position as sole entrepreneur and money-generating entity on the High Plains and in the Rocky Mountains, the Company had fallen on such hard times that it couldn't survive, even after its many reorganizations. Captain Thing, Wyeth's second in command, wrote: "The mountain men were all assembled on this river this season for Rendezvous and as crazy a set of men as I ever saw. . . ." Townsend, the greenhorn, recorded:

. . . Our own camp is with a heterogenous assemblage of visitors. The principal of these are Indians, of the Nez Percé, Bannock and Shoshone tribes. . . . There is in addition to these a great variety of personages amongst us; most of them calling themselves white men, French-Canadians, half breeds, &c., their color nearly as dark, and their manners wholly as wild, as the Indians . . . render our camp a perfect bedlam.

Fontenelle of the American Fur Company left Bellevue on the Missouri River the spring of 1835 with trade goods bound for the rendezvous. Accompanying him were two more missionaries sent out by the American Board of Commissioners for Foreign Missions. These men were Marcus Whitman and Samuel Parker, who originally were to establish missions among the Flathead and Nez Percé tribes. When they got to the rendezvous they changed their plans. Parker decided to go to the Oregon Country and, since the Flathead and Nez Percé seemed so anxious for missionaries, Whitman was to return to the United States and recruit more associates to come out with him the next year. Present at this gathering were 2,000 Shoshonis and 40 lodges of Flatheads and Nez Percés, a few Utes, 200 or 300 American Fur Company men, and a small party of Hudson's Bay Company personnel. The original complement of Ashley and his men had dissolved and broken up to the point that they were now free trappers or affiliated with the American Fur Company.

The concept of a sole supplier furnishing goods to a specific group of trappers on an agreed annual basis had broken down by this spring. The business was now back into the early American style — every-man-for-himself-and-the-devil-take-the-hindmost. Several companies were busy transporting goods to the rendezvous sites, and the trappers dealt and dickered for the best price offered for fur and the cheapest goods in the market.

Missionaries were at Bellevue, the jumping-off place for the rendezvous of 1836, in time to accompany the supply train to the mountains. Whitman was accompanied by his recent bride, Narcissa, Mr. and Mrs. Henry Spaulding, and William Gray, all intent on founding missions to serve the western Indians. These people were the first "swallows" presaging the horde of emigrants from the United States that would soon be clogging the trails and valleys. Nathaniel Wyeth, who had never been able to break into the supply business with any success, drove another nail into the coffin of the rendezvous when he sold his Fort Hall on the Portneuf River to the Hudson's Bay Company. This act insured that the rendezvous trade would have a next-door, persistent, knowledgeable neighbor cutting into its profits on a year-round basis.

The trade goods this year were supplied by the American Fur Company, the Hudson's Bay Company, and the ragtag successor to the Rocky Mountain Fur Company. The last-named company had money and personnel problems and, at this time, ceased to struggle for a place in the trade. They sold out to the American Fur Company.

Two things were converging at this time. The supply of furbearers, which a mere ten years before had seemed inexhaustable was now strikingly depleted by the unrestrained competition of the trappers, and the price of beaver pelts was plummeting due to the surge in popularity of silk hats.

It was all downhill from here on. The 1837 rendezvous on the Green River was a bedraggled affair stretching over several weeks and with several supply trains on the grounds, but only a few Indians. By this time permanent trading posts were being built throughout the country — Fort Hall on the Portneuf River, Fort William (later called Fort Laramie), Fort Union at the mouth of the Yellowstone River, Bent's Fort on the Arkansas River, and many other small posts were springing up like mushrooms, built by men trying to make a dollar. These latter lacked sufficient capital to survive the competition and falling fur prices. But all these businesses drew fur into them, fur that in prior times would have been taken to the rendezvous.

The Popo Agie River was the site of the 1838 rendezvous. The supply train carried along another group of missionaries headed for the West — William Gray, Elkanah Walker, Cushing Ells, Asa Smith, their wives, and Cornelius Rogers. All these missionaries, this year and previous years, made a point of writing home about the need to carry the Gospel into that vast stretch of wilderness and, incidentally, extolling the economic opportunities of the Oregon Country. All these reports got wide circulation in church publications, newspapers, and periodicals and added to the groundswell building up in the restless Americans.

The price of beaver had fallen so low that the traders were forced to raise the price of their goods this year to heights that the trappers could not tolerate. Many of the trappers could not even pay their prior debts at this new scale, and the traders refused to extend any more credit. The Hudson's Bay Company's representative reported that there were only 125 trappers there with a total of only 2,000 beaver. Faced with these conditions, many trappers slipped away without settling their debts or outfitting for another season. Some went back to their original homes, others took up ranching and farming around Taos or in the Oregon Country. Still others opted for jobs as meat hunters to supply the trading posts that had destroyed their way of life. A few took jobs in some capacity in governmental bureaus.

Some found employment as guides for the multitude of emigrant trains now making their way west. The members of these emigrant trains were, almost without exception, small-time farmers, store clerks, preachers, unsuccessful lawyers, and rosy-cheeked youths looking for new horizons. They had no trouble making their way from their homes in New York, Massachusetts, Virginia, and Pennsylvania through the settled part of the country. Having had contact with a few "tame" Indians back home, Indians who had been acculturated to the white man and his ways for 200 years, they thought they knew all about Indians. But when they reached the edge of the unsettled plains and came into contact with "wild" Indians, a different climate, and a strange terrain, they found that they were babes in the woods. They had to have someone to wet-nurse them from there on to their destination. The experienced and now jobless trappers, who knew the West and its Indians like the back of their own hands, were the perfect men for the guiding jobs. Most of the emigrant-train troubles, about which we read so much, were the result of the train members ignoring or rejecting the advice of their Mountain Man guides.

Pierre Chouteau, who was now the principal Saint Louis supplier, debated with himself, during the spring of 1839, about the wisdom of committing an inventory of goods to the rendezvous that was scheduled again for the Green River. He finally sent a small consignment of only four two-wheeled carts, each loaded with only 800 to 900 pounds and supervised by only nine men. Other individuals, including four more missionaries, swelled the total party to 27 persons, a vastly different entourage than a few years before. This small party accurately shows the decline of the rendezvous and its importance in the fur trade. Doctor Wislizenus, a member of the party, made some pertinent comments on the status of this rendezvous. Speaking of the trappers he wrote:

> But the days of their glory seem to be passed, for constant hunting has very much reduced the number of beavers. This diminuation in the beaver catch made itself noticeable at this year's rendezvous in the quieter behavior of the trappers. There was little drinking of spirits, and almost no gambling. Another decade, perhaps, and the original trapper will have disappeared from the mountains.
>
> The Indians who had come to the meeting were no less interesting than the trappers. There must have been some thousands of them. . . . The Indians had for the trade chiefly tanned skins, moccasins, thongs of buffalo leather or braided buffalo hair, and fresh and dried buffalo meat. They have no beaver skins.[15]

The year 1840 saw the last attempt by the Saint Louis suppliers to conduct a rendezvous. Again, it was accompanied by the forerunners of the exodus from the Eastern states. This year the missionaries were Father Pierre Jean De Smet, S. J., and three Protestant pastors — the Reverend Messrs. Clark, Littlejohn, and Smith, with their wives. This gathering found "times was certainly hard[,] no beaver and everything dull. . . ."[16]

Thus ended the institution of the rendezvous. It was born of necessity and died when the ailments that caused its birth caught up with it. The gluttony of the early traders and trappers who gave no thought to the morrow created a deadly, terminal malaise hastened along its course by the introduction of products of industry which undermined the world's dependence on fur. Even if these events had not taken place, the incipient western surge of all manner and ilk of Americans would have doomed the premise upon which the rendezvous was built.

So, the popular dramatization of the rendezvous as the standard, all-encompassing *modus operandi* of the fur trade is faulty. The rendezvous, as a force in the American fur trade, actually flexed its muscles only for a mere 13 years, 1824 to 1836.

Waiting for a parley. (Courtesy of Kamt-Mann & Co)

Chapter 7

A Reappraisal of the Blackfeet Hostility to the American Trader

The Blackfeet were nothing but trouble to the American traders in the early days of the fur trade. These Indians were a virile people naturally inclined to fight any one, any place, any time, and you name the terms. Their neighbors — the Sioux, Crow, Assiniboine, Flathead, Shoshoni — all bore voluble witness to that. But this bellicose attitude does not explain the unrelenting hostility with which they met the Americans. They rebuffed every attempt by the Americans to establish trade with them or be accepted by them.

The genesis of this hostility has been ascribed to their initial encounters with Americans. They drove Manuel Lisa, when he tried to trap the upper reaches of the Missouri River, back down to his post at the mouth of the Big Horn River, which was the limit of Blackfeet territory. When Andrew Henry tried to trap the three forks of the Missouri, they made life so miserable and the endeavor so costly that his party gave up the attempt. There was the Potts-Colter incident in which Potts lost his life and Colter staged his famous stark-naked footrace. Then there was the fight of the Blackfeet with the Crows, when Colter happened to be with the Crows and participated on the side of the Crows. But the well-known encounter between eight Blackfeet and Meriwether Lewis in 1806 is the main example cited for the Blackfoot enmity to Americans. Using these incidents to explain the hostility is only a convenient simplification.

The scuffle that Lewis had with the Blackfeet is typical of these various encounters. It occurred when Lewis and Clark were on their return trip from the Pacific Ocean. On reaching the mouth of Lolo Creek on the Bitterroot River, the party paused for rest and discussed its future course. It decided that it should split — Clark, with some men, going south to the Yellowstone River; Lewis, accompanied by the remaining men, going northeast to try the Indian shortcut by way of the Sun River to the Missouri River. The group split up for two reasons: first, to find out if the Yellowstone River provided a better watercourse to the west than the Missouri River, and second, to assess the potential value of a trading post in the Marias River area to siphon off some of the Indian trade that the Canadian traders were monopolizing.[1]

Even though the purpose of Lewis's course was to make an assessment of Indian trade potential, he was apprehensive when, on the evening of 26 July, he noted a party of eight Blackfeet watching his party's progress. Making the best of the situation, Lewis approached the Indians and established friendly relations. They selected a campsite, did the customary smoking, and had a friendly discussion concerning the trade of the Blackfeet with the Canadian posts for "arm amintion [sic] speritous [sic] liquor blankets &c."[2] The next morning the Indians slyly arose and tried to steal the guns of the whites. A scuffle ensued in which one Indian was stabbed to death. The Indians next tried to drive off the horses. Lewis foiled this, but another Indian was shot to death in the fracas. The Indians fled, and Lewis and his men quickly saddled the horses still available and struck out for the Missouri River. This tussle was no great disaster for the Blackfeet; it was a typical foray. The Blackfeet later remarked that Lewis and his men only got what was coming to them.[3]

None of these occurrences endeared the Americans to the Blackfeet, but neither did they cause an implacable hatred to develop. This Blackfeet animosity to the Americans was actually economic, originating in the tenets of Indian life.

In the course of intra-Indian trading, European trade goods were often known to remote tribes long before those tribes ever saw a white man. Goods passed through this intertribal trading system in the normal course of events and enhanced the trading position and power of each tribe involved. The white trader, realizing that the markups and profits accruing to the Indians affected his profits, constantly pushed his base of operations forward into new territory. The Indians always resisted those forward moves, sometimes benignly, sometimes vehemently, but they always resisted. Many statements to this exist in the literature.[4] Such statements are not confined to one tribe, one locale, or one time, but encompass the whole area and time of the fur trade. George T. Hunt wrote: "The Iroquois were out of fur, and would not permit the other Lake tribes to come through them to the Dutch traders, nor would they permit the Dutch traders to go through them to the farther tribes. The Iroquois were savages, but by no means simple."[5] Bernard DeVoto admirably sums up this Indian bias:

> A tribe that traded directly with the whites was in the most favorable situation, fully supplied and better armed than its customers and possessing the power of any monopoly. Consequently, there were trade rivalries, trade diplomacy, and trade wars. For most Indian tribes war

had always been a sport, a cult, and a vocation. But the trade with Industrial Europe made it for three centuries a fundamental condition of Indian society.[6]

The Blackfeet were not fur traders and made no attempt to be. They lived off the buffalo. It supplied all their daily needs. The only things they wanted from the white man were guns, trinkets, a few butcher knives, and awls. Guns had become a necessity for war, even though they were often put to other uses. Strange as it may seem, they still preferred the bow and arrow for buffalo hunting because of the ease with which this Stone Age tool could be handled during the heat of a buffalo chase. It was just as lethal as a gun and on horseback could be maneuvered much more readily. Six or eight arrows could be shot while one muzzle-loader gun was being reloaded.

The Blackfeet satisfied their needs by furnishing the Canadian companies with fresh meat, pemmican, and what few furs they might haphazardly acquire. The trade in pemmican was larger than may be imagined. Pemmican was the reserve food supply for the northern trading posts and was the principal sustenance of the Canadian brigades that took the round trip out with their furs from the winter posts every summer, either to York Factory or Grand Portage, returning to their posts with the next winter's supply of trade goods.

In 1755 Anthony Henday, a Hudson's Bay Company employee who was the first white man to make effective contact with the Blackfeet, reported that he had little success trying to persuade them to become Hudson's Bay Company customers. He wanted them to bring their furs directly to York Factory on Hudson's Bay, rather than depend on intermediate Indian traders. In one of his talks with the Blackfeet, they said:

> [York Factory] was far off, & they could not live without Buffalo flesh; and that they could not leave their horses &c; and many other obstacles, though all might be got over if they were acquainted with a Canoe and could eat Fish, which they never do. The Chief further said that they never wanted food, as they followed the Buffalo & killed them with the Bows and Arrows; and he was informed the Natives that frequented the Settlements were often times starved on their journey. Such remarks I thought exceedingly true.[7]

Successive tries by other traders were no more successful. Various journals, through the years, bemoan that no amount of cajoling would change this Blackfoot attitude and make trappers of them.

Because of this Blackfoot attitude their culture did not undergo the radical change that occurred in other tribes when European goods became available. Other tribes not only welcomed those goods, but adopted them to the exclusion of the native counterparts. The European products ameliorated living conditions; blankets were just as warm, lighter, and more easily dried than robes of animal skins: copper pots were more efficient and longer lived than clay pots; woolen leggings made of blankets, unlike leather counterparts, did not shrink and become clammy to the skin when wet; steel traps were more efficient than deadfalls; hatchets, as opposed to stone axes, revolutionized wood-gathering; butcher knives and steel awls lightened the household chores of the Indian women. In succumbing completely to these amenities, other tribes became dependent upon the white trader. But guns, geegaws, butcher knives, axes, awls, and a few items to trade to their neighbors were all the Blackfeet wanted, and their pemmican trade supplied the wherewithal for those items. The Blackfeet were fiercely independent as well as being self-sufficient. They insisted on maintaining their station in life as Lords of the Plains, ahorseback and hunting buffalo, not as menial trappers.

It is now time to place the Blackfeet *vis-à-vis* with the American traders within this context.

What did cause this constant hostility on the part of the Blackfeet to the American trader but not to the Canadian trader? Over the years, they maintained amicable (for Blackfeet) relations with the Canadians, who were the source of supply for what items they wanted. The question becomes especially interesting when it is realized that, suddenly, the American was accepted and permitted to start trading operations with them. McKenzie, in charge of Fort Union on the Missouri River, accomplished this acceptance in 1831 when he sent an interpreter named Berger to build Fort Piegan at the junction of the Marias River and the Missouri River. (An example of Blackfoot cantankerousness — after one season's trade they burned the post.) Commercial relations were thus finally accepted by the Blackfeet, and they patronized Fort Union on a regular basis from then on.

The answer is supplied by David Thompson and Peter Fidler. Thompson was a partner in the North West Company based in Montreal and had traded all over the Canadian fur-trade area from east of Winnipeg to the foot of the Rocky Mountains. For several years before and immediately after 1800, he was trading out of posts on the eastern slope of the Rockies. In this capacity he was intimately associated with the Blackfeet and became conversant with most of their activities and people.

One of his experiences with their embargo of trade to their western neighbors occurred in October 1800. At this time a band of Kutenais crossed the mountains in an attempt to reach Rocky Mountain House, where they could obtain European goods. Thompson heard of their presence in the area and, knowing the Piegan antipathy toward allowing the Kutenais to establish trade relations with the white man, rushed to meet them. Even with Thompson escorting them the Piegans harassed the party with every mean trick they knew and threw every obstacle they could think of in the Kutenais' path, calling upon Thompson's reservoir of stratagems to thwart the Piegans. The Kutenais and Thompson managed to reach the post and trade. Immediately after the trading, Thompson dispatched the Kutenais homeward because of the Piegan hostility.[8]

In 1807, in preparing to carry the trade westward across the mountains, Thompson was prevented by Blackfoot force of arms from taking his departure until they were drawn off by an alarm of other white men trying to slip by them to the southward (Manuel Lisa's attempt to trap the headwaters of the Missouri River).

In his *Narrative*, when he had the advantage of hindsight, Thompson was very clear as to their reason. He wrote: "I have already related how the Peeagans [*sic*] watched us to prevent our crossing the Mountains and arming the Natives on that side; in which for a time they succeeded."[9] The Blackfeet, masters of light cavalry tactics, weren't going to be outflanked and outfoxed by letting one opponent hold them in one position while another slipped around their exposed flank.

In narrating a later incident that occurred after he had crossed the continental divide, Thompson further illustrates this Blackfoot ban on transmontane trade by white traders. A war party to smash Thompson in his new location was being organized by the Blackfeet. During the discussion the civil chief, who was the instigator of the idea, told the assembly: "They the Kutenai have always been our slaves (prisoners) and now they will pretend to equal us. No, we must not suffer this. We must at once crush them. We know them to be desparate [*sic*] men, and we must destroy them before they become too powerful for us."[10]

Peter Fidler was employed by the Hudson's Bay Company principally as a surveyor and mapmaker. He and Thompson were contemporaries. After several years of this trading-mapping work Fidler wrote a letter to London describing some of the new country he had been over several years previously and enclosed a map that portrayed that country. A portion of that letter, dated 10 July 1802, reads:

> . . . Of all those different tribes in the Indian map only the Tatood & Cottonahow [Arapaho and Kutenai] Indians have been at any of our houses to trade, the former only this winter & the latter 2 years ago. But the Southern [Cree] Indians, with the Blackfeet, Blood and Muddy River [Piegan] Indians will still prevent them or any of the other Tribes from coming to trade regularly, it is not in our powers to make or persuade the tribes last mentioned to let them come safe to our Houses to Trade, they are so very jealous of their being supplied by us with either Guns or ammunition. . . .[11]

The Blackfeet were well aware that if traders succeeded in getting a foothold on the western slope that those Indians would have a direct supply of guns, affecting the military balance of power, and trade goods, which would eliminate one set of Blackfoot customers. They were protecting their middle-man position by forcing Thompson to go farther north and use Athabaska Pass on his trips to and from the Columbia River drainage.

By the same token, the Lisa and Ashley trapping ventures that were so emphatically driven back from the Yellowstone and upper Missouri Rivers were thus treated, not because of the potential loss to the Blackfeet of beaver pelts through trapping by Americans or by a distinct dislike for Americans, but because the Americans were on a direct water route to the western slope Indians which bypassed the Blackfoot control of trade.

After Ashley had created the rendezvous, with its overland supply route up the Platte River, as the practical way to conduct trapping ventures in the Rocky Mountain region, the Blackfeet could no longer maintain their Iron Curtain. The transmontane tribes such as the Flathead, Kutenai, Shoshoni, and Nez Percé began obtaining their supplies at this new trade center or through traders who operated out of the rendezvous.

At this same time, the Americans were beginning to encourage the trade in buffalo robes. The boat transportation provided by the Missouri River afforded the Americans the means to economically handle these heavy, bulky hides as opposed to the problems the items presented to the Canadian traders, who had to rely on packhorses and canoes.

This new market for buffalo hides fit right into the Blackfoot lifestyle. The hides were readily available to them, often being a surplus by-product of everyday life, and, if the desired number of hides was not on hand at a particular time, the acquisition of more suited the Blackfoot idea of proper employment.

These two factors, the buffalo robe market development and the bypassing of the Blackfeet by the opening of the rendezvous, rendered the Blackfoot position in the trade obsolete.

The Blackfeet then acquiesced; they started trading with the Americans.[12]

Their original enmity, which they expressed through force of arms rather than through treaties, import duties, and similiar modern devices, was caused by economic considerations. They possessed an enviable economic position and, being human, weren't going to sit idle and watch it deteriorate. Their grievance was economic, not homicidal per se.

Chapter 8

The Jeremy Pinch Enigma

A new chapter in the exploration of the Pacific Northwest by Americans will be written when someone succeeds in solving the mystery of the ghostly Jeremy Pinch. Jeremy popped up in 1807 when he wrote two letters to David Thompson and then faded into the mists of time.

Jeremy had to be the first American west of the continental divide after the Lewis and Clark Expedition and he may have been in the area prior to them. He is a nebulous, ephemeral character who has never been identified. He did exist, as the two letters to Thompson prove, but who he was, where he came from, what his purpose was, what happened to him, are all unknown.

David Thompson was a partner in the North West Company, a large fur-trading enterprise based in Montreal, Canada. In 1806 the North West Company instructed Thompson, who was stationed at the time on the headwaters of the Saskatchewan River, to find a practical passage over the Rocky Mountains and to open trade with the Indians on the western slope. This action was merely a company expansion program. It was not a secret, but, as a business matter in a highly competitive business, neither was it broadcast to the world. After some delay occasioned by the Blackfoot Indians, Thompson, in the spring of 1807, crossed the Rockies by what is now known as Howse Pass. He chose a site near the headwaters of the Columbia River and started building his first trading post, Kootenae House, on 18 July 1807. This date is important to what follows. Soon after his arrival the two Jeremy Pinch letters enter the story and form the puzzle. The letters, written in an official tone, ordered Thompson out of United States territory. The trouble with that was that the area was still a no-man's-land. The international boundary went only as far west as the Rocky Mountains at that time and Thompson knew it.

The two letters are a mystery in themselves as there is no ironclad connection between Thompson and the letters or between the letters and the author. While Thompson never mentioned receipt of them, a copy of the first

letter is in the Hudson's Bay Company's archives, and a copy of the second
letter, along with Thompson's reply, is in the Public Record Office, Surrey,
England. The copier of them made a note on the copy of the second letter that
Thompson's reply to it was in Thompson's handwriting. So, beyond a doubt,
Thompson did receive them.

The Hudson's Bay Company's Edmonton House journal for 10 November
1807 states that some Hudson's Bay Company men had recent contact with
North West Company men at either the North West Company's Rocky
Mountain House or the Hudson's Bay Company's Acton House. The journal
explains that these North West Company men had just come from Thompson's
new post on the headwaters of the Columbia River and reports that Thompson
had received a letter there, borne to him by the Kutenai Indians which was
". . . given them [the Kutenais] (when on a visit to a more southerly Tribe), by
the Americans, of which the following is a copy."[1]

Why should Thompson's men be carrying the letter? Was Thompson
forwarding it to company headquarters at Fort William? If so, there is no
record of it. And why should those three men show the letter to their
company's business rival? Even though Thompson accorded little import or
value to the letter, why should he make it available to his company's archrival?
Perhaps it was to scare them off from trying to follow in his footsteps. The
route the letters followed to come to rest in the two archives is unknown, but
they are there.

While Thompson never mentions the letters in his *Narrative*, his journal,
and a letter by him have remarks in them that surely must bear on these two
letters. This connection must be assumed because of the existing copies and
the remarks in the Hudson's Bay Company journal. And following this line of
reasoning, they had to come to him by way of Indian postmen as there was no
other way. Thompson's journal for 13 August 1807 reads:

About noon 2 Kootenas [*sic*] men from the great Band arrived, the news
they brought caused much crying and shrieks among the whole that we
thought an attack at hand & ran to arms but they informed us it was on
account of the Battle between the Flat Heads and Peagans [*sic*] in which
13 of the latter & 4 of the former were killed — that the Americans in
number abt 40 are settling a military and trading post on the south
Branch of the Columbia, whither the Flat Heads after the Battle had
retired.[2]

A month later Thompson wrote a letter to his company in which he
expanded those remarks, perhaps from additional conversation with the
Indians. In part, he wrote:

. . . they also inform me that about three weeks ago the Americans, to a number of about 42, arrived to settle a military and trading Post at the confluence of the two more southern & considerable Branches of the Columbia, & that they are preparing to make a small advance Post lower down the River; two of those who were with Captain Lewis were also with these, of whom the poor Kootenaes [*sic*] related several dreadful stories.[3]

While these passages do not state or infer that the first letter was received at this time, it is the only mention by Thompson of any occurrence that could be so construed. And they indicate Indian knowledge of another party of whites in the area. The presence of another such party is necessary to establish the validity of the letters.

The first letter was dated 10 July 1807 (eight days before Thompson started building Kootenae House) and was signed by James Roseman, Lieutenant, and Zachary Perch, Captain and Commanding Officer. Their location was given as Fort Lewis, Yellow River, Columbia. The letter purported to be official, as it stated that the authors' authority was "delegated to us by General Braithwaite Commander of all the newly ceded Territories northward of the Illinois." Its ten long paragraphs spelled out, in detail, regulations imposed on all traders, their conduct while with the Indians, and specific restrictions for traders who were not "native Americans" (see Appendix A, Letter 1).

That letter is a curious document. Diligent search by many persons has failed to identify any General Braithwaite in the American Army. In fact, General Wilkinson of conspiratorial fame was the only general in the army at that time, and he was stationed in Saint Louis, Missouri. That would be a logical location for a general commanding "all the newly ceded territories northward of the Illinois," and perhaps there is a connection. There is no record of a Captain Zachary Perch or of a Lieutenant James Roseman. There was no location named Fort Lewis in the whole Northwest at that time. The name Fort Lewis may have been used to indicate a recent official honoring of Meriwether Lewis, and Yellow River may have been a play of words on Yellowstone River. Both terms may have been concocted to give a ring of authenticity to the letter. Thompson's matter-of-fact reference to Meriwether Lewis sounds strange since Lewis and Clark did not return to Saint Louis until 23 September 1806. Thompson was in the area of present-day Calgary, Alberta, on that date, leaving the next spring to start on his jaunt over the mountains. For the information about Lewis and Clark to have reached Thompson under these circumstances seems farfetched, yet Thompson, matter-of-factly, accepts the information about the men who had been with Lewis and Clark. Since Lewis and Clark, on their return trip, stopped at the Mandan villages on the Missouri River from 14 to 17 August, the information about their trip was available to the North West Company's posts on the Souris and Assiniboine Rivers and probably spread throughout the Company's domain by means of their routine dispatches and correspondence. Thus, Thompson's apparent knowledge of Lewis and Clark is not surprising.

Thompson ascribed little value to the letter, since he didn't keep it, forward it to his company (as far as is known), copy it in his journal, or remark on it. It is certain that he did not reply to it. In December 1807 he received a second letter rebuking him for his failure to reply to the first one.[4]

This second letter was dated 29 September 1807, the place given as Paltito Palton Lake, and signed Jeremy Pinch, Lieutenant. In it is a statement that a chief of the Paltito Paltons told the author of the letter that the first letter had been delivered to Thompson. This second letter threatened Thompson with military reprisal if he did not conform to the instructions in the first letter and chided him for neglecting to reply to it. Thompson, on 26 December, made a tactful reply to this second letter, stating that he would submit the matter to his company as the problem's scope was greater than he was authorized to handle on his own (see Appendix A, Letter 2).

Jeremy Pinch's connection with this whole affair is limited to this last letter, and he, too, cannot be identified in any army lists. But the whole episode is usually called "the Jeremy Pinch letters."

The affair ends here, but the enigma begins.

The first letter is startling in that as far back as 1796 a trader by the name of J. McKay, operating out of Saint Louis under a Spanish license, penned a letter which he gave to a North West Company trader, who was at the Mandan villages, and instructed that the letter be delivered to the trader in charge of the North West Company's Brandon House on the Assiniboine River. That letter specifically forbade British traders from entering Spanish territory that the King of Spain claimed extended north to the divide between the water that flowed north to Hudson's Bay and the waters that emptied into the Gulf of Mexico.[5]

Correspondence concerning this ultimatum continued between Brandon House and the Saint Louis traders who were in the Mandan-Arikara area until 16 January 1797. Without doubt, this exchange of views became well known, a subject for gossip and speculation among the English and French-Canadian traders in the Great Lakes area.

Again, in 1806, another letter of similar content was addressed to the North West Company. In the fall of 1805 Lt. Zebulon M. Pike had been sent by General Wilkinson from Saint Louis northward on a reconnaissance of the Mississippi River headwaters. In February 1806 Pike reached Leech Lake in northern Minnesota and west of Lake Superior. There he found a North West Company post under the direction of Hugh McGillis. In a lengthy letter Pike reminded McGillis that the post was in United States territory, that it existed only by sufferance of the United States government, and that business could be conducted only under certain restrictions imposed by the United States.[6] And the first Pinch letter is patently paraphrased from this Pike-McGillis letter; so much so that credence cannot be given to a belief in mere coincidence (see Appendix B).

Thus Pike's letter to McGillis probably was no bombshell, merely a reiteration of the McKay letter of ten years before. Thus, the Pinch-Thompson letters probably did not cause Thompson any consternation. McGillis had spread the word of Pike's letter to his fellow Nor'Westers, so Thompson was familiar with that and, probably, with the McKay letter.[7]

Thompson knew that he was in a no-man's-land over which jurisdiction and sovereignty had not been decreed. He could readily have made the assumption that the Pinch letters were merely more of the same wrangle, and, if there were any basis for argument, it was a matter for the two governments to solve.

Pinch, whoever he was, had definite knowledge of Thompson. His first letter was dated eight days before Thompson started building Kootenae House. Pinch also knew just how to get the letters delivered; which Indians to use as postmen. He wrote the first letter on 10 July and it was delivered on 13 August. That was good time for Indian transmittal and indicates that Pinch did not rely on catch-as-catch-can delivery.

When a reply by Thompson had not been received by 29 September, Pinch wrote Thompson the second letter which was delivered, Thompson says in his reply to Pinch, on 24 December, but it could have been the 21st according to Thompson's journal, which records the arrival at Kootenae House of a Kutenai, two Salish, and two Nez Percé on that date.[8]

On top of all this, the second letter was addressed specifically to "The British Mercht. Trafficking with the Cabanaws [Kutenais]." In contrast, the first had a to-whom-it-may-concern tone as it was directed to "Foreigners who may at present by [*sic*] carrying on a Traffic with the Indians within our Territories for Peltries, &c."

Pinch knew the lay of the land. He was no johnny-come-lately to the area, nor was he operating from some remote place attempting to forestall or bluff a competitor. Pinch further pins down his knowledge of the area and his familiarity with the situation in his second letter. In that letter there are three definitive items — a chief of the Paltito Paltons had informed him that the first letter had been delivered to Thompson, the "Pilchenees" (most likely Atsina of the Blackfoot Confederacy) had raided the Paltito Paltons, and his knowledge that Thompson was in Kutenai territory. All this evidence forcefully indicates Pinch's existence in the area.

It is unbelievable that Thompson fabricated the letters for some dark reason of his own. He was not familiar enough with American policies to have couched the letters in the phrases and terms that are distinctly American, and he was not yet familiar enough with the country and its inhabitants to have been as precise as the letters were. And what purpose would such subterfuge have accomplished?

Up to this time, only three parties of white men had left any record of crossing the Rockies. The first to cross was Sir Alexander Mackenzie, who made a quick trip down the Fraser River in 1793 and an equally quick return to his base at Fort Chipewyan on Athabaska Lake. The second man was Simon Fraser, who built a post on McLeod Lake in 1805, too far north to have any bearing on the locale concerning Pinch. And since Mackenzie, Fraser, and Thompson were all working for the same company, there was no need for such a letter. The third party was the Lewis and Clark Expedition.

While the literature of the period indicates that there were many "free men," men not bound to any company, who had crossed the divide prior to this time and were familiar with the western slope of the Rockies, those men were exclusively Iroquois, métis, and French-Canadians. To a man they were illiterate, roving, happy-go-lucky types who gave no thought to trade or tomorrow.

In 1801 Thompson had dispatched two of these, Le Blanc and La Gasse, to return home with a band of Kutenai Indians who had come to trade at Rocky Mountain House on the Saskatchewan River.[9] The instructions given these men were to spend a year with the Kutenais, learning their language and making friends with them, then to return to Rocky Mountain House, bringing the Kutenais with them to trade. Kutenai folklore indicates that these two men continued to associate with the Kutenais, off and on, for several years.

In 1806 Jocko Finlay was sent from Rocky Mountain House to cut a trail for packhorses across the Kutenai country in preparation for Thompson's journey scheduled for 1807. Finlay would not have been sent on such a mission if he were not familiar with the country.[10]

By no stretch of the imagination could any of these *engagés* and free men be involved in the Pinch letter writing. Their background eliminates them. The two literate Canadians who are known to have crossed the Rockies before Thompson belonged to Canadian companies, and no known American had yet made the crossing, other than the Lewis and Clark party. They had returned intact to the lower Missouri River in 1806. Trading ships of American and British interests had frequented the Northwest Coast for 20 years or so, but the sailors didn't venture very far inland.

In the light of all this hazy information, who was the author of the two letters? An American? A Briton? A Spaniard?

The idea of a Spaniard seems beyond reason, but Duncan McGillivray, at Fort George on the North Saskatchewan River under the date of 22 February 1795, recorded in his journal: "that the Coutonees [Kutenais] a tribe from the Southwest are determined to force their way this year to this Fort or perish in the attempt; rumor reports that their Cheif [*sic*] has got a parchment Roll written by the Spaniards to the traders in this quarter, the contents of which are unknown."[11] There is no explanation for this statement; who, where, and why are fathomless. There are, though, vague references to a party of Spaniards, but these references seem to refer to a time prior to this. Upon analysis, they have to be relegated to the status of Indian legends.

Thompson, in reminiscing about his experiences on the Saskatchewan River in the winter of 1787-1788, tells of a war party returning to camp and relating their encounters with "the Black People" (the name they gave to the Spaniards) from whom they had taken a great many horses and mules.[12]

There is still another hazy reference to Spaniards having been in the general area at this time. There is a "Spanish Mound" in the Similkameen country of British Columbia. It received the name, according to legend, as the burial place of a band of white men who wore metal clothes and came into the area in the middle 1700s, "long before 'King George's men.' " They are supposed to have set up camp in the Keremeous Creek valley where they had an altercation with the local Indians.

They then went over the divide to a place near the present town of Kelowna, British Columbia. The next spring they retraced their route, being ambushed along the way by the Similkameen tribe. They and their accoutrements were then buried in the Spanish Mound.

There may be some substance to this tale. Indian pictographs in the area show mounted whites wearing what could be Spanish helmets, and old Indian graves yield hammered-copper Indian body armor similar to Spanish mail.[13]

Another bit of folklore ties shadowy Spaniards into the Montana-British Columbia area at a very early date. Duncan McDonald, the son of the factor at the Flathead Valley Hudson's Bay Company post, recounted that Yellow Bull, a Nez Percé who escaped from the surrender of the Chief Joseph (or Looking Glass) band, had a small brass cannon in his possession. When Yellow Bull was killed by another Indian he was buried on the bank of either Pincher Creek or Cut Bank Creek (the story is confusing on this point). The grave is said to be marked by a rock pyramid and covered with choke-cherry bushes and was "taboo to all Indians." The cannon was definitely supposed to have been obtained from "Black Men."[14]

All these vague references to "Black Men," and Duncan McGillivray's remark in his journal, leave a big question mark concerning Spaniards at the time and region here involved. With tongue-in-cheek, we must concede that Spaniards may have been in the area, and they may have still been there in 1807, and may have written the Jeremy Pinch letters.

Pinch's identification of his Indian associates as Paltito Paltons seems to refer to the Nez Percé of today. His Paltito Palton Lake can not be identified. Perhaps it was Pend d'Oreille Lake, Coeur d'Alene Lake, or even Flathead

Lake. The Nez Percés, Kalispels, Flatheads, Coeur d'Alenes, and Pend d'Oreilles were all closely associated and intermingled at this time. It would not be surprising to find that Pinch applied Paltito Palton to this whole group, or that he was with a band of Nez Percés who happened to be out of their usual territory and at one of these lakes.

We now start groping for identities, men who could have been in the area at the time. The Indian reference to 42 men, two of whom had been with Lewis and Clark, is the first lead. While all the activities of the Lewis and Clark men are not accounted for — some just dropped from sight — none of them had the attainments necessary to compose the Pinch letters. Some of them, however, are known to have returned to the upper Missouri River with the Manuel Lisa party in April 1807.[15]

Manuel Lisa was a leading spirit in the embryonic fur trade developing out of Saint Louis. He was shrewd, competent, energetic, competitive, and ruthless (some have called him a rapscallion). The Saint Louis fur trade had been desultory up to this time, but the Louisiana Purchase and the Lewis and Clark expedition crystalized it into a driving enterprise. Lisa seized this mood, organized a company, and started out with a party of 42 men in April 1807 for the mouth of the Big Horn River to found a trading post.

Since Pike had returned to Saint Louis in April 1806, the information about the Pike-McGillis letter was available to Lisa, who, in his shrewdness, may have had sly thought about using a copy of it during his stay on the upper Missouri. But he didn't arrive at the mouth of the Big Horn until 21 November 1807. Even though his party had 42 men, including some Lewis and Clark men, as the Indian report to Thompson stated, the time element rules out Lisa as the author of the Pinch letters.

Lisa was not the only entrepreneur responding to this new lure of the Missouri River. Every man jack on the river seemed to want to try his hand at trading. Lewis and Clark reported that on their return trip they met 11 different parties going upstream to trade.[16] And Larocque, stationed by the North West Company at the Mandan villages, reported in October 1805 that 14 boats passed that point headed upriver.[17] On 18 May 1807 William Clark, by then Superintendent of Indian Affairs at Saint Louis, wrote the Secretary of War that two large bands of traders had started up the Missouri River the first of the month, another had set out in March, and that he had reports that another party had left the Mandan villages early in the spring for the headwaters of the Missouri River. Documentation of this multitude of traders is almost nonexistent; they must have been mostly small fry.

At one point in the first Pinch letter the statement is made that "By information received at the Manden [sic] Village on the Mississoure [sic] we were given to understand that, some of the Subjects of Great Britain are about to carry on a Trade and traffic with the western Indians. . . ." This passage clearly indicates that, within a relatively short time prior to this first letter, the author had obtained knowledge of the North West Company's instructions to Thompson to cross the divide, and, also, that Pinch's route had been by way of the Missouri River. Further confusion on this point is contained in a letter from Pierre Chouteau to William Eustis on 14 December 1809. It mentions a rumor that the North West Company had erected a fort at the three forks of the Missouri River and that Chouteau gave some credence to it because 30 Americans who had frequented the Mandan area had not been heard from for the last 18 months.[18] There is no verification of the existence of such a North West Company post, but it could have functioned as a base for those Americans.

One of the upstream-bound parties met by Lewis and Clark was commanded by former army captain John McClallen.[19] The two parties met just below the mouth of the Platte River. McClallen said that he was bound for Santa Fe, New Mexico, by way of the Platte River, on a private trading venture sponsored and financed by General Wilkinson. This is interesting. Wilkinson had been pestering Washington officials with reports of British activity on the Missouri and Mississippi Rivers, and he wanted permission to take summary action to control this encroachment. In two of his letters to Washington he mentioned that he was sending a small, private venture to the Yellowstone River and that he had engaged a Captain McClallen to go to Santa Fe.

By the time McClallen met Lewis and Clark he had resigned his commission, so he was on a private venture and such would not be subject to any official reports or authorization. Wilkinson was involved at this time with Aaron Burr's dream of a southwest empire and was also the commanding general of Lieutenant Pike. Pike had just completed his tour of the Mississippi River headwaters of the Arkansas River. Why would Wilkinson send two parties, Pike and McClallen, into the same area at the same time?

Perhaps here is another of Wilkinson's intrigues — utilization of a rehash of the Pike-McGillis letter by a man ostensibly on his way to Santa Fe, but actually on his way to the Oregon Country. McClallen may have gone up the Platte River, but he was to continue west to seek the Columbia River drainage. The encounter of McClallen with Lewis and Clark is the only written record of any Wilkinson scheme along this line. When called to account, as he was, for his various activities, Wilkinson may have destroyed all notes and records, if any, of this project. Be that as it may, McClallen was never heard of again.[20]

It is barely possible that Thompson made one last reference to him in a letter of 21 December 1810 when he wrote ". . . As the Peeagans [*sic*] killed an officer and eight men out of a tribe of 12 do."[21] (The "do" is an abbreviation commonly used in that day for "ditto.") This incident may have occurred in present-day Montana, but that is all there is to it. If McClallen is the officer referred to by Thompson, where had he and his party been for the four years between the time that Lewis and Clark met him and his demise in Montana in 1810?

There is another incident that can't be tied into anything. On 24 February 1810, Indians informed Thompson, who was at his Salish House on the Clark Fork River in Montana, that a Courter had been killed by the Piegans.[22] Thompson, in his only reference to Courter, identified him as "a trader and Hunter from the U States." A few days later he notes that "Rive" came to his camp with "word from the White Hunters" requesting Thompson to come to Courter's camp to settle Courter's accounts and to keep the Indians from absconding with Courter's goods. Courter must have been the leader of this group with "Rive" and *engagés* with no authority, or they wouldn't have called on Thompson to settle the estate.

"Rive" was Francois Rivet, who had accompanied Lewis and Clark on their outward journey as far as the Mandans. In the spring of 1805, Lieutenant Warfington took a detail back down the Missouri River from the Mandan villages with various reports for Washington. Rivet went with this detail as far as the Arikaras. When Lewis and Clark got back to the Mandans on their return in 1806, they found Rivet again with the Mandans. Later, he somehow got from the Mandan area to the Flathead area where Thompson found him with Courter. Rivet had a buddy, Degie, who also had been with the Warfington detail and ended up, years later, in the Oregon Country with Rivet. He could very well have been with Rivet in Montana. These two men are possibly Lewis and Clark men, mentioned by the Indians, in the Pinch party. These men, though, were not the authors of the letters, since they were both illiterate. But the "White Hunters," from whose camp Rivet came to see Thompson, are another matter. It indicated that Rivet was not a lone trader, or an *engagé* of a lone trader, but that an organized party was in the area.

Thompson does not elaborate on this incident, even when he recounts the disposition of Courter's goods. He prosaically closed the accounts and went on about his business. And this is all we know of Courter.

Could a "Courter" have been in the area in 1807? There was a Courtin in the fur trade on the upper Mississippi River, a Courtois who did business with the Clamorgan-Loisel supply house in Saint Louis, and a Corton reported by Robert McClelland of the American Fur Company to be trading on the Missouri River. Similar names such as Courteau and Ceantoin are found in the literature. They may all have been the same man with French, anglicized, or phonetic spellings.

Since Courter is known to have been in our special area at about the right time, did he have the necessary information, education, and attributes to have written the Pinch letters? If he were Pinch, Thompson surely would have identified him as such during Thompson's extended stay in the area — from 1807 to 1810 — but then Thompson completely ignored the Pinch letters, so he may have ignored Courter and any connection of his with Pinch.[23]

It is possible that Courter had some connection with the band of French-Canadians that Thompson found living in the Flathead Lake area in 1809. These people had come from the Illinois country, according to Thompson, and had drifted westward until they finally settled around Flathead Lake.

They told Thompson that they were a party of 350 men when they started their hegira, but, due to old age, accidents, war, and disease, they had dwindled to 25 men when Thompson found them.

Their origin may be rooted in an event of 40 years before. After England defeated France on the Plains of Abraham and imposed the Union Jack on French territory, there were many French permanently domiciled in the Old Northwest, the "Yllinois [sic] Country" of Spanish Upper Louisiana. A large number of these French did some soul-searching and, rather than live under the Union Jack, they moved west across the Mississippi River.

They had been residing in the Illinois country for many years and were classed as traders, but they had no connections with Montreal or any steady source of supply. They functioned in the trading fraternity as temporary engagés for regular outfits coming into the area or as freelances obtaining supplies out of New Orleans by way of Cahokia or Kaskaskia. The rest of the time they just lived off the country. Their discontent and disillusionment with the turn of events at Quebec led to a "gathering of the clan" and a decision to get out from under British rule. They probably found that they had jumped from the frying pan into the fire. The surprise awaiting these French who moved to the French (western bank) territory was that the French had secretly ceded Louisiana back to Spain just prior to the signing of the Treaty of Paris in 1763. Thus, unknowingly, they were moving into not French, but Spanish land and were under Spanish colonial policies which were as hateful to the French as British rule. They probably then continued their drift on west up either the Missouri or Platte Rivers.

Thompson, in discusssing their origin, states that they were under Spanish rule on the Illinois River, but after the Revolutionary War the United States "insisted on their becoming settlers or retiring elsewhere. . . ." That remark isn't correct according to the sequence of historical events, but by the foregoing modification it becomes very plausible and renders obsolete the usual belief that the first white settlers in the Flathead Lake area arrived several decades later.[24]

A few more fragments of information bear on the above hypothesis. A letter, written in 1766, seven years after the battle on the Plains of Abraham and four years after the Treaty of Paris which ceded all the French possessions east of the Mississippi River to England, stated: "It is said many of the French in Canada & Numbers of those settled on the east side of the Mississippi, near our posts [British], intend to remove to the Settlement belonging to the French on the opposite Shore." The writer of the letter went on to remark that he thought there were about 400 French families in the Illinois territory.

A crude census a year later came up with about 1,200 French (men, women, and children), 300 to 350 slaves, and 168 "strangers." The latter were French inhabitants of the area with no fixed, settled domicile. They were footloose vagabonds, *coureurs de bois*.[25]

The same year a British army officer on a tour of inspection went through the area and reported that at Cahokia: "The inhabitants of this place depend more on hunting, and their Indian trade, than on agriculture, as they scarcely raise enough for their own consumption. . . ." In describing the small village of Saint Anne near Fort de Chartres he wrote: "In the following year when the English took possession of the country, they abandoned their houses, except three or four poor families, and settled at the villages on the west side of the Mississippi, chusing [*sic*] to continue under the French government."[26]

Thirty years later an American, writing about Vincennes, penned: ". . . but its two hundred houses were small and badly furnished, one fourth of them empty, for after the arrival of the Americans Many of the Most respectable and Wealthey [*sic*] families (had) left the place and Either went to Detroit or the Spanish side of the Mississipi [*sic*]."[27]

It is conceivable that out of that French population of the Illinois area, especially the 168 "strangers," 350 dyed-in-the-wool French could have made that move across the river and into the iron hand of Spanish colonial administrators. Unhappy with this situation, they drifted onward looking for an unhampered existence.

Thompson's remarks about their presence on the shore of Flathead Lake in Montana are borne out by a grave headstone unearthed a few years ago on Ashley Creek, a tributary of Flathead Lake. The stone is inscribed "J. B. Roth (or J. Broth) 1741." The figures are in the European form and discredit the supposition that the stone is a hoax, the result of a schoolboy's idle time coupled with a fertile imagination. A schoolboy of quite a few years ago would not have known the European form of 1 and 7. Furthermore, Mr. Thane White of Dayton, Montana, an authority on the Kutenai, says that Kutenai superstition forbade mention of death or death dates; that only birthdates were acknowledged.[28] Thus, a French-Canadian, born in 1741, would have been around about the time that Thompson found them living there. The stone validates Thompson's remarks that they were there.

If our man Courter were connected with these people as a supplier of European goods, it seems strange that Saint Louis business records have no reference to him. The French-Canadians surely did not revert to the Indian Stone Age way of life. They must have received a supply of white man's amenities on a somewhat regular basis.

And then there was Josh Jones, another man shrouded in mystery. Some carvings found on an old aspen tree provide the only clue to his existence. In 1940 Mr. George Shoup of Tendoy, Idaho, an old-timer in the area, was off the usual trail across Lemhi Pass when he found an old aspen six miles up Agency Creek that bore an inscription carved in the bark reading, "Josh Jones 3-16-1810." Accompanying this inscription are also carved two Indian signs which have been interpreted to mean "Take notice. Eight persons camped at this place."[29] At the Narrows in Birch Creek Canyon he also found several Indian pictographs which he believed were connected with the inscription on the aspen tree. They were translated as meaning: "Eight persons in companionship with twelve other persons, all being well with them, and they are going upon the mountain and travel eastward."[30]

Mr. Shoup was so fascinated by this tantalizing bit of information that he cut the tree and took home the portion of the trunk that contained the inscription. That trunk still exists in the possession of the George L. Shoup family of Tendoy, Idaho.

Ring counts and an appraisal of this portion of the tree have been made by the University of Idaho and the U.S. Forest Service. While these two assessments do not completely agree on the age of the tree, they both indicate that the tree could be old enough to have existed at the time of the inscription. This fragmentary note on Josh Jones is the only reference to him that is known.

Mrs. Tex Kauer of Lemhi, Idaho, has surmised a possible explanation for the Josh Jones carving. But nothing has surfaced about the Indian carvings and pictograph. Mrs. Kauer's research has established that in the summer of 1910 a Wilber and Walter Jones cut firewood on the creek where the aspen was found. Walter Jones' nickname was Josh. Josh could have been a practical joker who decided to leave a memento of their presence on the creek in such a way as to make future generations go away mumbling in their beards. While in this mood he may have deliberately carved 1810 instead of 1910. On the other hand, Josh may have been a circumspect individual and actually carved 1910 on the tree, but the tree, in its attempt to repair the wound and in its natural growth processes, may have deformed the 9 until it looks like an 8 today. With this speculation we may go a step further and guess that Josh discovered the pictograph and realized that it would be a perfect foil for a practical joke.

Still another man comes into consideration. An Anthony Bettay wrote a letter to President Jefferson on 27 January 1808 in which he recounted a journey just completed.[31] He claimed that he was in the West for three years, during which time he had reached a point some 1,700 miles beyond Saint Louis, and that he found a silver mine on the Platte River, a passage across the Rocky Mountains, and a westward-flowing river. Was Bettay a glory hunter seeking notoriety with wild claims? Was he an original member of McClallen's party who made it back to Saint Louis? In this case, why did he not mention the connection? It would have lent validity to his claims.

Since Wilkinson's papers are devoid of any accounts of McClallen, other than those mentioned previously, the McClallen trip may have been a Wilkinson scheme that Wilkinson hid when called to account. He may have told Bettay to forget any connection with McClallen. Perhaps Bettay was a member of one of those parties that William Clark mentions leaving Saint Louis and the Mandan villages in the spring of 1807. But that doesn't allow Bettay to have been gone for three years. In any event, that is all that is known of Bettay.

As a final possibility, the legendary Jacques Houle or Hoole comes into focus. There are passing references to him made by several writers, but no concrete data concerning his activities in the area have as yet surfaced.

The passing references to him are for the years around 1810 and relate that he was killed by the Blackfeet in 1814. He is spoken of as an old, white-haired man who had been in the area for some time. One writer guessed that he was about 90 years old in 1808. Another writer gives a summary of his life which indicates he may have been slightly younger. That writer recounts that he was a soldier in Scotland in 1745, moved to Canada, and fought with the French at the Battle of Quebec. Various things then caused him to go into the Indian trade, but just how or when he arrived in the Flathead, Spokan, Kutenai area is not known. He seems to have been content to have settled there and live with the Indians.

He seems an unlikely suspect as the author of the Pinch letters. He was an old man, happy where he was and with no overriding concern about the fur trade. His background would lead him to welcome Canadian traders rather than try to repulse them. For him to have written the letters would have served no conceivable purpose.[32]

The only name remotely resembling Jeremy Pinch, Zachary Perch, or James Roseman that has turned up in the searches for Pinch's identity is Jeremiah Painsch. This man was an early resident of the Cape Girardeau district of Missouri. The census of 1790 lists no such name, but in 1801 a listing of persons then living in the area shows a Jeremiah Paynisch in the "German settlement." The census of 1803 picks up the name "Jeremiah Banish with a household of two men, four women, sixty minots (the French measurement for a little more than an English bushel) of corn and nine cattle." On 1 May 1806 and on 8 May 1809 he recorded before a board of commissioners a claim to 400 arpents (340.28 acres) of land in the White Water River district. These records list him as Jeremiah Paynisch alias Boening. In 1818 an official survey of the 400 arpents of land certified the grant to "Jeremiah Paynish otherwise Boening by the Lieutenant Governor of Upper Louisiana on 20 January 1800." The Cape Girardeau County Book A, page 6, records the death of a Jeremiah Panish on 5 March 1825.

This information definitely locates a man with a name similar to Jeremy

Pinch in the early days of Missouri and close to the fur-trade emporium of Saint Louis. In the sparse settlement of those days he was doubtlessly known as far away as Saint Louis, and many men of his Cape Girardeau and Saint Genevieve districts became involved in the fur trade. William Ashley and Andrew Henry were the best known of those men. But there is no indication that our man ever became a trader; he stayed home and tended to his 400 arpents all during the time of the Jeremy Pinch episode.

My conclusion is that this man was known locally in the vernacular as Jeremy Pinch and that some of his acquaintances forged that name to the Pinch letter, knowing that the letter could not be tied to Paynisch because he had never left home.[33]

Along this line of conjecture, were both the first and second Pinch letters signed by the same man? Transmittal by Indian carrier left much to be desired. Sweat, fording of streams, rain, smoke, and the wadding of messages into any convenient receptacle, all took their toll. Is it possible that Zachary Perch and Jeremy Pinch were the same signatures but upon receipt by Thompson, deciphered differently each time, with James Roseman being left off the second letter? In this case, why the demotion from captain in the first letter to lieutenant in the second letter?

Since the search for an identifiable man leads nowhere, is it possible to identify sites of old trading posts and thus work backwards to Pinch's identity?

Thompson never mentions encountering Pinch's post or hearing Indian rumor concerning Pinch. Of course, he didn't mention Courter either except to record Courter's death and the settlement of his accounts. Nor did any of the other traders who came into the area soon after Thompson mention anything about Pinch's prior presence or the site of his post. Since gossip was a strong Indian trait, it is strange that Indian gossip concerning Pinch was not still alive when these other men came into the area.

In various journals, letters, and reports of the early traders there are vague references to an American post on the Clark Fork River in Montana. Others refer to a North West Company post at the three forks of the Missouri River. Finan McDonald, writing about the Hudson's Bay Company's "Snake Country" trapping venture of 1823, mentions that ". . . they [Americans] had a fort there fue [*sic*] year agoe [*sic*] about ½ mile beloe [*sic*] Corta is old fort."[34] This remark ties in with Pierre Chouteau's statement in his letter to William Eustis on 14 December 1809, mentioned previously, which alluded to a North West Company post at the three forks of the Missouri. The "Corta" of McDonald's remark could have referred to Courter. Alexander Ross conjectures that the old ruins of a post he found in the Flathead Lake area were the remains of Joseph Howse's post of 1811. It was not Howse's as the site is at the wrong end of Flathead Lake.[35] It probably was Courter's. And, maybe, Pinch's? One report has it that this last site was Jocko Finlay's site when he was a free trapper during the fall of 1809.[36] But all these identifications are just speculations since the house has not been tied definitely to any one man.

In reviewing all this information, we find that Courter is the only man known to have been in the proper area at about the proper time. The others are possibilities. But none of them can be pinned down as *the* man. Pinch, or someone masquerading as Pinch, existed because someone wrote the two letters. Was it just one man or several men with a party? Where did they come from? What was their purpose?

The solution to this mystery must involve several points: (1) probably a person or persons associated in some way with Lewis and Clark, (2) a literate person, (3) a person who was on the Missouri River between the Mandans and Saint Louis, or in Saint Louis, during the period April 1806 and July 1807, (enough time must be subtracted from the latter date to allow the person to travel to the Pacific Northwest by July 1807), (4) a person intimate enough with the trade and officialdom to have a knowledge of the Pike-McGillis letter and an intimation that the North West Company was going to send a party across the Rockies in the spring of 1807, (5) a person who had been in the Pacific Northwest long enough to have established communication with the Indians since that person found out immediately of Thompson's crossing of the Rockies and knew how to route the letters to him.

I lean toward accepting either McClallen or Courter as Pinch. McClallen fits all the above criteria except the one requiring Lewis and Clark personnel. But then, why did he drop from sight after meeting Lewis and Clark at the Platte River? We have no idea which direction he went or how far, nor any clue to his future whereabouts.

As for Courter, we are plainly told that he was in that country a short time after the letters, and that he was an Indian trader. We don't know where he came from, or when, or what his connections were.

Maybe McClallen and Courter were members of two different detachments of Wilkinson's which met in the Northwest with Courter staying in the Montana locale, while McClallen died or drifted on.

The question remains: Who was Jeremy Pinch?

Chapter 9

On the Dalliance of David Thompson

Much criticism has been leveled at David Thompson for his failure to reach the Pacific Coast in advance of the founding of an outpost at the mouth of the Columbia River by the Pacific Fur Company. This carping attitude is due to a lack of appreciation of the ramifications of Thompson's task.

Thompson was confronted with a strange and confusing topography when he crossed into the northern part of the Pacific slope of the Rockies. It is a mountainous country with broken ranges and spurs angling off in all directions through which the rivers have to meander. It is not like the eastern slope, to which all the fur traders were accustomed. There a river will break out of a defile in the mountains and then go in a more or less direct eastern course across the prairie. The rivers of the western slope are tortuous in their course around and through this jumble of mountains. Sometimes two rivers only a few miles apart run in opposite directions, and then circle and join together a few miles downstream. In other cases, two rivers may run parallel for a way, then abruptly diverge emptying into two different streams. This tangle of mountains and rivers has no rhyme or reason and befuddles all newcomers to the area. Thompson was no exception, and this, as much as anything else, explains Thompson's long sojourn in the trans-Rocky Mountain area before he undertook his trip to the mouth of the Columbia River.

Although the criticism of Thompson covers his whole transmontane period it can be distilled into separate charges. First, he was dilatory in his penetration of the Pacific Northwest in the period of 1801 to 1810. If he had

The original version of this essay appeared in the Winter 1972 issue of *The Beaver*, published by the Hudson's Bay Company. It is reprinted here by the kind permission of that publisher.

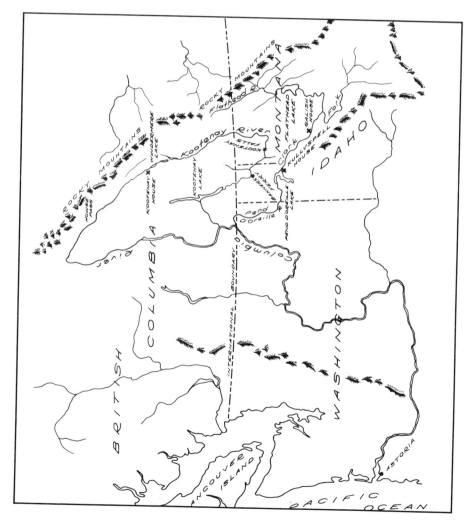

Map of the contorted and confusing terrain confronting David Thompson in his effort to establish trade west of the Rocky Mountains. (Courtesy of the *Beaver* magazine of the Hudson's Bay Company)

been more aggressive and followed the example so admirably performed in 1790 and 1793 by Sir Alexander Mackenzie on his treks to the Arctic and Pacific Oceans, he would have reached the mouth of the Columbia River in plenty of time to have forestalled any attempt by John Jacob Astor to gain a foothold there for his Pacific Fur Company. Second, on Thompson's final dash for the Pacific in 1810 and 1811, he was exasperatingly and unconscionably slow. I can present no defense of Thompson on this last charge as he did dilly-dally, and the evidence bearing on those tactics can show no reason.

I can only speculate on his reason.

He had been a conscientious employee of the Hudson's Bay Company for several years when he inexplicably left and joined the North West Company. This action was completely out of line with his past and future employment. There must have been some unrecorded, maybe embarrassing, reason.

However, he did faithfully serve the interests of the North West Company during the period from 1797 to 1811, when he retired, except for this trip to the mouth of the Columbia River to thwart Astor's plan for a trading post at that place. I think this probably was out of pique.

On 28 June 1810, at Terre Blanche House on the North Saskatchewan River, Alexander Henry, the Younger, recorded in his journal: "Mr. Thompson embarked with his family for Montreal in a light canoe with five men and a Salteur."[1] Thompson was en route to Montreal to avail himself of an overdue leave. Then no further mention is made of him in any of the records until Henry again records on 12 October of the same year: "I was astonished to hear that he [William Henry, a cousin] came from below and had left Mr. Thompson near the north branch waiting for his people."[2]

At Rainy Lake Thompson had been met by emissaries from the just completed annual meeting of the partners of the North West Company at Fort William. The details concerning Astor's Pacific Fur Company venture and what explicit instructions Thompson may have received at Rainy Lake are unknown. Surely, though, a course of action was discussed at that meeting since Astor's intentions and preparations were well known to the North West Company. This message received by Thompson could only have been an express dispatch of explicit orders. The only mention of this episode is found in six foolscap pages in Thompson's handwriting in the Public Archives at Toronto, which reads:

> April 14. Set off to recross the Mountains with the furs & to Lac La Pluie [Rainy Lake] where we arrived July 22nd, 1810. Mr. Astor, having engaged some of the clerks of the N.W. Co'y, formed a company and sent a vessel around Cape Horn to the Columbia. Everything was changed. . . . I was now obliged to take 4 canoes and to proceed to the mouth of the Columbia to oppose them. Accordingly I set off from Lac la Pluie.[3]

Thompson was the best-qualified man in the company for that purpose, not only from his years of experience in traveling, trading, and surveying, but from his inclusive and intimate knowledge of the area to be traversed. Upon receipt of these orders, it is conceivable that Thompson was downhearted, even to the extent of feeling persecuted or imposed upon, and he adopted a sullen attitude. This could explain the desultory manner in which he performed the first part of his mission, but it doesn't justify it. Professor Glover, in his introduction to Volume 40 of the Champlain Society's reprint of *David Thompson's Narrative*, goes into great detail in trying to find the reason for Thompson's actions, concluding that it is a blot on Thompson's character.[4] On the other hand, an opposing analysis is presented in David Lavender's *Fist in the Wilderness*.[5] A reader interested in delving into this display of capriciousness by Thompson is referred to those two discussions.

To the first charge outlined above — that Thompson was dilatory in pursuing a route to the mouth of the Columbia River between the years 1801 and 1810 — we have a horse of a different color. In all fairness to Thompson, we cannot let his actions in 1810 and 1811 tar his actions during 1801 to 1810 merely because it was the same man in the same location. He was seeking two different goals and he must be appraised in that light.

When Alexander Mackenzie had descended the Mackenzie River to the Arctic Ocean in 1790, the Company routinely accepted it and mundanely noted that it set topographical limits to further thoughts of expansion in that direction. After they had examined his experience,

> . . . there remained to be organized the territory of the Pacific Coast drainage basin. The advantages of this trade had been recognized after voyages of Captain James Cook. Alexander Henry's letters to William Edgar dated Montreal, September 1, 1785 and March 5, 1786 insisted on the possibilities of a route from the Northwest to the Pacific, but Pond and Mackenzie had shown no overland route was feasible. After the amalgamation with the XY Company in 1804, however, it became necessary to find new territory for the large number of partners. Moreover, the expedition of Lewis and and Clark was regarded as a forecast of the possibilities of American competition. . . .[6]

In 1793, when this same man made his renowned trip up the Peace River, down part of the Fraser River, then overland to Bella Coola on the Pacific Coast, he didn't accomplish much in the eyes of his fellow traders. "Although contrary to Pond's expectations, no feasible transport route to the Pacific had been found."[7] It brought no immediate financial return, nor did it show any promise.

The Company seemed to feel this trip to the Pacific Ocean was pure folly. If

Mackenzie had had any practicality, he would have turned back in the early stages. The prevailing feeling in the fur trade was that it was a business and had to show profit. There might be times when the assessment of a certain situation called for action, which would result in a small or temporary loss to meet competition or unusual circumstances, much on the order of a "year-end sale" or a "fire sale," but the overall, year-in-year-out business must show a profit.

Thompson had been well grounded in this concept from the time he was first sent inland from York Factory by Humphrey Marten in 1786, through his years of service under William Tomison, "inland chief," down to the time of his departure from the Hudson's Bay Company and employment by the North West Company. William Tomison exemplifies this concept of the fur trade from a strictly financial approach. As E. E. Rich states: "William Tomison, with his great experience in the founding of Cumberland, Hudson House, the South Branch, Manchester House, and Buckingham House, was intent upon the organization of the trade on the Saskatchewan in opposition to the Pedlars. In this he was purposeful, energetic, and sensible."[8]

Catherine M. White writes:

> At his first post on Sipiwesk Lake, Thompson was forced to compete not only with the rival Canadians but also with the Company's [HBC] traders from Churchill Factory. As previously noted, the York and Churchill posts were directly responsible to London, and being thus independent of one another, they often entered into such strenuous competition that it was necessary for the Board of Directors in London to intervene.[9]

With this background and frame of mind, Thompson, in 1801, participated in the first feeler put out by the North West Company for a way to establish trade with the Pacific Coast Indians and a practical route to the Pacific Ocean. He knew, probably intimately, of Mackenzie's Fraser River journey and that that river was not the Columbia, and that the route had no practical application. He must also have been familiar with both Vancouver's and Gray's identification of the mouth of the Columbia, which had been discovered in May 1792. With the information that this great river came out at this known point, the traders had an indefinite area for its source, as they were familiar with the Rockies and it was obvious that the Columbia did not flow through them.

If the river which Mackenzie had followed in 1793 did happen to be the Columbia, which all their assessments contraindicated, perhaps there were some tributaries of it that were navigable. Or perhaps the Fraser was a tributary of the Columbia. In any case, a more southerly and direct route would have to be found to have any value to the fur trade. "The route discovered by Alexander Mackenzie was already authenticated, but it was too difficult; Thompson's task was to seek an easier and more southerly route, by which a constant flow of trade to the Pacific Coast and so to China might be maintained."[10]

The first try by the North West Company to penetrate the Rockies was in 1801. It was unsuccessful, but its importance, according to Arthur S. Morton:

> . . . does not lie in any discoveries he [Duncan McGillivray accompanied by Thompson] may have made so much as in the fact that he and the North West Company were feeling their way to the Columbian enterprise as early as 1800-1801. . . . The Columbia enterprise was not pushed in the years immediately subsequent to McGillivray's first attempt. This was doubtless due to the need of men and capital during the fierce struggle with the XY Company, but also to the fear that the enterprise would bring financial loss, if the furs were to be carried all the way across the continent to Montreal. In his "Some Account of the Trade carried on by the North West Company," written by Duncan McGillivray in the months before his death in April 1898, and when Fraser's posts in New Caledonia had been built he says, "The trade as it is carried on at present beyond the mountains, instead of getting any profit, is a very considerable loss to the company, as the furs did not pay for the transport to Montreal, where they were shipped. . . ." It says much for the eagerness of Duncan McGillivray and the North West Company for the Columbian enterprise that, despite their failure to secure the short line of transportation, they went on with the policy of advance across the Rockies and to the Pacific Coast. They must have been confident that careful management would overcome their difficulties. In the light of this, reforms and economies recorded in the so-called Minutes of the North West Company may well be noted.[11]

Over the next three or four years, the North West Company made many changes in its operation, attempting to increase its financial return. The Company was not unduly concerned or overly eager to open the transmontane trade but was cognizant of its possibilities if it could be developed economically.

After the first attempt to cross the Rockies in 1801, the idea was allowed, not to lapse, but to lie fallow while other problems were wrestled with. The problems and haggling caused by

> the outrageous conduct of the Indian trade absorbs attention and obscures the fact that the two Montreal concerns were absorbed in

rivalry for something of greater significance than their race to secure the hunts of the Athabaskan (and other) Indians. Mackenzie's route to the Pacific was indeed of no serious value to the fur trade. It must be improved on. But any new route would still start from Athabaska, or perhaps from the upper reaches of the Saskatchewan, and would lead into the Rockies in a southwesterly direction. If, as was inescapable, both North West Companies accepted that the all important brigades for the Pacific must start out from Athabaska, then they were forced also to accept the fact that the long haul from Montreal to Athabaska was a handicap.[12]

In 1806 the project was reactivated, maybe because Mackenzie rejoined the company in 1804 when the North West Company and the XY Company amalgamated. His known enthusiasm for the idea of development of the Pacific trade, coupled with Duncan McGillivray's, could have been the overriding influence at the Fort William meetings of the Wintering Partners. Arthur S. Morton gives credence to this thought. He wrote:

It has been argued that the Columbian enterprise was the result of the American expedition to the Pacific commanded by Lewis and Clark. Rather, it rose out of Alexander Mackenzie's spectacular voyage to the Western Sea and his scheme to go in and take possession of the coastal fur trade. The subsequent expedition of Lewis and Clark could be no more than an additional incentive. The enterprise was the fixed policy of Duncan McGillivray when he was a Wintering Partner on the Saskatchewan and during his years as agent for the Company, and it was launched in his last year but one, for he died on April 9, 1803.[13]

As a direct indication of the general trend of thought within the trade, James Bird, in a letter of 1806, wrote:

Mr. David Thompson is making preparations for another attempt to cross the Mountains, pass through [the Kutenai country] and follow the Columbia River to the Sea. He is to have eight Men with him, and the object of his enterprise is said to be, to ascertain positively whether a trade can be formed with that Country valuable enough to be worth persuing [*sic*] through the difficulties with which it must be attended, and, if it should, the uniting of the commerce of the two Seas.[14]

Along this same line of thought, Thompson himself in a letter to his company on 23 September 1807 wrote: ". . . our so long delayed *settling* of this Country."[15] (Italics mine).

Tobacco Plains. The valley lies just west of the Rockies in northern Montana and southern British Columbia. The Kootenai River, down which David Thompson cruised in 1808 in the first exploration of the area, lies in the far background at the foot of the mountains. The valley received its name from the fact that the Upper Kutenai Indians raised native tobacco here. (Photo by Winton Weydemeyer)

All these comments are conclusive evidence that Thompson's transmontane project was no crash program — merely a pilot project. He had to determine to the satisfaction of his company that it was worthwhile and economically feasible.

After Thompson had made it across the continental divide in 1807, he was in new country — the country described at the beginning of this essay. He had no road maps, no tourist information booths, no filling stations for ready reference and direction, and he found himself on a northward flowing river. He must have thought of Mackenzie following a northward flowing river on the other side of these mountains and ending up at the Arctic Ocean.

In addition, he may have had some of Lewis and Clark's information as there were close personal and financial ties between Saint Louis, Montreal, New York, Michillimackinac, and Fort William. It is extremely unlikely that he had any published work on Lewis and Clark since the first work, the *Gass Journal*, was published in 1807.

This nebulous information, from all these sources, including the known mouth of the Columbia River and Mackenzie's trip down the Fraser River, convinced Thompson he had to go south and west. Therefore, he went south, up this river that he had stumbled upon, which happened to be the Columbia before it turns west and then south. Just south of the headwaters of this river, with a one-and-one-half mile portage, is a southward-flowing river, the Kootenay. He then backtracked and built Kootenae House on the headwaters of the Columbia River just below present-day Lake Windermere. He stayed there the rest of 1807 trading with the Kutenais.

In the spring of 1808 he started feeling out this new country, traveling down the Kootenay River, over to Lake Pend d'Oreille, up the Clark Fork River, and over to Flathead Lake. In the course of this exploration he built two more trading posts, Kullyspell House and Saleesh House.

By 1810 he had promoted a good trade, each summer taking his traded fur back over the mountains and exchanging it for a new supply of trade goods.

The remainder of the years he spent traveling the rivers and lakes of the region, trading and familiarizing himself with the complexities of these mountains and the courses the rivers followed through them, searching for a southerly route that would put him on the upper reaches of the Columbia River. The rivers, though, continually confounded him — they all seemed to go north. Indian information led him, in 1810, to try the Pend d'Oreille River even though it flowed northwesterly. The river became boisterous and was leading him astray, he thought, even though it would have taken him to the Columbia River. He abandoned it and returned to Kullyspell House where he finished the trading season.[16]

In the spring he started for the Company's headquarters at Fort William on Lake Superior to take a promised leave and, probably, make a detailed report on his experiences and the lay of the land.

He got as far as Rainy Lake where he was met by an express message to turn around and go back to the mouth of the Columbia River to forestall Astor's planned opening of a post at that point.

Some have called all this time he spent in Montana and Idaho dilatory. Since there was no emergency when he was sent there, and it was incumbent upon him to ascertain the lay of the land so that the best route to the coast could be used, get the friendship of the Indians, and, above all, to pay his way to prove that the area promised a profitable venture, reflection brings the realization that he accomplished his mission admirably in this maze of mountains and rivers.

Thompson has been maligned for this period in his life even though he did what a careful, prudent man would do in similar circumstances and did it in a workmanlike manner. His achievement has been misunderstood by persons unfamiliar with his problems which were a combination of topography and economics.

Chapter 10

Spy and Counterspy?

A little over 150 years ago the United States and Great Britain became involved in a territorial dispute. It was an issue almost as inflammatory as the Revolutionary War and the War of 1812, but it was resolved by cool heads before anyone started burning gunpowder or letting blood.

It was the Oregon Question. Like Uncle Tom's Topsy it just "growed up" and during its growth two blurred episodes took place. It is these two episodes with which we are concerned.

Prior to these two events, many white sailors — Cabrille, Hecate, Meares, Cook, La Perouse, Kendrick and Grey, Vancouver, Bodega y Quadra, and many more — had been roaming the northwest Pacific seas for 100 years, but they had done nothing toward proclaiming unquestioned sovereignty over the coastal area. Their interests were maritime trade and expansion of empire. The land area lay fallow awaiting the future.

This land area had no future. It was unknown and unattainable from the land-based eastern establishments, and its potential was unrealized. No one wanted it. No one was concerned about it.

In 1763 when France, by the Treaty of Paris, ceded all her possessions east of the Mississippi River to England, and by secret treaty, all her land west of that river to Spain, there had never been a boundary between the English colonies and the French colonies on the eastern shore of this continent and now, after that ceding, there was no need for one. But when 1783 came along and the treaty ending the Revolutionary War was signed, that need became necessary.

The Canadian-Maine boundary was left in limbo, but in the West, where all the confrontation between Canadians and Americans occurred, it was of pressing moment. The diplomats, relying on imperfect knowledge and crude maps, agreed on a boundary for that area. It was to run through the Great Lakes to the northwest corner of the Lake of the Woods, and thence to the

Henry Vanderburg, a *bourgeois* of the American Fur Company operating out of Fort Union on the Missouri River, had been dogging a trapping party of the Rocky Mountain Fur Company for some time. He abandoned what proved to be a fruitless chase and struck out to employ his men in serious trapping. The trappers soon ran into a hunting party of Kainahs (a tribe belonging to the Blackfeet Confederacy and known today as Bloods). In an ambush by the Kainahs Vanderburg was killed. (Courtesy of the University of Montana)

headwaters of the Mississippi River. Of course, one of the results of the Revolutionary War was that the American colonies received all the English land east of the Mississippi River, so by taking the international boundary just to the headwaters of that river gave what was to become the United States a definite territory. This arrangement was satisfactory for many years as the northern Maine area was only a wilderness.

But growth, restless expansion, and fur trade pushed against the western boundary — the Mississippi River. When the Louisiana Purchase opened the trans-Mississippi West to Americans, it opened a can of worms. What were the boundaries of Louisiana? They were ill-defined. No one knew for sure. Some persons assumed that the western boundary was the Rocky Mountains, others that it extended to the Pacific Ocean. The southern boundary between what France had sold to the United States and what Spain was still claiming, after all her dealings back and forth with France over the territory was, to say the least, hazy. And the northern limits? They weren't even guessed at; the area was *terra incognita*. Fur traders, both Canadian and American, were roaming the northern plains with no thought of boundary lines, jurisdiction, or sovereignty.

Into this passive vacuum stepped the North West Company of Montreal, John Jacob Astor of New York City, and the War of 1812. What had been a *laissez-faire* attitude over the Great Plains suddenly became a burning issue. Astor was one of the major fur dealers in the world and had a vision of collecting western furs at a convenient spot in the West (saving the long trip overland to the East), of taking them to the avid Chinese market where they could be exchanged for Chinese wares, and of hauling the new load of merchandise to the London or New York market. He would be killing two birds with one stone; getting two payloads out of one round trip. The North West Company knew what he had in mind as he had proposed that they participate in the scheme. They declined, but Astor went ahead with the idea, hiring some of the Nor'Westers as part of his personnel.

The plan matured. In 1811 Astor sent a party by sea and another party by land to establish a post at the mouth of the Columbia River. The two contingents joined and built a post which they named Astoria. The North West Company lost no time in coming overland to oppose the post and brought with them the news of the outbreak of the War of 1812. Part of the news was that Great Britain had sent a warship on its way to seize Astoria. The Nor'Westers offered to buy out the post before it was seized. The Astor men decided to sell. (This little transaction has caused a great deal of musing by historians concerning the honor and integrity of both the buyers and the sellers.) Be that as it may, this little byplay and the treaty ending the war initiated the Oregon Question.

Great Britain, in the treaty, agreed to restore all the places that were seized during the war. The United States maintained (egged on by Astor) that Astoria, way out there in the boondocks, fell under this provision. Great Britain denied that interpretation, claiming that Astoria was sold before the warship arrived to seize it and, therefore, Astoria was not a prize of war. The argument was settled by agreement in 1818 awarding title of Astoria to the United States, but leaving it occupied by the Nor'Westers.

While that little bit of drama was taking place, unnoticed and unremarked, in a remote corner of the world, diplomatic negotiations were going on concerning the boundary through the Great Plains.

There was Canadian insistence that since the Treaty of 1783 stated that the line should run from the Lake of the Woods to the headwaters of the Mississippi River, that was where it should go, even though it had been found that the headwaters were considerably south of where they had been thought to be in 1783. The Canadians felt that the line should run west from the Mississippi to the coast in the neighborhood of the 45th parallel. Such a line would have put the northern two-thirds of the present state of Minnesota, all of North Dakota, the northern third of South Dakota, all of Montana, the northern half of Idaho, all of Washington, and a sliver of Oregon under British sovereignty.

The Americans took the position that, at the time the first line was laid down, the Mississippi River was thought to head much farther north, and the intent of the treaty was to make a straight line west from the Lake of the Woods, and that the approximate location of such a line would be the 49th parallel. The Americans also insisted that the line continue straight through the continent to the Pacific Ocean, including part of Vancouver Island. The British, because of their fur-trade interests in the Oregon Country, would not hear of that solution. They insisted that if that line were adopted it should go west only until it intersected the Columbia River and then follow down the middle of that river to the sea.

The commissioners could not resolve this problem, so, to quiet it, they agreed to a line running along the 49th parallel to the summit of the Rocky Mountains with a ten-year joint occupation of the disputed territory beyond the mountains. This solution satisfied the commissioners and diplomats as it seemed an equitable line through the land that was being used and which held all the promise of the future. The country beyond the Rockies was unknown, too distant for any practical purpose, and all fragmentary information indicated it was good only for Indians and furs. "Everything . . . [was] under the iron domination of time and distance."[1]

The disquieting and irritating question of the southern boundary of the Louisiana Purchase was also settled at this time. In 1819 Spain and the United States agreed to a line between their respective territories. The boundary was set from the Gulf of Mexico, up the Sabine River, then up the Red River of

The United States-Canadian boundary in northwestern Montana and southeastern British Columbia. Shows flooding of Tobacco Plains by the Libby Dam Reservoir, "Lake Koocanusa." (Photo by Winton Weydemeyer)

Texas, then across to the Arkansas River up to its headwaters, thence north to the 42nd parallel, which it would follow westward to the sea. That left only the northern boundary to be decided between Great Britain, Russia, and the United States.

Russia, in expanding her Aleutian fur-trading domain, had extended her activities as far southward as San Francisco Bay. But this expansion had not profited her. The increased overhead had more than offset the gain. To retrench and still accomplish some of the objectives that had prompted her expansion she withdrew to the Alaskan region and, in 1824, entered into two separate treaties — one with England and one with the United States. In both treaties Russia gave up all claims to any territory south of 54° 40′.

The southern boundary settlement with Spain stirred up no criticism, but the northern boundary agreement was another matter, especially in light of the Russian withdrawal northward. The believers in Manifest Destiny and the radical Anglophobes started beating their drums in the cadence that the diplomats had been derelict in agreeing to extend the boundary only as far west as the Rocky Mountains. Such was a surrender of wholly American interests.

Arguments, claims, and counterclaims went on in Congress and the press for an immediate and favorable solution (*i.e.*, favorable to the United States). The English, characteristically, maintained a low profile, insisting in all discussions and public remarks that they had a just claim to all or part of the area in question. The brouhaha was finally settled by an agreement on 8 August 1827 for joint occupation, subject to cancellation by either party giving 12 months notice to the other party.

That agreement quieted diplomatic and Congressional discussion, but the American public continued to propose schemes for trade and colonization and propounded thunderous nationalistic propaganda. Public clamor kept increasing, reaching a crest in 1840. People began to emigrate to the Oregon Country, thinking that land grants would be forthcoming, and that they had the governmental and public response in England. A demand arose to resist this encroachment by American homesteaders and merchants as such an increment would load the issue in favor of the United States.

In 1843 the Oregon enthusiasts held a convention in Cincinnati, Ohio, which went off the deep end by adopting a resolution that the United States immediately claim and occupy the Oregon Country up to 54° 40′, even if it brought on war. By the time of the presidential campaign of 1844, the fever was so high that James Polk ran and was elected on the slogan of "All of Oregon or none" and "54° 40′ or fight." Congress again revived the issue with the fire-eaters demanding that notice be given Great Britain that the 1827 joint-occupancy agreement be terminated, that troops be sent to the territory, that land surveying be started so that the squatters in the territory could have their holdings confirmed, that the settlers be armed, that mail routes be started, that commercial regulations be drawn up (to deprive the Canadians of their foothold), and that Indian agencies be formed. War fever was building, and bills were introduced in Congress for increasing the navy and militia. As a sign of the times, abrogation of the 1827 agreement passed the House on 27 April 1846.

Cooler heads in both the United States and Great Britain did not want war.

Great Britain stood to lose all of Canada in any such war, because of the long land boundary across which the United States could mount offensives at about any point before England could get troops transported, positioned, and provisioned. And the awesome British Navy would be useless in such a war. On top of all this, she had to contend with a famine in Ireland, a war in India, and widespread dissatisfaction at home. The United States was in no better position. She had other issues coming to a head — the annexation of Texas, the war with Mexico that was brewing, the occupation of California, the slavery question with its ramifications, States' Rights, free trade and monopoly arguments, and the future course and disposition of the public domain. Above all, war over the Oregon Country would cause a consolidation of British, Spanish, and Russian Pacific interests that would destroy the foothold of the United States in the area.

In the face of all these factors, President Polk adopted a hard-nosed attitude. He wanted to twist the British Lion's tail, but the public mood took one of those quick shifts centering on a quick victory in the Mexican War and the consolidation of the occupation of California. The Senate, responding to the shift, refused to go along with the cancellation of the mutal occupation agreement with Great Britain. Senator Benton, up to this point one of the foremost firebrands on the Oregon Question, made a Senate speech in May 1846 conceding that the Oregon Question had taken a back seat and the 49th parallel was a practical boundary. Great Britain, sensing an opportune opening, immediately made a formal offer to settle on that basis. On 15 June 1846 the treaty was signed making the 49th parallel the boundary, leaving open only the question of Vancouver Island. Finally, 25 years later, the line was drawn through Puget Sound among the San Juan Islands.[2]

All the preceding discussion sets the stage for the entrance of two men who may have been undercover agents for the two governments. Their activities are opaque. One wonders why they acted as they did. But history is replete with the lengths to which governments will go to accomplish undercover missions. In the light of the excitement and passions aroused by the Oregon Question, these two men were possibly spies.

The two men were Benjamin Louis Eulalie de Bonneville, Captain, United States Army, and George Frederick Ruxton, a one-time lieutenant in the British Army.

Bernard DeVoto, in *Across the Wide Missouri* (page 417, note 6), wrote that Captain Stewart, a British nobleman who spent six years, off and on, hobnobbing with the trappers and traders in the Rocky Mountains, could have been a British agent. A close study of that man's activities gives no reason to suspect that he was a spy — only an itchy-footed Scotsman. In the same note DeVoto also wrote: "It has turned out that George Frederick Ruxton was acting as a British agent in 1846 and 1847. . . ." Regrettably, DeVoto cites no documentation to prove his statement, leaving it as conjectural as it always has been.

Let us take up the story of Captain Bonneville first. His actions whet our curiosity. He was born in France of French parentage on 14 April 1796. Thomas Paine, the renowned pamphleteer and promoter of democracy, was living in France at this time and was a close personal friend of the family. He was aiding the cause of the French Revolution. The political unrest finally forced the elder Bonneville to send his family to America in 1803. The family lived with Paine, who had returned to the United States, until the elder Bonneville came over to the new land in 1807 or 1808. The family was well known and well thought of in France, and soon earned recognition in the United States as a creditable and acceptable family.

On 14 April 1813, at the age of 17, Bonneville, the son, entered the United States Military Academy. He was graduated on 11 December 1815, and appointed a brevet second lieutenant of light artillery. In January 1817 he was promoted to second lieutenant. Until 1819 he performed routine service in the New England area. Then, in 1820, he was assigned to a road-building project in Mississippi. In June 1821 he was transferred to the Second Infantry and served on various details at Fort Smith, Arkansas, and San Antonio, Texas. In 1824 he helped build Fort Gibson on the Grand Fork of the Arkansas River.

When the Marquis de la Fayette, an old family friend in France, paid his social visit to the United States, renewing acquaintances and visiting friends, he arranged for Bonneville to be appointed his aide during the tour, and to be granted a leave of absence for one year to accompany him back to France. While in France, Bonneville was promoted to captain and upon his return, reassigned to Fort Gibson. Until 1831 he served in the Arkansas and Missouri Rivers area where he met many Indian traders and became accustomed to the frontier.[3]

On 21 May 1831 he requested a two-year leave of absence to engage in a private fur-trading venture. This was a strange step for a career army officer to take. To interrupt his career, lose seniority, and cause higher authority to speculate on his dedication and perhaps put a blight on his future can only be called strange. He, apparently, was well considered; probably one of the "fair haired boys" of the army hierarchy due to his family background and connections, as well as his ability.

The army, in accordance with the standards and practices of those days, normally would have refused to even consider such a request from one of its career officers. But it granted this leave with some provisos. One was to forward "every information which you may conceive would be useful to the Government."[4] Another was to study the country, its characteristics, the Indians' economy and habits "within the limits of territories belonging to the United States between our frontier and the Pacific."[5] Everything was to be at his expense, but he was to keep the War Department informed of his "position and progress" (see Appendix C). Of particular interest is the reference to the Pacific Ocean. The American fur trade did not extend that far at that time. Onely a few hardy souls were venturing over the continental divide in trapping forays, and these forays were just stabs westward from bases on the eastern slope. But the Oregon Question was confronting the government.

Upon receiving his leave, which was granted for the period of May 1831 to October 1833, Bonneville went east to spend six months studying astronomy at West Point, buying instruments and equipment, and securing financial backing. In delving into the financial arrangements we get a glimmering of why Bonneville spent six months before setting out to trade with the Indians. Any such venture required capital, the larger, successful operations being backed by tens of thousands of dollars. All indications are that Bonneville and his family did not have that kind of money, so he had to secure outside subsidy. Did Bonneville have an inkling that his family's connections would assure him of such support, or did interests involved in the Oregon Question choose him as their undercover agent? If his family's background were such as to bring his name to mind in search for such an agent, and his occupation and experience on the frontier were such as to make his endeavor a logical employment, he may have been approached as an emissary. Or, if the proposal was strictly his own conception, the Oregon Question proponents may have seen a Heaven-sent opportunity to obtain some first-hand information and ammunition for their cause.

In any event, during his stay in the East

> . . . he had the good fortune to meet with a gentleman of high respectability and influence, and who cherished a school fellow friend-ship for him. He took a general interest in the scheme of the captain; introduced him to commercial men of his acquaintance, and in a little while an association was formed, and the necessary funds were raised to carry the proposed measure into effect. One of the most efficient persons in this association was Mr. Alfred Seton, who, when quite a youth, had accompanied one of the expeditions sent out by Mr. Astor to his commercial establishments on the Columbia [River]. . . .[6]

So wrote Washington Irving, who was a good friend of Astor's. Can we read between the lines here? Can we speculate upon and try gropingly to assess the connections and interrelations that may have existed between Bonneville (with his family background and occupation), Astor (the wily, shrewd, wealthy man of power), Irving (trying to protect his good friend Astor's machinations), the War Department (under constitutional civilian control), the President and members of his cabinet (who had diplomatic problems), and influential senators (who were confronted with public demands)? We are dealing here with raw power and politics in all its aspects of demagoguery, backscratching, and smoke-filled rooms. The rigamarole of a boyhood friend and Seton stepping into the breech to furnish the financial aid could have been camouflage to conceal any direct governmental interest in Bonneville's expedition; it was strictly a commercial venture with not even Astor, who had vast interests in the fur trade and the Oregon Country, having any connection with it. Washington Irving, who published his account in 1849, went to pains to mention that he just happened to meet Bonneville at Astor's home at the conclusion of Bonneville's sojourn in the Far West and again happened to meet Bonneville in Washington at a later date and that Bonneville generously put his manuscript and journals in Irving's hands.[7] It was all mere happenstance, but why was Bonneville at Astor's house if Astor had no involvement in the affair?

But let's go back to the actual affair and see how Bonneville performed his trading effort and/or mission.

Bonneville was back on the frontier recruiting men in the spring of 1832. He left Fort Osage on the Missouri River on 1 May 1832 with a party of 110 men recruited locally. These men were nondescript with the exception of Joseph Rutherford Walker and Michel Cerré, who were experienced Mountain Men. He employed 20 wagons to transport his goods rather than using the usual packhorse train. In this innovation he followed the lead of Sublette, who had used wagons a couple of years previously to go to the rendezvous, but Sublette did not cross the mountains with them as Bonneville succeeded in doing. This use of wagons may have been dictated by the need to know if a military force, which by its nature needed wagons, could accomplish a journey to the Oregon Country. His route led up the Kansas River to the Big Blue River, then to the Platte River, striking it just below Grand Island, Nebraska. He went up the Platte River, cut over to the Sweetwater River, then crossed over to a branch of the Green River, arriving at Pierre's Hole on 27 July 1832 in time for that year's rendezvous.

He immediately went a few miles up the Green River and built a permanent base camp close to present Daniel, Wyoming. It was a poor location for Indian trade as it was not readily accessible or a site frequented by Indians, and the winters were severe. While most accounts call it Fort Bonneville, the experienced trappers promptly labeled it Fort Nonsense and Bonneville's Folly. De Voto wrote that Bonneville, a West Point-trained strategist, chose it because ". . . it was a strategic center of the mountain area and as such could serve as a base and supply depot for armed forces moving into the Oregon Country, block any invading army coming from the Columbia River, cover the route into South Pass, hold the key to the interior basin, and the routes to California." I can't agree. The winters would have rendered untenable any such strategic use. Bonneville, being a greenhorn and unfamiliar with the country didn't crank into his calculations the environmental factor.

E. S. Topping, in his *Chronicles of the Yellowstone*, wrote: "Bonneville came overland from St. Louis this same year and made his headquarters on Green River; but he received his supplies from Fort Cass." I can find no other such statement, but Topping was an early pioneer of the area and presumably spoke from an accumulated store of local oral history.

Bonneville should have been able to carry considerable supplies in his large wagon train, so why should he have needed a supply depot? Washington Irving, in his detailed account, doesn't even suggest such an arrangement. Since Fort Cass was one of Astor's trading posts, maybe Irving deliberately ignored such an arrangement to protect not only Astor's involvement but any indication to an outsider that this was more than a mere trapping party.

But, if the above is true, why? The trip up and down the Big Horn River would be tedious and hazardous, and the rendezvous' purpose was to supply the mountain trade over the expeditious Platte River, Sweetwater River, South Pass route. If Bonneville were a bona fide mountain trader, why should he deviate from the accepted mode of trade?

Bonneville soon found out that his Green River site was not desirable and moved to winter quarters on the Salmon River about four miles west of Salmon, Idaho. Before he left his first post though, he established a pattern that he would follow throughout his time in the mountains. He broke up his band of trappers, sending one party to the Bear River north of Salt Lake and another to the Crow Indian country in the Wind and Yellowstone River drainages. This proclivity of his — sending out parties to great distances from him — was followed consistently and assured that his trapping and trading efforts would suffer, being out from under his supervision. But if his purpose in so doing was to assemble the maximum amount of information concerning the country, he couldn't have followed a better plan.

From the Salmon River site he traveled up the Green River to Jackson's Hole and then over to Pierre's Hole, where he set up quarters for the winter. He almost starved that fall, so he broke camp and went back to the north fork of the Salmon River. The day after Christmas he left, going south to the Snake River and then west to the Three Buttes. For five months he had been prowling around the edge of the Oregon Country and may have thought he was in the heart of it. The two seasoned Mountain Men in the party had been sent off on the other jaunts, and he had only fragmentary maps of the area and the rumors and gossip, which constituted the verbal description of the country, to rely upon.

After a month he returned to the Salmon River cache and reequipped his party for trapping on the Malade River. He stayed there until 15 June when he went back to his cache on the Salmon River and then on to the general rendezvous on the Green River.

His several detachments, coming in from their various areas, reported to him at this time. They related nothing but bad news — horses had been stolen, caches rifled, they had been outwitted and outtraded by Hudson's Bay Company men, had been in Indian fights that forced abandonment of goods, and so on. These reports are examples of Bonneville's "bad luck," "inexperience," "lack of commercial sense" with which he is often charged. But if viewed in the light of a deliberate attempt to garner all the information possible in the shortest time, it makes sense. In furtherance of this view, we must remember that Bonneville offered high wages to keep his party roster at full enrollment and seemed to be content to put anyone on his payroll, even the drifters and vagabonds. If his primary motive was profit from furs, he surely would have had the idea forced upon him by this time that he must keep some sort of control over his party and that he would be better off with a few reliable men than with many drifters. But if his idea was to put many parties in the field to gather information on the country he needed many men.

While at the Green River rendezvous, in spite of all the bad news he had just received, Bonneville put still more extensive plans in motion. One was "to establish a trading post on the lower part of the Columbia River, near the Multnomah Valley, and to endeavor to retrieve for his country some of the lost trade of Astoria."[8] Another was to explore the Salt Lake country. The third was to go back into the Crow country. He put Walker in charge of the Salt Lake enterprise with instructions to keep a minute journal and to make maps. Walker was furnished with one year's supplies and told to be back for the next summer's rendezvous. The remainder of the men were divided again, some being sent back into the Bear River country, with Bonneville taking the rest back into the Wind River area.

He fiddled away the summer, then started south for the Colorado River, but, after a few days, turned west for Bear River. From there he went down the Snake River again and put up a winter camp at the Portneuf River. On Christmas Day he left this winter camp for the Columbia River.

On 4 March 1834 he arrived at the Hudson's Bay Company's Fort Walla Walla which was in charge of Pambrun, an experienced Hudson's Bay Company man. He was regally received and the utmost hospitality extended to him, but when he tried to buy supplies to continue his trip, Pambrun emphatically refused to let him have anything. Pambrun, no doubt, knew of Bonneville's army position since Bonneville made no secret of it. He was commonly referred to as Captain by the Mountain Men and Indian gossip concerning him, very likely, preceded Bonneville to Fort Walla Walla. Pambrun, knowing the army connection, must have been even more apprehensive about furnishing Bonneville with succor than he would have a run-of-the-mill Mountain Man nosing around Hudson's Bay Company territory. So, on 6 March, Bonneville started back for his post on the Portneuf River.

On 14 May he left that winter camp and started, with the rest of his brigade, for the rendezvous on Bear River. All his detachments were to report to him at that place. (All this scurrying around brings to mind the action of army reconnaissance patrols.) Walker checked in at the rendezvous from his Salt Lake excursion and reported that he had meandered around beyond Salt Lake until he finally ended up in Monterey, California, where he spent the winter ogling the girls and participating in fiestas. Washington Irving, following Bonneville's lead, was extremely critical of Walker for wasting the trade goods without acquiring any fur, thus putting the whole enterprise in financial jeopardy. The question arises, was this a convenient handle for explaining Bonneville's financial failure, or was it another subterfuge to cover Walker's failure to explore the country beyond Salt Lake, hunting for the mythical Buenaventura River or the headwaters of the Multnomah River? Of course, Walker was derelict in wining and dining away the winter in Monterey, rather than trapping a few beaver and finding out the lay of the land. He might have included a little sideline sashay into California in the line of duty.

At this 1834 rendezvous Bonneville's lieutenant, Cerré, reported in from a trip to Saint Louis where he had taken fur from the previous year's rendezvous. From there he had gone East and visited Washington, D.C., where he had delivered Bonneville's letter written in 1833, to General Macomb of the War Department. Part of the letter read: "The information I have already obtained authorizes me to say this much; that if our Government ever intend[s] taking possession of Oregon the sooner it shall be done the better."[9] He then went on to state the number of men required to carry out this intention plus conditions at various Hudson's Bay Company posts. This was one way to get a report into Washington without causing comment — send a known Mountain Man into Saint Louis with fur which would cause no interest and then let him drift east, perhaps to purchase further supplies, and while he was roaming around, just happen to visit Washington to see his Congressman or someone.

Bonneville, at this 1834 rendezvous, made still another set of plans. One party was to trap the Yellowstone and Wind Rivers during the fall, then go down to the Arkansas River and set up a winter camp. Bonneville, himself, set out again for the Columbia River, to return in the spring to the Arkansas River where he could rejoin his main party.

When he reached Fort Walla Walla he, again, received the same welcome and the same refusal to render any assistance to him. He tried trading with the Indians to obtain sufficient supplies to continue his journey. The Hudson's Bay Company, though, had explicitly forbade the Indians to do any such thing. If the Indians wanted to continue their relationship with that company, they had only one course open to them — obey. Bonneville's only recourse was to turn back into the mountains where he could obtain game. If he continued he faced starvation.

On 17 November 1834 Bonneville was back on the Wind River and canceled his order for the Arkansas River meeting. He took the party back to Bear River where they went into winter camp. The next spring, he moved back to Wind River, sent out two parties to trap, and on 5 July started back to Independence, Missouri, arriving on 22 August 1835. By this time he was almost two years overdue on his leave of absence.

From Independence he went to New York. Why to New York is not explained. One would think he would make a point of first reporting in to some Army installation, but he didn't. Washington Irving found him at Astor's home. Apparently, it was more important to report to Astor than to the Army. When he finally reported at Washington, he found to his dismay that he had been dropped from the Army rolls on 30 May 1834. He immediately applied for reinstatement, but the Army refused to consider it. General Macomb said that he was under the impression that Bonneville had intended to resign anyway at the end of his leave.[10]

The wrangle between Bonneville and the Army continued with Bonneville getting no place until President Jackson stepped in on 5 January 1836 and submitted a request to the Senate for Bonneville's reinstatement.

All this uproar was good camouflage for Bonneville's activity. Or, it may have been that General Macomb and the War Department were not privy to the plans and purposes of the President, the secretary of war, the secretary of state, or the diplomatic corps. Astor's ways were devious ways, and he had the ears of the most influential men in and out of government.

While all this maneuvering was going on, Bonneville notified the Adjutant General of the Army on 8 May 1836 that he had to close out some business affairs in the West, and, on 19 April of that year, he obtained from William Clark, Superintendent of Indian Affairs in Saint Louis, a license to trade at "Laramais Point" on the Platte River. (The time element bearing on these two incidents is inexplicable.) Five days after the date of the trading license the Army issued General Order No. 25 which reinstated Bonneville to the rank of captain in the Seventh Infantry and assigned him to Fort Gibson.[11] Whether or not he made the trip to Laramais Point is questionable. In 1838 one of his former employees, Montero, who had been with the Yellowstone River trapping party, was taking steps to recover for himself some disputed furs in cache at the "Portugese Houses" on the Yellowstone River.[12]

Bonneville returned to duty at Fort Gibson in August 1836. His subsequent career was not remarkable. He participated in the Mexican War where he was both breveted lieutenant colonel and court-martialed for misbehavior before the enemy. He blamed the court-martial on the envy and malice of his fellow officers. His life after that was routine. He commanded Fort Kearney on the Oregon Trail, served as commandant of the Military District of New Mexico, and so on until he became ill and was retired on 9 September 1861. During the

Civil War he was called back for duty in minor administrative posts and promoted to brevet brigadier general. He died in 1878.

He started with everything going for him in the Army. Suddenly he abandoned routine for an activity unimaginable for a career Army officer and contrary to standard Army procedure. Was he granted leave on orders from on high for mysterious purposes and reinstated in the same manner? Such action could very well have soured his contemporaries and predicated his future obscurity in the Army. But in that astonishing and irregular break in his career he had reconnoitered the approaches to the Oregon Country. From his military training and experience, plus the wagons he had taken with him, he must have formed an opinion on the practicality of marching an army to the Oregon Country. Since no route presented an open road, he surely had suggestions for alternative operations.

Immediately after his return to Washington the United States Navy sent out an expedition under the command of Lt. William A. Slacum. There was nothing secret about it. It was a routine naval survey of our Northwest Coast. His official instructions were "to generally endeavor to obtain all such information, political, physical, statistical, and geographical as may prove useful or interesting to this government."[13]

He arrived in the Columbia River in December 1836 in an American ship and spent a month talking to the settlers in the Columbia and Willamette River valleys plus the few he found around Puget Sound. As a result he became an extremist in his views, especially of British claims to the territory and their attitude toward Americans. The commercial potentiality didn't impress him, but he did acquire an antipathy toward the Hudson's Bay Company's policies and personnel. He was so rabid in that bias that he reported to the Senate, contrary to fact, that the Hudson's Bay Company incited the Indians to attack Americans.[14]

Two years later, in 1838, pressures and interests in the problem caused the United States to officially dispatch another expedition to the Pacific Ocean. This one was composed of four navy vessels under the command of Lt. Cmdr. Charles Wilkes. Its purpose was described as a survey of the Pacific Islands and Singapore for commercial and scientific objectives. Wilkes's instruction contained a specific charge to examine "the territory of the United States on the seaboard" and "the coast of California with special reference to the Bay of San Francisco."[15]

The trip was planned to cover four years. Thus, Wilkes didn't arrive at the mouth of the Columbia River until the summer of 1841. The hazards presented to vessels by the bar at the mouth of the river caused him to downgrade the suitability of that river for seaborne traffic, but he, like Slacum, was enthusiastic about Puget Sound and San Francisco Bay.

He did a more thorough job of investigation than Slacum had done. He split his men into four parties and explored the coast from Puget Sound to San Francisco Bay and the interior as far as present-day Spokane and Walla Walla. At the conclusion of the exploration he started the ships for San Francisco and sent a party overland up the Willamette River and down to San Francisco, where it rejoined him.

His report, though voluminous, did little to clarify the vague information about the Oregon Country. Bias, prejudice, and extraneous material were so interlarded into the report that pertinent facts could not be extracted with certainty.[16]

Those two expeditions, Slacum's and Wilkes's, were not espionage in any sense of the word. They were open, official acts, but they expressed continuing and active interest by the United States in the Oregon Country. Perhaps Bonneville's report had stimulated that interest and had shown the need for more information on the interior of the country to evaluate the Oregon Country propaganda.

As the American public's hue and cry over the Oregon Country increased the British became concerned. The Hudson's Bay Company, in particular, was making insistent pleas for more British concern about the problem.

In the early winter of 1845, Sir George Simpson of the Hudson's Bay Company was in London. He met with the Prime Minister and Foreign Secretary to discuss the defense of Canada in the face of this increasing American bellicosity. Simpson suggested that some regular soldiers be sent to the Red River Settlement at Lake Winnipeg and that they be reinforced by native militia recruited on the spot. Also, he suggested that four shiploads of Marines be dispatched to the mouth of the Columbia River and that they be augmented there by 2,000 local militia. These were to seize and hold Cape Disappointment at the mouth of the river.

In response to Simpson's plea, the diplomatic state of affairs, and the Duke of Wellington's pronouncement that the Canadian border was indefensible, the British government sent two lieutenants of engineers, Mervin Vavasour and Henry Warre, to Canada for an inspection and to make recommendations.

Simpson and the two lieutenants met in Montreal and went on to the Red River. On the way Simpson continually stressed the need for garrisons at several points. Vavasour and Warre, though, recommended only a detachment of cavalry and artillery for the Red River and went on west in company with Peter Skene Ogden. On arrival at Cape Disappointment they found it preempted by some Americans. At the same time, four British warships arrived to show that Great Britain was determined "not to allow their rights to be encroached upon." The British officers, some of them sons of the nobility, were unimpressed by the country and its prospects; it seemed a howling wilderness that could never achieve the amenities of civilization. Lieutenant Pell, the son of the prime minister, dutifully and speedily carried all the combined reports back to London.[17]

This British activity was not a secret any more than the American naval expeditions, but it highlights the worry of both governments and bears on the activity of the next man we are going to consider.

George Ruxton was born on 24 July 1821 at Eynsham Hall, Oxfordshire, England, to middle-class parents. He had a normal boyhood, but at an early age showed an independent turn of mind, being intolerant of discipline. This characteristic led to more than the usual trouble with school authorities. At the age of 14 he was enrolled in the Royal Military Academy at Sandhurst. This transition did not quell his rambunctious nature, which led to his expulsion from the academy after two years.

For some reason he left England in 1837, at the age of 16, to enter the civil war then raging in Spain. He made the journey at a more or less leisurely pace. His family was not wealthy, but perhaps they defrayed his expenses in the hope that the experience would satisfy his wanderlust. In an account of that journey he wrote of his need to proceed more rapidly because of a "fast consuming purse." He finally reached the forces supporting the royal family and enrolled with them. In the course of the fighting he was commissioned, made a knight of the Order of San Fernando, and decorated. That war drew to a close in 1839, and Ruxton returned to England — a battle-decorated officer just ready to turn 18 years of age.

In some way, he managed to secure an appointment in the British Army as a lieutenant on 2 August 1839. He served at various postings in England and Ireland until he was sent to Canada, where he arrived on 8 July 1841. His new posting was to Amherstberg on the Detroit River. Finding military life at that station boringly routine, he availed himself of every opportunity to hunt and associate with the Indians and white residents of the area. His restless character still was not satisfied, so he obtained leave and went back to Great Britain. The next spring he returned to Canada and rejoined his regiment. In a few months his fidgety, impatient nature reasserted itself, and he applied for permission to sell his commission. Permission was granted. He then changed his mind and requested that he be permitted to withdraw his request. For some reason, perhaps the disgust of higher authority for his lack of steadiness, this last request was refused.

Now free to indulge his capriciousness, he went on an extended hunt in Ontario with some Indian friends. En route he took passage on a ship from Buffalo to Detroit. An incident illustrating the mood pervading the American public at that time over the Oregon Question occurred on that ship. An American fellow passenger remarked to Ruxton, "You Britishers will never keep the Canadas, anyhow you fix it. They was meant for the States and the States will have it, that's what they will."[18] Ruxton spent that winter on this hunt, returned to Lower Canada and took passage for England sometime in the spring of 1844.

By June of that year he was on his way to Africa. His reason or motive is unknown. The same blank applies to the necessary finances. Any savings he may have had from his army pay surely were used up by this time. He had had to pay his own way to and from the hunt in Ontario, pay his expenses and buy equipment while there, and then his passage back to England. His expenses for the couple of months he was in England were probably minimal, since he could fall back on his family for board and room. Under these circumstances, how did he finance this latest trip?

He reached Morocco about 1 September 1844. Within a few weeks he was back in England. An interesting sidelight to this episode is that France and Morocco were at war at that time, and the minute peace was declared, Ruxton went home. With his known fidgety feet, army experience, and with the constant antipathy between England and France, he may have been sent by England as an observer of French logistics and tactics.

After only a couple of months at the most, he was again on his way to Africa, saying that he wanted to explore the Zambesi River and cross over the continent to Mozambique. At this time the English and Dutch weren't getting along too well over colonial aspirations in Africa, and Ruxton's proposed itinerary would have been through the northern edge of the Dutch dreams.

Ruxton's equipment for this trip included 125 pounds of bar lead, 25 pounds of tin, 50 pounds of gunpowder, 10,000 caps, 12 muskets, 12 dozen gunflints, 500 musket balls, 1 single rifle, 1 double rifle, 1 double shotgun, 1 elephant gun, 2 pistols, and bullet molds. Apparently this was a bona fide expedition, whatever its purpose.

He made a more or less exploratory jaunt down the west coast of Africa, leaving one ship and tramping a few miles before hailing another ship for passage to another part of the coast. He finally disembarked at "Walwich Bay" (Walvis Bay?), which put him in a position to start his cross-country exploration. His farther progress was stymied by some Portuguese traders and a missionary, who blocked his efforts to hire natives as guides and porters.

Frustrated, he returned to England and contributed a paper to the Ethnological Society on the Bushmen of Africa. At the same time, he applied for governmental assistance for another trip to Africa. That request was referred to the Geographical Society for an opinion. The various requests, opinions, and referrals to governmental bureaus became bogged down in red tape. All efforts to cut the red tape were fruitless. It all could have been a smoke screen to make a subsequent journey to Africa by Ruxton appear to be strictly a scientific trip in which military intelligence had no interest.

While the governmental machinery was grinding away, Ruxton suddenly embarked at Southampton on 2 July 1846 on a ship bound for Vera Cruz, Mexico. This quick decision to go to Mexico happened to coincide with the outbreak of the Mexican War.

Ruxton, after his arrival in Mexico, represented himself as an agent for British commercial interests. He had never been or represented himself as such before this time, nor, as we shall see, did he conduct himself as such during the stay in Mexico. Instead he went pell-mell through Mexico and its northern area. Also, the timing of this trip leads to speculation. The Oregon Question cry of "54° 40' or Fight" by the Americans was in crescendo. Among his possessions after his death was found a pamphlet on the Oregon Question.[19] In the preface to his serial published by *Blackwood's Magazine* (and subsequently brought out as a book), he obfuscates his reasons for the journey. He wrote: "It is hardly necessary to explain the cause of my visiting Mexico at such an unsettled period; and I fear that circumstances will prevent my gratifying the curiosity of the reader, should he feel any on that point."[20] Why should he feel any compunction about naming his principals if he were truly a commercial agent?

The thought occurs that, if he were an espionage agent, he might have as his primary goal an assessment of American military preparedness, execution, training, and know-how so that, if the Oregon Question came to blows, the British government would have a firsthand account of these military factors and their application by the Americans in a remote stretch of country. Ruxton's military service plus his Canadian experience would make him a natural choice for such an assignment.

When Ruxton arrived at Vera Cruz, he spent no time furthering commercial contacts in that important port, but left immediately for Mexico City. When he arrived at that capital, he spent a few days equipping himself for a journey to the northern provinces, and, maybe, authenticating his status as a commercial agent. But he certainly did not spend enough time to further any major commercial contacts. He didn't stop any place in Mexico, then or later, to go into a song-and-dance for the benefit of merchants. The fact that he was supplied with substantial funds is shown by an incident during this part of his journey. At one town his lodgings were burglarized. The culprits were apprehended and his belongings, including $3,000 in cash, were returned to him.

He left Mexico City on 14 September and proceeded northward as rapidly as possible, through Durango, Chihuahua, El Paso, and on to Santa Fe with scarcely a pause. Chihuahua was in a state of martial law as Colonel Doniphan's forces were poised at the Rio Grande River. Ruxton, though, obtained an immediate pass through the lines by virtue of his British passport and papers attesting to his status as a commercial traveler. At El Paso the authorities attempted to detain him, but, once more, his credentials cleared him. He encountered the outpost of the American Army at Valverde. Again, his credentials opened all doors for him, in spite of the fact that he had arrived from Mexico and had no commercial goods with him. In contrast, the well-known, genuine American merchants with an actual assortment of goods were held in abeyance. He was so well received by the Americans that he went on to Santa Fe with Lieutenant Abert's party.

All these incidents detract from the credibility of Ruxton's insistence that he was acting as a commercial agent. He must have had some other skit that he used on the Americans and glossed it all over with this recital of commercial connections. Especially so, since at one point in his journey, he wrote that his papers showed that he not only had British connections, but was also a commercial agent for the Mexican government. Would the American Army receive him with open arms under that circumstance? And the role of commercial agent does not tally with his activity after he reached his journey's end; there was no commercial activity at that point.

He arrived at Santa Fe on 21 December 1846 and left there in January 1847 for Taos, New Mexico. At Taos he was advised to proceed no farther north because the passes were closed by snow. He ignored the warning, explaining he could find no pasturage for his animals at Taos, while Mountain Man hearsay assured him of winter pasturage on the upper Arkansas and Platte Rivers. If he were on a business trip his insistence to proceed ever northward, despite all impediments, seems inconsistent. But he left Taos immediately for the north and suffered severely from a storm in the mountains. Once through the mountains, he stopped at "The Pueblo" on Fontaine-qui-bouille Creek, where he spent the rest of the winter. Now he seemed satisfied; apparently he had reached his objective.

During the winter The Pueblo was visited by Harwood and Mark Head, two experienced Mountain Men.[21] Concerning Mark Head Ruxton wrote, ". . . whom I had intended to hire as a guide to the valley of the Columbia [River] the ensuing spring."[22] But Mark Head was killed during the Taos uprising shortly after this meeting.

At the end of March 1847, he left Taos and went north along the Front Range in Colorado. He returned to the Arkansas River after a couple of months without attempting to go on to the Oregon Country. Perhaps he couldn't find another qualified guide to replace Mark Head as the Mountain Man era had fallen on hard times. By far the most of the dyed-in-the-wool Mountain Men had left the business, taking up land in Oregon, settling in New Mexico with a family on a farm, hiring out as meat hunters for emigrant trains or trading posts, going back home to Missouri or Kentucky, or acting as Indian agents. He may have been in a quandary if his objective was the Oregon Country, or maybe it was time for him to make a report.

On 2 May he started up the Arkansas Valley for the States, joining up at Bent's Fort with an Army quartermaster train bound for Fort Leavenworth, Kansas, where he may have heard that the Oregon Question was settled. At

Fort Leavenworth he boarded a river steamer for Saint Louis, thence went to Chicago and New York, where he took passage to Liverpool, England.

The Oregon Question treaty had been signed in Washington, D.C., on 16 June 1846 while Ruxton was preparing to sail from Southampton. If he were a spy sent out to probe the potential of the Oregon Country and assess American military capabilities, he was a little late, but word of the signing probably had not filtered back to England in time to countermand his orders. If his purpose were to ferret out information to help Mexico in her war with the United States, why did he hurry through Mexico and the opposing armies and on up to the edge of the Oregon Country? His remark about Mark Head and the Oregon Country, as well as his delay and gathering of resources on the Arkansas River, seems to give a definite clue as to intentions.

He spent his time in England, after his return in 1847, writing up an account of his experiences for *Blackwood's Magazine*. It was so well received that he wrote a companion piece which was published as a book entitled *Life in the Far West*. Both are entertaining and authoritative accounts of the time, and excellent sources of information. By spring 1848 he was complaining of ill health and, in a letter to his mother, told her that he could spare her only ten pounds. This indicates that the family was not monied. Shortly after this, he sold his royalty rights to the book and used the money to pay his way back to the United States. Upon reaching Saint Louis, his health took a turn for the worse and he died there on 15 August 1848.

Why did he come back? If he had been employed by the British government, maybe they had no further need for him. Perhaps his health foreclosed any such future activity. Maybe he was enamoured of the West and saw a future in writing about it, since his style and subject matter had been so well received by both the public and the critics. No one knows why he returned.

In casting our thoughts back over this essay — the Oregon Question, Bonneville, Ruxton — we find three seemingly unrelated affairs; unrelated on the surface, that is. But when we indulge in a little conjecture, we begin to wonder if there wasn't more to them than meets the eye.

Bonneville may have been sent out at the instigation of the radical proponents of "All of Oregon or None" with the stipulation that whoever was selected for the job should be able to assess the military side of the routes, logistics, and topography so that plans could be formulated for an occupation of the Oregon Country by force. Bonneville's restless traipsing, making only a token effort to trade, lends credence to this premise. He was gathering information of the above nature. There were no problems for a military force up to the continental divide since that was a well-known, open, straight-shot route. But the western slope route for the seizure of the Columbia Valley presented unknown hazards for a military traverse (otherwise, why did he take the wagons?), and that is the area in which Bonneville himself spent all his time.

A review of Ruxton's activities leads only to questions. Suddenly and with no apparent reason he abandoned an interest in Africa and set off for Mexico at the outbreak of the Mexico-United States War. If his interest was, as he insisted, strictly commerical, why did he hie himself as rapidly as possible through Mexico without applying himself to commerical relations? If he was determining how Great Britain could extend help to the Mexican government in the prosecution of the war, why did he not spend some time with the Mexican authorities in Mexico City and the Mexican troops in the field? If his intent was to assess American military strength and capability why did he not pause at Valverde and Santa Fe? He did none of these things.

He seemed to be obsessed with the need to reach the American Far West, and as soon as he arrived there he was content. Why did he spend only a few months in that location and then return to England? He may have had only a private, personal desire to sample that life and then reduce his experiences to writing. Since his prior writing on the Bushmen of Africa had been so well received, he may have gotten an idea from that effort to expand his field.

If so, why did he not proceed from Liverpool to New York, to Saint Louis, and on to the headwaters of the Arkansas River, rather than taking his roundabout route? If he had nothing to hide he went the long way around and expended a lot of unnecessary time and exertion.

On the other hand, if he were an English agent why should he approach the Oregon Country from the east? If war came, no English army could use that approach. Also, in the event of war, England could not transport troops and supplies to defend Canada's border, land them on the East Coast, and then dispatch a portion of them for the Oregon Country; they would have been forever getting there.

But, if England dispatched a force by sea to be landed on the Pacific Coast, firsthand knowledge of the terrain, routes from the east, and the problems such routes might pose for an American Army going to Oregon would be of inestimable help to the British. They already had information concerning the interior of the Oregon Country. Their extensive fur-trading operations throughout the area had revealed the interior topography, but from what direction, pass, or river would the Americans make their thrust? If the British had this information they would have a base for formulating a strategy and could make intelligent deployment of their forces.

His short stay in the West, sort of a once-over-lightly sampling of a new land, may have been dictated by orders to render a report to England at stated intervals so that his government would have current and up-to-date information. In going back to some settlement from which he could forward that report he was trying to meet that deadline. His arrival at the settlement would raise no questions; merely some sort of wanderer who had come in for fresh supplies and guides.

When he arrived at Fort Leavenworth he probably heard that the Oregon Question had been settled, so his mission was finished.

His remark about getting Mark Head to guide him to the Columbia River indicates that his original task had not been completed when he arrived at Fort Leavenworth.

This evaluation of his activity is creditable in light of Polk's inauguration and Polk's fire-eating proposal of "54° 40' or Fight" and the mounting public clamor to do something about the Oregon Country. Beyond doubt, the British government was concerned over this state of affairs. Ruxton's emergency assignment was aborted by the unexpected reversal of the American attitude and the satisfactory solution of the problem.

Piegan camp on the move. (Courtesy of Kamp-Mann Co)

Chapter 11

In Defense of the Indian

Most of the books about and accounts of Indians that we have read and listened to are flawed, even though we listened to an old-timer, or the book was written many years ago by someone in close contact with Indians. The storyteller saw Indian customs and society through European eyes. He might have been a second or third generation American, born and raised on the frontier, but his parents and grandparents had imbued him with a European viewpoint. That viewpoint unconsciously flavored his interpretations and assessments of Indian life.

The Indians had a distinct culture with its own perspectives, traditions, and a highly organized society.

When the colonists came to these shores to make new homes and lives they brought with them their European concepts. They made no effort to understand the Indians' culture but condemned it because it was different. From this clash of ideologies and the stubborn colonial refusal to give an inch grew much of the subsequent Indian troubles in the United States.

Even before the colonists arrived, the early explorers, seeking something to exploit, the fishermen frequenting the Grand Banks, and the itinerant, cruising fur traders saw the natives of these shores as a barbarous, savage race. Many natives were kidnapped or enslaved, some brutally, some under duress, some blarneyed into coming aboard the ships for a journey to the wondrous land of the white man. Once in custody they were ridiculed and treated as spectacles. There was even learned discussion in Europe concerning their status; were they human, subhuman, or just a higher order of animal?[1]

The European concept, and thus the colonists', was that Europe was the epitome of civilization. Europe had scrutinized, tried, and winnowed all human traits from many cultures until it had harvested the true essence of life. Other societies or cultures were considered inferior. Bringing the peoples who were unenlightened into the fold of European culture and standards was the white man's burden.

The colonist made much of his "civilized" attitude and his meticulous consideration of Indian title to the land. He conscientiously entered into formal purchase transactions that complied with English law, but gave no thought, or at best a sneer, for the Indian formality, ritual, and ideas governing such transactions. The bargain was struck not "at arm's length between a willing and knowledgeable buyer and a willing and knowledgeable seller" as the Indian had knowledge only of his custom, and the Englishman paid no attention to it. The abstract principles of English law were beyond the Indian's comprehension. He related to the idea of community property and a religious belief that Mother Earth was inviolate. Man was permitted to utilize her bounty the same as the deer, the fish, and the birds, but Man could not own Mother Earth.

When an Englishman bought a tract of land from the Indians, he extinguished in his eyes, all Indian right to it. Then he built fences and posted no trespassing signs which the Indian could not understand. All the Indian had bargained away was permission for the colonist to abide in that territory. If the Indian complained about this usurpation of right, the Englishman self-righteously maintained that he had complied with the law — *his* law.

He said that he had found a band of Indians encamped along a stream in a small meadow fishing and gathering herbs, and that the location appealed to him. He had approached the Indians with an offer of two blankets, an ax, some beads, and a few steel arrowpoints and conveyed the idea that he liked the spot and wanted to buy it. The Indians could see no reason why the white man's living there would incommode them in any way, so they accepted the offer. The white man pulled out that magic stick that made marks on that funny birchbark the white man used and made some of the white man's chicken tracks on it. He then proffered it to the Indians to validate. The Indian complied with more chicken tracks of his own, thinking that this was part of the white man's strange rituals.

Then, later on, when the white man started running Indians off the property and perhaps taking a potshot at one of them, wounding him, or when a band of hungry Indians came by and shot one of the white man's cows for food, the white man immediately got up a posse and went in pursuit of the culprits. Catching up with some Indian band — perhaps a band completely ignorant of the incident — the posse killed the men, women, and children to teach "those marauding, irresponsible devils some respect for the law."

The Indian response was according to Indian custom. Incidental bloodletting was not a tribal transgression but a matter between the kinfolk of the murderer and the one murdered. Accordingly, the kinfolk of the murdered Indians descended on the white settlers and took blood toll. The white accounts of the incident were always unanimous in that the white action was just retribution and a sanctioned action according to the English law. In England a man could be hanged for stealing a load of bread, and those miscreants of Indians had shot and eaten a whole cow. But the Indian action in retaliation was just plain savagery.

Similarly, later on, when the whites had founded some little settlement composed of a store, a church, a backsmith shop, and a few houses, there were cases in which Indians came in to trade some furs. The storekeeper welcomed them with open arms, passing out gratuitous cups of whiskey, then giving them more until the Indians were well befuddled. At this point the storekeeper began trading whiskey for fur until he had all the fur in return for, at the most, a gallon of cheap whiskey. As the Indians were besotted, they might vent their exhilaration in vandalism. When the white men remonstrated, events sometimes erupted into wanton destruction by the Indians such as setting the village afire or killing a white man.

When the news of this confrontation got out, the militia was mobilized to punish the Indians for this wanton and unprovoked savagery. The militia, in righteous retribution proceeded to kill whatever Indians they could find and destroyed villages and crops in the vicinity. The militia's action was considered as sacrosanct, legal war, not white savagery.[2]

The encroachment upon tribal territories by English expansion, whether by purchase or squatter's right, had a two-fold effect upon the Indian. It lessened his range for food-gathering, meat and vegetable, and he was forced into either a marginal subsistence or dependance upon white charity. If he fell back into the latter he was called a shiftless, lazy, no-account Indian. If he chose the former he became a degraded, lowlife specimen of humanity. If he rejected the above options, he necessarily had to expand his activities into some neighboring tribe's territory. Logic and livelihood compelled the neighbor to object. When all these conflicts reached an impasse or boiled over, the Indian was called a bloodthirsty, murdering devil.

The colonists' blatant, self-righteous bias (bigotry, if you will) was crooned at the cradle, preached in the pulpit, and blared from books. It is no wonder that it became imbedded in American folklore and part of the national heritage. No patriotic American would dare subscribe to any other creed.

No American could admit that the Indians, in the main, were a friendly, compassionate, helpful people who would extend the hand of friendship and camaraderie whenever given the chance. No. The Indians were a base, deceitful people, lulling and gulling their way while waiting their chance for an act of treachery. This attitude, born in colonial days, was so firmly implanted in American mores that it caused three centuries of bloodshed, agony, and dishonor. As recently as 1907 the state of Montana published, as required reading for all school children, a *Pioneer Manual* which pinpoints the white man's bigotry. That bigotry accounts for much of today's Indian bitterness and rancor.

The manual read, in part:

> From 1803 to 1861, the territory included within the present limits of Montana was dominated by Indians and to some extent by hunters and trappers in the employment of the different fur companies. The entire territory from the eastern border to the Rocky Mountains was one vast pasture land grazed over by countless numbers of buffalo. Its mountains, plains, and streams abounded in many kinds of game and fish and the territory had been for a century the hunter's paradise. Civilization was then a stranger to Montana.
>
> The Sioux and Crow in the eastern and middle sections of the territory, and the Blackfeet, Piegans, and Flatheads in the west and south had been from time immemmorial [*sic*] the lords [and] masters of this region and were then holding all other tribes in subjection, awe, and terror. "Their rights to be there were none to dispute." Treacherous, cunning, thieves and cowards at heart, brave only when there was no danger of peril to encounter, hunting and fishing their occupation, feasting and reveling in times of plenty, starvation and death facing them in times of want; thrift, prudence and provision against famine forming no part of their inheritance, cruelty to a foe in their clutches always a prominent trait of their character, war upon inferior tribes their diversion and delight, scalp locks dangling from their belts and lodgepoles as trophies of their prowess and valor in war, nomadic in life, lazy, shiftless, improvident, having no fixed or permanent homes, these wandering tribes of Montana, like the Arabs of the desert, were the pirates and free booters of the western plains and mountains, and such indeed in this region and during this period was the life, character, custom, and occupation of these aborigines, differing little if any from the native races east of the Mississippi.
>
> The only [law?] then recognized and observed in this region was a peculiar kind of trapper's code and Indian custom effective only where they could be enforced; where "might was right and law was will." In all disputes, force was the only argument and submission the only alternative. This was, however, the period when our territory was slowly emerging from this condition of savagery and barbarism to law and civilization.[3]

With the philosophy expressed above pervading the American conscience, how can we blame the Indian for resisting the white man's ruthless debasing of the Indian's beliefs and way of life? Especially when the Indian's side of the problem was not even considered?[4]

An example of the American refusal to weigh, understand, or appreciate the Indian way of life is afforded by the standard appraisal of the male Indian as being lazy and throwing all the work onto the women. The Indian man is constantly portrayed as lying around in the shade, smoking, gambling, gossiping, letting his wife do all the cooking, the preparation of leather and fur, root and berry gathering, hoeing the corn and beans, butchering and drying of meat, and serving as a packhorse when camp was moved.

That assessment of work distribution fails to consider the man's role. Men were visible during the middle of the day around the camp, but they were just between chores. They arose early, some of them hunting (finding and killing game was no small chore), some looking for raiding parties of other Indians which would threaten the security of the camp. Horses must be tended, a chore usually delegated to the older boys, who had to be surpervised. Grazing available to the horses must be checked. When the game in the area had been driven away by constant hunting, or had drifted out of the vicinity, or the graze was exhausted, or the security of the camp was threatened, or when certain vegetables or berries ripened in another area, it was the men's job to select a new campsite, determine the best route to it, scout that route for enemies, evaluate the available water and wood, and organize the move. During the move, the men were responsible for the security of the band, giving protection to the head, flanks, and rear, standing ready to repel any attack no matter how sudden or from what direction. These routine chores of the men called for dawn and dusk activity. Thus, at midday, when the white man usually observed and evaluated them, the men were at leisure after a hard morning's work and were anticipating a hard evening's work. It was during this leisure period that the men discussed all their new assessments and made decisions as to their immediate and long-range situation while keeping their hands busy making bows, arrows, lances, shaping arrowpoints, repairing their buffalo-hide shields, and refurbishing their accoutrements.

An analogy can be drawn between the common idea of the role of Indian men and women and a visit to our present-day society by a Martian. If a few little green men from Mars landed at some American town, observed our society for a week without entering into that society, they would return to Mars with a report that would run somewhat as follows: The women of the Earth people are abused while the men lead an indolent life. The men arise in the morning, eat a meal prepared by the women then depart for a business section of the community where they spend the day gossiping, carousing, and eating. In the evening they return home to a meal prepared by the women, then disport themselves in a carefree manner until bedtime. On the other hand, the women are confined to homework and child raising, taking the children to school, cooking, housework, shopping, laundry, and attending to all the multi-tudinous details of married life. In other words, they are drudges while the men are lazy, good-for-nothings with none of the responsibilities of their society and contributing nothing to it.

A report such as this could be expected from someone unfamiliar with our society, who made no attempt to enter into it, but merely stood on a residential street corner making superficial observations. The majority of American commentators entered into Indian villages in this same frame of reference, and their remarks are just as invalid as the Martians' would be.

When the white man began to infiltrate Indian country many of them were dissolute adventurers — some immoral, some amoral, and some were renegades. They all professed to espouse Christian virtues and ethics, but the Indians observed their character and antics and drew conclusions. Later, when the settlers followed the adventurers, a mixed batch of characters and personalities were evident — some were good people, some were rogues, some were Sunday Christians who made a point of attending church every Sunday and praying the loudest but who spent the rest of the week cheating, defrauding, and lying to the Indians.

As the whites succeeded in imposing white culture upon a territory, the Indians absorbed some of the vices of the white man. The whites then berated the Indians as scandalous scoundrels. In truth, the Indian was only reflecting modes of behavior he had picked up from the white man's culture, and the white man found it unsavory. The shoe was ill-fitting when it was on the other foot.

Along this same line of thought, there has been much "tch-tching" and looking-down-of-noses because some Indians practiced polygyny. The existence of polygyny, to the disapproving people, is *prima facie* evidence of an amoral and lecherous character, no consideration being given to a different society, mores, or set of standards. If we assess the practice of polygyny by the Indian under the conditions confronting the Indian, we can understand that it was a practical solution to a problem imposed by his hard, strenuous life.

As the Laws of Nature dictate, young Indians of opposite sex were attracted to one another. Two individuals would formalize this attraction by marriage according to Indian ritual and custom. The marriage would endure and prosper similar to any other society, there being a mutual goal, division of labor, and enhancement of material well-being. If and when the husband began to achieve prominence in the band's affairs, the societal structure demanded that he provide food and accommodation for the persons who came seeking his advice and assistance. This requirement placed larger demands upon his family in providing larger, more commodious quarters, and a constant food supply in excess of the family's needs.

By this time the wife probably had children to care for, and these increased requirements taxed her beyond her ability.

As mentioned in the essay on Indian trade practices and concepts, all these increased societal demands posed a problem which could not be solved by merely hiring some additional help or buying some supplies, because the Indian had no idea of the abstract principle of money. To provide extra meat for the pot, more leather for a larger tipi, or more bedding the husband had to acquire an extra horse or two that he could lease out to some man who was just starting out as an adult or who was not well-favored in material advancement and who would share the results of the hunt with the horse owner. After the hunters returned with the kill, the wife now had more than a normal workload to contend with. If she had a sister, or niece, or cousin (the first wife preferred another member of her family who had the same background and upbringing) who was young and full of energy or widowed and needing support, she and her husband would approach that other woman for help in the butchering, cooking, leather-tanning, berry-picking, and vegetable-gathering.

This other woman then became a member of the household, an integral part of the menage. As such she was considered, by others and by herself, as a wife; this was her home. There was no way she could have a separate entity and take pay for her services (so many pounds of meat a day, so many beaver pelts a week, or so many buffalo hides a month). What would she do with it? She would have to try to barter it again for food and lodging, and who would be amenable, and for how long, to that arrangement? Especially so, since she would be contributing only this pittance to the routine of the other household.

There was often a surplus of women in a tribe. While worldwide, due to some compensating knowledge of Mother Nature, there were 105 boys born to every 100 girls, this ratio was not sufficient to even up the sexes in the mature years of Indian life. Even though both sexes were subject to childhood accidents and diseases, males suffered a higher rate of mortality. The risks of war, a horse stumbling and throwing its rider during a buffalo chase, exposure to severe storms, starvation during a scouting expedition, falling from a precipice or breaking a leg in a remote area during a solitary hunt, mauling by a grizzly bear — all these perils took a toll among the male population. About the only hazard an adult female faced was childbirth. Thus, Indian women often outnumbered men.

How could surplus women be supported? While they could make a contribution as single women to the distaff functions of a band, what man or men should assume the burden of supplying these women with the necessary raw materials? And if that problem were solved, how could the results of their labor be distributed? The problems would have been endless due to personalities, changing relationships and conditions, deaths among the adults, both men and women, and new girls reaching adulthood displacing or altering a previous arrangement.[5]

The natural solution was for extra women to become part of a family. Polygyny wasn't the result of lust by men, but was a tribal necessity.

Probably many women preferred the role of a second wife of a prominent, respected, well-to-do man than the bride of a young, unknown, untried youth.

Shamanism is another aspect of Indian life that has been depreciated. A shaman or medicine man fulfilled a function which was a combination of today's physician and a man of the cloth. This function was just as valid and achieved results just as effective as those of today's practitioners of medicine or spiritual counsel.

A medicine man's incantations, burning of herbs, rattling of gourds, making signs in the dust, and laying on of hands had as profound an effect on the Stone Age patient as our civilized session on a couch with a psychoanalyst or spiritual consolation by a man of God. Yet people who make much ado about their weekly session with their "head-shrinker" or their rapport with the teachings of a particular church are usually people who ridicule the role of the medicine man in Indian life. Solace is the result in all these cases.

We must also remember that at the time of the white man's encounters with Indian medical practices the white man's art and science of medicine was not very advanced. Blisters, poultices, leeching, bloodletting, and purges constituted the arsenal of medical lore. The white man had just left the era of dried frog eyes, powdered rhinoceros horn, and a dram of black goat's blood administered during the full moon. Why should we expect Indian medicine to have been more advanced? Many of the Indian remedies were scorned by the Europeans because the remedies were indigenous and suffered from the lack of a Latin name and inclusion in a European pharmacopoeia. Also, they were administered with incantations and hocus-pocus that smacked of witchcraft. But today many of those same herbs are recognized inclusions in modern medicine.[6]

This deplorable American attitude toward the Indian culture persisted until well into this century with no realization by the Europeans that the Indians, a hunting-gathering-fishing-horticultural people, lived in harmony with the land; they conformed to Nature's ecosystem. But the white man, in his conceited wisdom, ignored all this, saying, "These stupid Indians don't know beans about the proper use of land — look at all those idle acres!"

Using this premise the white man wrested the land from the Indians, confining them to reservations where they were forced to live under the edicts of the government and subsist, supposedly, on that government's charity.

The white man then plowed up every acre he could get a plow into and grazed the forage of the untillable land until it was ruined. He devoted his efforts to forcing the land to produce more grain and meat than the land could sustain. He then adopted "improved" practices to force it to produce even more. He impounded, diverted, and polluted the waters of the continent. All in the name of progress.

The Indians had lived a stable existence on this land for thousands of years.

The white man has had it for a mere century or two. But the Indian ended up with no taxes, no mortgages, no dustbowls, no debts, no bankruptcies, no government subsidies. These results beg the question: Was the Indian really stupid?

Striking proof of this thesis that the Indian has been maligned is offered by the Canadian experience. When the first French fur traders started foraging for fur out of their Quebec and Montreal bases, they immediately recognized the advantage of enrolling the Indian as a partner in the business. He could gather fur in the course of his everyday life and bring it to collection points. In this capacity he was important to the business and was treated accordingly. The French learned the Indian's language, his customs, his codes, his mores, and responded to them. The French accepted and accommodated the Indian. The communication thus established led to mutual respect, and when friction points arose the issue was resolved bilaterally. The result was that Canada never had the vicious (on both sides) Indian problems that plagued the United States.

Collosal Olmec head. Pre-Classic, 1100 B.C.

[The following plates in Chapter 12 show sculptures dating from the Olmec-Maya period of Central America. (From von Wuthenau's *Unexpected Faces in Ancient America.* Courtesy of Crown Publishers)]

Chapter 12

Blue-Eyed Indians

Years ago many stories were passed around about strange tribes of Indians. The tribes were always beyond the horizon, always seen by someone else, but the stories were accepted as true and passed on as fact. They related to blue-eyed Indians, bearded Indians, white Indians, red-haired, blond, and curly haired Indians. Those stories led to speculation, some of it serious and learned, as to the origin of the American Indian.

One of the most widely accepted theories claimed the Indians were direct descendants of the Lost Tribes of Israel. This theory invoked physical characteristics and serpentine comparisons of the Hebrew language and some Indian languages. Today, we know that the Indians had been on this continent long before the Asia Minor troubles arose that gave rise to that theory.

However, we cannot ignore the mass of folklore that came into being in Asia Minor about ancient seafarers who made contact with far and mystic lands.

The earliest historians, Pliny, Virgil, Strabo, Aristotle, told tales, handed down in the folklore of the Phoenicians, Egyptians, and Minoans, of seamen who prowled unknown seas 3,000 years before Jesus of Nazareth. They wrote of old accounts of a great landmass lying many days sailing time to the west of Africa. People tend to pass off these accounts as "poetic license" — someone embellishing an account of a mundane trading trip to some Near Eastern port. The teller of such a tale would thus enchance his fame as an entrancing spinner of yarns.

Perhaps we should give such legends and folklore more respect than we have in the past. Recent archeological and ethnological assessments of artifacts and cultures point to the very real possibility that there may have been contact between the Old and New Worlds many centuries, maybe millennia, before Columbus. Unfortunately, the scholars engaged in ferreting out, translating, and evaluating the information cannot agree. There is much acrimonious debate over the translation of a stone's inscription, the date and

Early Classic terracotta head from Vera Cruz.

origin of an artifact, or the diffusion or independent development of a phase of a culture.

Corroboration of some of these dim, blurred fables does exist. Thor Heyerdahl made a crossing from Africa to South America on a frail, reed sailing craft, proving the premise that such a journey in such a craft is possible. Many artifacts bearing designs and figures that are almost copies of Near Eastern and African artifacts have been found in the western hemisphere. Diggers and probers have found caches of Hebrew coins in the southeastern United States and Venezuela. Sculptures, other coins, inscriptions, and questionable implements have been discovered. Central American Indians had legends of bearded white men (transformed into gods) who came from and departed to the east. Fragments of ancient Chinese writings make references to voyages of 4,000 years ago eastward from China to a far land.

Out of this welter of information we must give serious consideration to the possibility that a portion of the American Indian heritage was a transplant from Asia Minor, Europe, and even China.

After we have given due weight to all this vagueness, we must come back to the unquestionable bloodline of the American Indian (a suggested better name would be Amerind but it has never caught on).

All hard evidence leads to the conclusion that the American Indian originally came from northeastern Asia; the migrations starting some 30,000 to 40,000 years ago.

At that time what we now know as Siberia was being used by bands of roving Mongols. These people were the ancestors of today's Chinese, Japanese, Turks, and the legendary Tatars (usually spelled Tartars). They were not a well-defined group or groups with fixed characteristics in the formative years, but drifted into and out of vast areas, coming into contact with and mixing with other developing peoples. Eventually, definite societies with distinct cultures and set values evolved.

The waxing and waning of the glacial ages was one of the determining factors in this primitive, nomadic era. As a glacial age matured it changed a large amount of the world's water into ice, which, in turn, caused a lowering of the oceans. Since the Bering Strait is shallow, this lowering of the seas exposed the land under the strait. Then the glaciers gradually crept down over that land, closing it to utilization as effectively as the water did. After a period of time that ice age began to recede, again opening a connection between Asia and North America.

These advancing and retreating glaciers, with their accompanying climatic changes, affected the land as well as the sea. As the ice moved down onto a landmass any people living there had to retreat. As the ice receded, people drifted back into the area. This ebb and flow of ice and people occurred not only in the Bering Strait area, but also in other regions as glacial ages varied in

A highbred Jalisco lady with truly noble Semitic features. Late Classic.

their encroachment on the land. Some changes were to the east and some to the west of the Bering Strait, and some affected the strait itself.

The glacial stages and the unstable Siberian population meant that at times people would wander over onto the North American continent only to be cut off and forced southward. Climatic changes often drove the parent Siberian peoples out of northeast Asia, leaving a void to be filled as conditions improved. When better conditions did arrive people again drifted into that Siberian corner of the world furnishing personnel for another migration to North America.

Over a series of glacial ages migrants to North America could well have been from different primitive tribes in different stages of development. But all were of primitive Mongol stock.

Since the American Indian originated from the early Mongols and came to North America in several separate migrations, the bloodlines were all the same even though, eventually, we had many tribes living here. After his arrival in the northwestern projection of the continent, he was probably content for the time being — the climate, food, and shelter was the same as he was used to. There was no way for him to realize that he had passed over onto another continent. Later, when population growth began to put pressure on his economy, the tribe would split, with a portion moving on to another location. When the next migration arrived in the area the same problem arose; some of the people had to move on.

As the next glacial period approached, with its accompanying climatic changes, the food problem would become acute. All the peoples would begin to search for a better livelihood, and the only direction they could go was south and east. Some probably worked their way around the northern end of the Rocky Mountains with the rest continuing down the Pacific Coast.

Another period favorable for migration would arrive. Those people would go through the same set of trials as the first group. This progress to the south and east by successive waves of people must have occasioned armed clashes from time to time, with the vanquished, in a shattered state, being forced to seek another homeland. Some segments would have scattered to the four winds.

In this manner the continent was populated, but the situation was not static. Famine, droughts, wars, disputes within a tribe, flight from the evil spirits deemed responsible for a contagion — all contributed to a constant fracturing of societal organizations. As these fractures took place some intertribal mixing must have been inevitable; two small bands trying to establish themselves but constantly harassed by larger bands would, for mutual advantage, coalesce. A victorious army would take home captured children either to replace their comrades who had fallen in battle or as slaves, or as casual romantic interludes, and so through the whole gamut of human activity.

Distinguished Semitic head from Vera Cruz. Late Classic.

For thousands of years the Indian roamed and multiplied until he embraced the whole of his hemisphere. During this time Nature had not been idle. Climate, food supply, and the environment of a particular region with the type of life and physical exertion it demanded, dictated the development of distinct characteristics in various regions. Yet the Indian retained his basic ancestry. All this means that while an Indian was an Indian, tribes and individuals exhibited slight differences, especially so when we remember that the original Siberian stock may have come from different primitive Mongols crossing the Bering Strait at different times.

When the white man came into contact with one segment of these new, strange people, he stamped into his mind an unvarying impression. He forgot or failed to consider the variances that exist among Europeans, a people and area with which he was familiar. He forgot that all Europeans are not identical; not all Swedes are husky, blond men and buxom women, nor are all Spaniards brunettes with slight, agile frames. Since the first Indians encountered by the white man had more or less common physical attributes, he mindlessly thought that all Indians were identical.

But they were not identical. Occasionally, someone would say he had seen a redheaded Indian or two, or one with blue eyes, or curly hair, or a tribe that was taller or stockier or lighter skinned than the accepted stereotype. Such reports caused wild speculation; those Indians were freak Indians, and what was their ancestry?

Considering the wanderlust that is ingrained in the human, we find ourselves floundering in the mists of time. While we have authentic accounts of Genghis Khan, Attila the Hun, Xerxes, and the Tatar hordes that overran vast stretches of country, in the process scattering their seed through many peoples, they do nothing for our story except to authenticate the worldwide propensity of man to roam, to seek new lands, or to satisfy an urge to expand. That propensity may be the backbone of the ancient legends of the Near Eastern mariners who voyaged far beyond the Pillars of Hercules and returned with iron, tin, dyes, spices, gold, wondrous tales of sea monsters, and storms of horrendous ferocity until the gods were pacified by sacrifices (Caribbean hurricanes?).

These legends sound like pipe dreams until certain items found in the western hemisphere are considered.

In the last few years there have been enough investigations and discoveries unearthed to make the scholars who were skeptics begin to revise their thinking. Those who insisted that since there are no accounts in European libraries or governmental records to substantiate pre-Columbian voyages, such, therefore, did not take place. They are beginning to reassess their adamant fixation.

By 300 B.C. the Iberians (Spaniards) had compasses, ceramic bowls in which a lodestone was floated, as well as a crude astrolabe with which to navigate. This knowledge spoils the conventional opinion that sailors, even as late as Columbus's time, had no means of knowing where they were, where they were going, or where they had been, that they sailed by dead reckoning. If the Iberians had such sailing aids by 300 B.C., how long had they been in existence, and what other peoples had used them before that time?

The cynics who refused to consider any journeys before Columbus's are having to retreat and at least consider some of the newfound evidence. There are bronze artifacts found in New England which are fashioned in the European manner and date from the period of 200 to 300 B.C. And there are the bronze weapons found in the Mound Builders' sites in the Mississippi and Ohio Valleys which date from the period of 200 B.C. to A.D. 400. Bronze is an alloy of tin and copper. While there is much copper in this country, and the Indians used it extensively, there is no time. Thus, how could the prehistoric Indians have fashioned bronze? The same applies to an iron battle ax, apparently of Norse origin, found at Rocky Nook, Massachusetts. The smelting and fashioning of iron was also unknown to the prehistoric Indians. When the later explorers — Columbus, Cabot, Cartier — made contact with the historic Indians, they found those people avid for anything made of iron, a substance unknown to them and from which they shaped many objects.

The moot question of Norse settlements on this continent has been laid to rest by the uncovering of authentic Norse villages on Greenland and at L'Anse aux Meadows in Newfoundland.

Then, there are the multitude of inscribed stones such as the Kensington Stone, the Bat Creek Stone, the Metcalf Stone, the Paraiba Stone, and on and on. In addition, there are many inscriptions on canyon walls and around doorways of crude stone huts. Originally, they were all dismissed as hoaxes because the examiners were not well enough versed in ancient languages and the changes that occurred over the years in those languages (as even our language is changing from day to day). But today there have been translations of many of those inscriptions by more advanced linguists who can point out the confusing points in the inscriptions, that an ill-schooled person did the writing, or that it was done in a transition period between two forms of the language, or in a language unknown until a few years ago.

Furthermore, Roman coins of A.D. 200 and A.D. 135 have been found at three different places in Kentucky. Other Roman coins of the second century A.D. have been found in Tennessee. Mixed in with some of these Roman coins were Hebrew coins of the same period. They were found in an undisturbed grave containing nine skeletons and a stone inscribed in the Canaanite language.

There is still another point that cannot be ignored. Archeologists have spent much time digging in Central America, uncovering whole towns, pyramids, graves — you name it. These diggings have exposed many statues and wall carvings. Prominent among them are accurate portrayals of Phoenician noblemen with distinctive beard and headdress, Negroes with all the typical negroid features, and Asiatics with the high cheekbones and almond-shaped eyes. It seems unlikely that such authentic depictions are merely the exercise of an artistic temperament. To me, there is only one explanation — the Aztec sculptor had actual models to guide him. Otherwise, the carvings would only suggest or remotely resemble such persons.

All the above remarks do not mean that Assyrian or Phoenician kings mounted large naval expeditions to the New World thousands of years ago and founded colonies on American shores which overran and superseded the native cultures and societies. Any such arrival of Near Eastern people was probably accidental; a bad storm carried a ship bent on a coastal voyage along the western shore of Africa or Europe clear across the Atlantic Ocean. Eventually, buffeted and damaged, the sea cast it up on some Caribbean or American shore, with only a few survivors managing to reach land. Those castaways were stranded. In time they blended into the native population but were too few to cause any radical change in the native culture. Their presence was accepted and some of their ideas and culture may have been modified and adapted by the natives.

Along this line of thought we may conjecture that some ship, blown far off course but surviving, made a landfall on some Caribbean Island or the coast of South America. The crew landed to make repairs, get fresh water and firewood, and, while there, stocked up on local products such as gold, silver, native dyes, pearls, logs of promising wood, fruits, and vegetables. Then they reembarked to beat and find their way back home. If they made it, their king would immediately impound all the knowledge thus gained and use it for his own profit and ends.

The king might then have outfitted regular convoys to this new wonderland, making regular trips to bring back those exotic things. In this case, he probably set up "agents-in-residence" to remain in the new land between trips to gather supplies. Such men, naturally, would enter into the life of the natives.

If any of these encounters did take place, it would not mean that whole cultures or societies of Indians were wiped out and that the Near Easterners substituted their own mode of life in an area. What strangers may have arrived under those circumstances would have been only grains of sand on the seashore as compared to the numbers of the natives present. But those few strangers would leave their genes in the population.

If logic compels us to consider these possibilities, however farfetched they may seem, then we must consider that genes of Mediterranean peoples could have been introduced into the bank of Indian genes at the same time these artifacts were made. Once genes are introduced, they remain to be drawn upon by succeeding generations. Here was a source of curly hair, heavy beards, and acquiline noses. Colonists often cited these features as presumptive evidence that Indians were of a certain, recent, modern extraction.

* * *

Skipping several centuries we find legends bearing upon northern European ventures into the uncharted seas to the westward. St. Brendan was an Irish monk who, around A.D. 500, sailed westward from Ireland on a voyage that lasted seven years. He was searching for the Isles of the Blessed, a refuge for pious, God-fearing men where it was always summer, the trees always laden with fruit, green glades with murmuring brooks filled with "she-goats with full udders" waiting to be milked, and where there were no worries or intrusions upon the enjoyment of a simple life. In those seven years he is said to have visited many islands, large and small. Some of the islands were inhabited by recluse Irishmen, others by mysterious beings.

Then the legends jump 500 years to the Norsemen. Conditions had become such in Norway and Denmark around 800 that people began to seek other homes. Many of them moved to Iceland, which became settled by 900 to 950. Those sea rovers then began to feel out the small islands that stretched westward from Iceland. By 980 they found the eastern shore of Greenland, and in 985 Eric the Red, upon being declared an outlaw in Iceland, took some followers and founded a colony on the west shore of Greenland.

But during the Norse settlement of Iceland they had made life so miserable for the Christian Irish, who were trying to establish themselves in Iceland after fleeing from the Norse invasion of Ireland, that the Irish fled again. According to legend, they were called Westmen. The Norse sagas lend substantiation to this folklore. They mention Hvitramannaland, which translates into White Man's Land. This Norse reference is a continuation of the Irish legend about Ireland the Great. The White Man's land was supposed to be inhabited by white men who carried banners in processions and chanted in a tongue unknown to the Norse. The same sagas mention that Eric, upon arrival in Greenland, found remains of boats and houses built after a European manner.

Those Norse settlements in Greenland persisted for about 300 years. Then, after several years in which there had been no communication between the settlements and the mother country, the Norse sent a ship to investigate. The settlements were found to be vacant. Where the inhabitants went and why, no one knows. There is no evidence or reference to a pestilence or invasion destroying the communities. The people must have just abandoned their homes. Climatologists believe that at this period the climate of Greenland was warmer than it is today, but about 1300 it began to cool off . Such a shift may have forced the Norsemen to change their mode of life, perhaps infiltrating Indian tribes, contributing blond and red hair to the Indian bloodline.

If there is anything to these legends, and recent archeological findings have proved the existence of those colonies, we are forced to assume that the Norse (and Irish?) had contact for several centuries with the natives of that area. Also, it is logical to assume that the Norsemen, rovers by nature, did not erect fences around their settlements and never ventured outside.

We are all familiar with the story of the English colony on Roanoke Island. It was started, then abandoned, then reestablished with the promise of help and supply from England. When the succor failed to arrive regularly as promised, due to English troubles in Europe, the colony disappeared. When providers did come all they found was the word "Croatoan" inscribed on a post. There was no evidence of an epidemic killing all the people, or of a battle in which everyone was slain, or of anything else. The colonists were just gone.

Those people in a strange country and climate and dependent to a large extent on the generosity of the neighboring Indians may have found life as English colonists to be unbearable and had drifted, singly or in groups, into Indian tribes and had been assimilated. Here is another possible source of strange genes.

Going back to the Greenland colonies, they depended, to a large extent, upon the export of fish to Iceland from where it could enter the European market. They had found immense quantities of codfish off the southern tip of Greenland where the Labrador Current and the Gulf Stream meet. Years later, Cabot recorded that in the Gulf of Saint Lawrence he encountered schools of cod so compact that they impeded the progress of his ship, and Cartier wrote that by lowering a basket over the side of his ship a basketful of fish could be brought on the deck at each dip of the basket. This new supply of fish that the Norse brought into Iceland excited the English, Breton, Basque, and Portuguese fishermen who were, by then, frequenting the waters around Iceland.

Those fishermen were not long in following the Greenlanders to this treasure trove of cod. In so doing they had to land from time to time for fresh water, firewood, to dry their catch, or to repair their ships. Surely those fishermen, while on shore, did not completely ignore the Indians. This contact in the thirteenth to sixteenth centuries provides yet another source of strange genes to be incorporated into the Indian's reservoir.

No specific, definite record exists of the trade of the European fishermen on the Grand Banks, but there are enough fragmentary references in letters, custom records, folklore and vague innuendos to lend credence to this activity. The most concrete of these references are in Lescarbot's *History of New France* (vol. 2, pp. 22-23 of the Greenwood Press 1968 reprint). Lescarbot states: ". . . For from remote times and for several centuries our seamen from Dieppe, St. Malo, Rochelle, and other mariners . . . are wont to make voyages into these countries in search of codfish . . . sail year by year to carry on their fishery, which, as I have said, dates back for several centuries. . . ." In the

John Day letter, written in the winter of 1497-1498, in Cumming, Skelton, and Quinns' *Discovery of North America* (McClelland and Stewart, 1971, p. 80) he writes: "It is considered certain that the cape of the said land was found and discovered in the past by the men from Bristol [an English fishing city]. . . ."

This dearth of information on European fishermen is understandable for several reasons — merchants did not want to publicize their sources of supply for a competitive edge, the times and era did not lend themselves to printed matter for general distribution, and the participants were not only illiterate or semiliterate, but had their minds concentrated solely on fish and its marketing.

This long period of time, from B.C. until the time which we have been considering, provided ample opportunity for the Indians to have acquired new inheritance characteristics.

The early colonists and fur traders were fascinated, obsessed might be a better word, with the Indians who deviated from the white man's stereotype of them. A good example is the furor that attended the "positive" identification of a tribe of white Indians someplace in the Spanish "Yllinois [*sic*] Territory above Saint Louis." The speculation, after years of stories about freak Indians being thither and yon, over the next hill, or around the bend of the river, solidified into a firm conviction that these Indians were of Welsh descent.

Much effort was expended, funds were raised even in Wales, to locate that tribe so that the facts could be pinned down. The Welsh legend of Madoc and his difficulties with his brothers and half-brother — and Madoc's legitimacy or illegitimacy — was revived.

The legend revolved around the accession to the throne of a Welsh kingdom in the late 1100s. Supposedly, as the result of all the politics and power-plays, Madoc sailed from Wales with some followers, landed at Mobile Bay, left his cohorts, and returned to Wales, where he picked up another 120 Welsh, and then disappeared.

After the passage of a few years, the legend goes, native pressures around Mobile Bay forced the Welsh to move up the Mississippi River. It seems that the more they moved, the more pressures they encountered. After being continually forced upstream for a century or so, they found a spot on the banks of the Missouri River in what is now North Dakota, where they could live in peace.

When this tribe was actually investigated by knowledgeable men, the Welsh Indians turned out to be Mandans, conventional Indians speaking a Siouian dialect. To be sure, they were lighter skinned and had a little more facial hair than their neighbors, but these deviations from the Indian norm were no greater than the deviations found in other tribes, clans, or individuals.

In this maze of legends, folklore, and history is it any wonder that the early Europeans, from time to time, encountered redheaded, blond, bearded, or blue-eyed Indians?[1]

Chapter 13

Topography's Influence on Colonial Mores

The colonies and settlements on the North American continent did not spring full-fledged from Columbus's journeys to the West Indies. They had to evolve into a viable form over a period of years. Old World politics, New World politics, human frailties, foibles, cupidities, aspirations, economics, a strange climate, a completely new environment, and, last but not least, topography shaped their destiny.

Strictly speaking, Columbus was not the discoverer of the western hemisphere. His journeys occurred at an opportune time. The prior contacts with this continent had failed to elicit Europe's interest since that continent had not developed to the point of needing extra resources. But by Columbus's day Europe was desperate, from depleted resources and the needs of an increasing population, for an outlet for its pent-up energy and the need for new resources. Columbus's reports of the new route to the wealth of Cathay and Cipangu provided such a release, and Europe scrambled to take advantage of it.

But Columbus was a latecomer. The early Norse use of these shores did not lead to any development, and the fishermen using the Grand Banks were a single-minded folk engrossed in supplying the vast European market. They had no interest in colonization, or the building of empires, or the salvation of souls, or the founding of new commerical ventures — just fish. Their use of the area and their undoubted contact with its shores induced no realization on their part or the part of their backers as to the new potential presented.

We must go back into European history to understand why Columbus's return to Europe with some gold, a few pearls, and a little spice touched off such a mad melee. Why should all Europe jostle and push for a place at this new fount of wealth when all prior contacts had produced no reaction?

The answer lies in the development of cities and the emergence of a merchant class. The Industrial Age meant increased prosperity for all classes

A map showing the jumbled terrain confronting the English colonists in their efforts to penetrate to the north and west and the ease enjoyed by the French by means of waterways and prairies in their expansion to the west and south. (Courtesy of Richard Aquila's reprint of the 1775 Evans' map in his *The Iroquois Restoration*)

and a subsequent demand for raw materials and finished products to satisfy the new purchasing power. Add to this, the depleted state of European material resources and the start of a rapid population growth.

When Columbus opened the door to this wondrous warehouse of new wealth, Europeans feverishly embarked on a course to utilize it. Europe was asking for trouble because colonies were an unknown operation. She had had no experience with such outposts. The colonies grew up by trial and error as no one had the foggiest notion of how they should be handled. No one had any blueprints to follow, nor did they have any conception of the size, diversity, distances involved, or the climate of the continent.

An analogy can be drawn from this experience to the backcountry man going to a circus where he saw an elephant for the first time. He opined, "There ain't no such animal." Even though the beast was before his eyes, he was dumfounded. It was beyond his wildest imaginations. He had no idea how to feed or care for it and could imagine no way anyone could put it to a profitable use. The Europeans, when challenged by this new continent, were as perplexed as that man was by the elephant.

The rising maritime powers — England, France, and Holland — were emerging nations plagued by many problems. While they wanted to exploit what Spain had uncovered in the Caribbean area, they were denied access by Spain's seapower. This circumstance forced them to channel their efforts to our eastern seaboard. If Spain had not controlled the Gulf of Mexico, with bastions ringed around those waters, the story of North America might have been astoundingly different. If these other countries had first taken root in the Mississippi Valley who knows what might have developed? Here topography first raises its head.

While Spain had been lucky in uncovering the Inca gold in her search for the Orient, those treasures were still a goal much desired. The denial, by Spain, of the southern area for search was not too much of an imposition on the other budding maritime countries. They were not blocked in their searches. The fishermen's route was known, and France and England had visions of finding a shortcut to the Orient.

The French were the first to establish outposts in this search for the Strait of Anian as their fishing interests led them to locate in the Gulf of Saint Lawrence. The English, thus, were left the stretch of coast between the French holdings and the Spanish domain.

This chance allocation of territory influenced the future of the continent more than is generally realized. The two peoples mainly concerned, the French and the English, were antagonistic because of differences generated in Europe. But since the area open to exploitation by these two peoples was contiguous and presented, in general, the same problems and the same overall thicket of the new and unknown, it would seem that the two, having the same general cultural background, would come up with the same solution. But they didn't. Topography was a large factor in the future political development.

The French, in their search for the Strait of Anian, were led up the Saint Lawrence River where they awoke to the fur-trade possibilities, eventually adding it to the fish trade. The success they had in this new trade led them farther up the Saint Lawrence River to the Great Lakes. From there the southern tributaries of Lake Erie provided them access to the Ohio River watershed; by way of Green Bay and the Fox and Wisconsin Rivers the Mississippi River was reached. From the western end of Lake Superior, through Rainy Lake and Lake of the Woods, they reached Lake Winnipeg, the key to the best fur country on the continent. Still pursuing the beaver, they traveled up the Red River of the North to the area drained by the Assiniboine with its easy access to the upper Missouri River, and to the tremendous drainage of the Saskatchewan River, whose farthest reaches finger the Rocky Mountains. In a relatively few years, the French were utilizing half of this continent, albeit on a roving, helter-skelter, transitory basis.

The French eagerly embraced the far-ranging fur trade to the practical exclusion of other lines of endeavor. Several reasons caused this concentration of effort. Fur was a cash crop; agriculture, such as they knew it, was not profitable (witness Lord Selkirk's attempts in Assiniboia); the Indians gladly assisted in the fur-gathering; and the topography induced, aided, and abetted the trade because of the waterways.

The fur trade was a ready-made way to earn a living, but the people did not consider themselves colonists. They viewed themselves as businessmen trying to turn a profit. The French government and merchants did not understand how to cope with the situation. Should it be a strict commercial enterprise, supported and supplied from France on a day-by-day basis as returns might justify? Or, should there be a deliberate effort to found a self-supporting entity with its commitment of capital? Or, something in between? In any event, what should be the attitude of the government and mercantile interests? How much control and supervision should be necessary and how should the colony be tied, if at all, at the great distance from the mother country? No one knew.

The French at Quebec were concerned not at all with these abstract matters. Their concern was money and prestige, and as long as enough support, either local or from overseas, was available they were satisfied. They were building a community and founding a society, but not intentionally. The details had to be hammered out over time.

While this activity produced a large revenue in the aggregate for the French, both in Canada and in France, the coffers of the crown got little of it as no built-in mechanism had been contrived to siphon off a share of those returns. Moreover, this fur economy was not producing staples of commerce needed by the populace of France, nor was it heeding directives which would directly benefit the Crown. These circumstances were contrary to the French Crown's concept of the function of what should exist — furthering the glory of the motherland.

Confronted with this multifaceted problem, the Crown decided to institute control over colonial activities and to extract what it thought was a properly due revenue from this new trade. A system of licenses and taxes was devised with a military-type administration to oversee the new rules. This embryonic government had its work cut out because it had to police the far horizon as well as regulate the centers of population. Its control had to be all-encompassing since there was no civilian "chain of command" or recognized lines of authority.

Putting aside all the resulting frictions, evasions, changes of direction, and recriminations, this policy resulted in a direct tie between each trader and the government in Quebec and on to the Crown in Paris. Though the populace of Canada was engaged almost entirely in the fur trade in some capacity and most led a roving, footloose existence, roaming from post to post as they pleased or the demands of the trade required, this new system of government meant that the king's writ ran to the outermost trading post and his scepter cast as dark a shadow over each *habitant, hivernant, voyageur,* and *courieur de bois* as if he lived in Paris or Lyon.

The English, after their conquest of Canada, did not change this broad, far-flung commercial activity with its tenuous line of communication between individuals and organizations. The system was working and producing as good results as could be expected. There was nothing closeknit or cohesive about this Canadian pattern. Years of this system led to an acceptance of the English parliamentary form of government — allegiance to a crown as a symbol of sovereignty, and a parliament, existing under the sufferance of that crown, through which the common man could resolve his problems and desires. Since the crown assured continuity and stability and the common man was thus shielded from despotism, each member of parliament was privileged to veer in his position as he saw fit, and, by the same token, he was subject to recall at any time.

This form of government was acceptable to, and perhaps was the only form of government suitable to, these far-ranging, loosely associated Canadians. In other words, the early fur-trade mode of life made up of men scattered over half a continent with no cohesion or settled debate over issues, even issues that had been defined prior to an election, called for a government subject to change as issues changed or the direction of government became distasteful. Topography induced this viewpoint.

The English colonies are a different story. The American people evolved a government from a different set of circumstances. England, in her forced confinement to the Atlantic Coast, soon abandoned hope for a Northwest Passage. Of a mercantile bent, she did not make the mistake of France whose colonial policy fostered a hand-to-mouth existence on the part of any true colony. Rather, England began to concentrate on trade between the colonies and the motherland.

Realizing that a prosperous colony made a more prosperous motherland, England operated her colonies through chartered companies of proprietors and stockholders who were concerned with making a profit.

While some of the American colonists were malcontents, in the main they were adventurers responding to the lure of profit. Recognizing this situation, the English performed some screening of persons who wanted to emigrate to the New World, stressing the need for hard work. Some men, their imaginations inflamed by stories of life in the colonies and comparing it with the prospects of their future in their station of life in Europe, feverishly embarked for the land of opportunity. Thus, a stable, industrious set of immigrants was the core of the colonies.

Men bound for the English colonies brought their wives, children, shovels, plows, cattle, and household goods. Each family promptly claimed a plot of land and put down roots. The man built a house, cleared some land, planted a crop, sheared his sheep, and made plans for the future. He became a "solid citizen." When the next shipload of immigrants arrived, they located as neighbors to the first settlers and duplicated the first family's activity.

To be sure, a few men of the colonies became Indian traders — men like Sir William Johnson, George Croghan, and Conrad Weiser — as contrasted to the merchants who conducted Indian trade as a sideline. But those men were beyond the pale. The majority of English colonists considered them deviants from the accepted norm. Instead of welcoming them and their activities as contributions to the welfare of the colony and an extension of the colony's influence, they were classed as troublemakers. Their activity generated Indian problems which interfered with colonial business and plagued the serenity of the community. And who cared about a few rascally Indians out there in the hinterland? The Indians were "furriners" anyway. They didn't dress properly, speak a proper language, or think in terms of English common law. By consensus, those traders were just a thorn in the side of society. The internal problems of the community came first and the feeling was "if only those pesky traders would just stay home and hoe their corn as God-fearing men should, the rest of us could get on with our business."

There evolved communities of kindred souls with common problems, common goals, and common aspirations. The communities became enclaves, self-contained and self-sufficient. When one enclave became unwieldy, another was started in the vicinity, but this natural growth could not progress up a waterway that continually beckoned the settlers onward such as the Canadians had wherever they happened to be.

The English were not lured into new ventures, new experiences, or new ideas. They were confined to their environs with their contemporaries since no river existed that could lead them onward.

The terrain confined all these enclaves to a narrow coastal strip with the Atlantic Ocean on one side and the forbidding Appalachian Mountains on the other. Constructing roads through those forested mountains was an imposs-ible task and traveling over them would have been economically prohibitive. That left cheap, easy water routes as the only means for an expansion of settlement, but no river led through the mountains. The Hudson River, stretching north from Long Island Sound, was the only waterway that would eliminate the mountain barrier. By traveling up the river to its headwaters, then working around the end of the mountains and utilizing the tributaries to Lake Erie the English could have entered the Ohio River drainage and expanded their area. This route would have been time consuming and costly, and squelching any possible use of that route was the fact that the headwaters of that river were the home of the Iroquois Confederacy. The Iroquois, sitting between the French and English fur markets, were conscious of their middle-man status, were jealous of it, and protected it with all the means at their disposal.

Under these limiting conditions the English colonies developed a narrow, self-centered view of life. The problems invariably were of a local nature — food, shelter, security, and who was responsible for what. This preoccupation with problems of mutual concern on a small scale caused the social and elemental political life of the individuals to be tied to the enclave. Their thoughts were directed first to their individual problems, next to their particular colony, and only finally to the Crown. The Crown was a distant symbol similar to a church spire seen in the distance but with no bearing on the task at hand like digging out a stump.

The development of this parochial attitude is revealed in the bickering among the various communities over Indian troubles and the relations of each community and colony with England, and it carries down to the present time in maxim of States Rights that flavors American politics.

Wives, cows, Indians, and topography were not the only things tying the English colonist to the eastern seaboard. This political philosophy was necessarily based on the selection of leaders who were pledged to advocacy of viewpoints agreed upon by the settlements. The main concern was the aims or impact of some situation upon that particular enclave. A representative was selected because of his espousal of and dedication to the wishes of the majority. He was given a definite mandate to pursue a defined course.

This dedication to particular objectives doesn't mean that each enclave became single-minded and absorbed in a single topic to the exclusion of all else. The case of Massachusetts provides a good example of one topic assuming a position of alignment with another community, while a different topic arising at the same time would cause still another alignment.

In 1690 Massachusetts was faced with a growing problem of an acceptable, readily available medium of exchange. There wasn't enough English sterling in circulation to give the average man a few coins to use in his daily business. So, the colony issued paper money backed only by faith in the government. The status of this money was no different from today's monetary medium — an alloy quarter dollar and a paper ten dollar bill, neither backed by gold, silver, or any tangible asset, merely the word of the government that a certain coin or note has a certain value.

Some of the people did not have much faith in the government's ability to make good on their promise. In a few years a group of men with large land holdings issued their own notes in various denominations which were backed by land as security. A man with, say, a 100 dollar "land bank note" could surrender it and claim a certain number of acres.

About the same time a group of merchants in Boston issued their own notes, known as "silver notes." These notes were backed by the assurance of the merchants that they had sufficient cash flow to be able to meet at any time a demand that the note be redeemed for silver. The merchants' idea was that these notes would circulate in lieu of cash and conserve their supply of the English sterling, so difficult to come by.

These three monetary schemes received varying responses. A portion of the population was skeptical of all forms; other people were partial to just one of them. Fishermen close to Boston who had constant dealings with Boston merchants would much rather have a "silver note" than a "land note" which merely gave them a claim to a number of acres in the wilderness. On the other hand, the farmer settler, who was trying to develop a paying farm miles from Boston, preferred "land notes" as he could trade them in for a desirable piece of land. A "silver note," to him, was far from home.

While the people were wrestling with this monetary problem, church problems came along. There is no need to burden readers with another recitation of the Salem witch hunts, Increase and Cotton Mather, Anne Hutchinson, Roger Williams, the scope of authority the church should have, or exactly how much departure from the rituals, dogma, and authority of the Anglican Church should be permitted. It suffices to say that the enclaves took an active part in religious dissension.

From these two problems, money and church, to say nothing of other discords, the reader can infer how one enclave would align itself one way on one problem, but differently on other problems. In each case it sought to promote its particular view and to reserve to itself its own attitude.

There was no broad division of opposing opinions throughout a whole colony. No cleavage into two or three camps of widespread concurrence occurred within the colony, each side exposing a difference in concepts such as we have today in our Republican and Democratic parties. The enclaves remained as individual entities for many years.

With the passage of time and the rapidly increasing immigration, the isolation of enclaves broke down. They ceased to exist as the new inhabitants filled the voids among them, both geographically and ideologically, and a polymorphic community took shape. But the imprint of the enclave persisted. Men were elected to office who represented the opinions of a region or particular interests and were pledged to promote those views for a specific term of time.

It is a far cry between these two concepts of government. The responsive Canadian government, which can react to changing tides and affairs, versus the stable United States government which is committed to a course for a definite period. Topography had a major role in the forming of these divergent postures as the early settlers of each country were subject to the conditions imposed by the locale in which they found themselves.

They had to make the best of what they had and molded their structures, economic, social, political, and philosophical, according to the dictates of the conditions confronting them. Walter Prescott Webb summarized it: "Politics is an opportunist, coming forward to lay its eggs after the nest has been fully constructed. The frontier [in this case the eastern seaboard and the Saint Lawrence waterway] had built a nest, and built it well, before politics and statecraft came to lay a new government which was called democratic. The fledgling found the nest just right and the whole social, economic, and mental environment suited to its growth." Topography played an important part in this nest-building.[1]

The peoples of the New World did not tumble willynilly into the future.

Notes

Chapter 1
Global Aspects of the Fur Trade
(pages 5-12)

1. Stephan P. Krasheninnikow, *Exploration of Kamchatka*, trans. E.A.P. Crownhart-Vaughn (Oregon Historical Society, 1972), xi. Oleks Rudemka, "Russia in the Pacific Basin," *Journal of the West* (Apr. 1976): 52-59. William Coxe, *Account of the Russian Discoveries between Asia and America* (University Microfilm reprint, 1966), 275-297. James Gibson, *Feeding the Russian Fur Trade* (University of Wisconsin Press, 1969), 4-8. George V. Lantzeff and Richard A. Pierce, *Eastward to Empire* (McGill-Queens University Press, 1973), 132-143. Robert J. Kerner, *The Urge to the Sea* (University of California Press, 1942), 30, 67, 75, 84-88.

2. W. J. Eccles, *The Canadian Frontier* (Holt, Rinehart and Winston, 1969), 105.

3. Paul C. Phillips, *The Fur Trade* (University of Oklahoma Press, 1961), 2: 105.

4. Excerpt from *A Century of Conflict*, by Joseph L. Rutledge, reprinted by permission of Doubleday & Co., Inc.

5. Account book of Andrew Hyde in possession of author.

Chapter 2
Principles of Indian Trade
(pages 13-23)

1. George E. Hyde, *The Life of George Bent*, ed. Savoie Lottinville (University of Oklahoma Press, 1968), 31, 32. John Upton Terrell, *Traders of the Western Morning* (Los Angeles, CA: Southwest Museum, 1967), *passim*. John C. Ewers, "The Indian Trade of the Upper Missouri before Lewis and

Clark: An Interpretation," Bulletin of the Missouri Historical Society (July 1954): 429-446. John C. Ewers, *Indian Life on the Upper Missouri* (University of Oklahoma Press, 1968), 14-33. Arthur J. Ray, *Indians in the Fur Trade* (University of Toronto, 1974), *passim*. Wilbur R. Jacobs, *Dispossessing the American Indian* (Charles Scribner's Sons, 1972), 9. John C. Ewers, *The Horse in Blackfoot Indian Culture*. Bulletin 159 (Smithsonian Institution, 1955), 8-14. John C. Ewers, *People and Pelts*, ed. Malvina Bolus (Winnipeg: Pegius Press, 1972), 1-24.

2. Harold E. Driver, *Indians of North America*, 2d ed., rev. (University of Chicago Press, 1969), 148, 213-215. Terrell, *The Western Morning*, 122-124. Ewers, *The Horse in Blackfoot Indian Culture*, 3-19.

3. Eccles, *The Canadian Frontier*, 12-13. H. P. Bigger, *The Voyages of Jacques Cartier* (Public Archives of Canada), 11: 21.

4. Ray, *Indians in the Fur Trade*, 68, 69. Jacobs, *Dispossessing the American Indian*, 34.

5. Arthur J. Ray and Donald Freeman, *Give Us Good Measure* (University of Toronto Press, 1978), Chap. 5.

6. George T. Hunt, *The Wars of the Iroquois* (University of Wisconsin Press, 1967).

7. David J. Wishart, *The Fur Trade of the American West: 1807 to 1840* (University of Nebraska Press, 1979), 94.

8. As quoted by Cornelius J. Jaenen, *Friend and Foe* (Columbia University Press, 1976), 92, 93.

9. Wilcomb E. Washburn, *Relations between Europeans and Americans during the Seventeenth and Eighteenth Centuries*. As quoted in Jaenen, *Friend and Foe*, 122.

Chapter 3
Tobacco in Indian Trade
(pages 24-30)

1.   The information in the foregoing essay was extracted and paraphrased from the pamphlet "The Naming of Tobacco Plains," which I published in 1975. That pamphlet was written for the tourist trade of my home area — the Tobacco Plains of northwestern Montana. Tourists are constantly questioning residents of the area as to why the name Tobacco Plains is applied to a mountainous terrain in Montana since everyone knows that tobacco is a southern crop. The information for that pamphlet was acquired over several years and from many scattered sources. It was recorded on tablet sheets, scratch pads, backs of envelopes, and handy scraps of paper. Upon completion of the pamphlet I gathered up that hodge-podge array and consigned it to the round file. For that reason I can give the reader only

references to certain books. In printing the pamphlet I felt that the tourist reader would not be interested in detailed references to particular statements. Yet I wanted to show that I did have some authority for my statements, so all I did in the pamphlet was to list some of the books that were consulted. Those sources are:

American Tobacco Company, *The American Tobacco Story.*
American Museum of Natural History, Anthropological Papers, vol. 21, 1924.
Brown, Young, and Murray, *Local History by First Women's Club, Eureka, Montana*, typewritten paper of 17 pages (n.d.).
L. J. Burpee, *Journals and Letters of Pierre Gaultier de Varennes de la Verendrye*, Champlain Society, 16 (Greenwood Press reprint, 1968).
J. Carver, *Travels through the Interior Parts of North America in the Years 1766, 1767, and 1768* (Ross and Haines, 1966).
Elliott Coues, *New Light on the Early History of the Greater Northwest*, 3 vols. (Francis P. Harper, 1897).
Alfred W., Crosby, Jr., *The Columbian Exchange* (Greenwood Publ. Co., 1972).
Driver, Indians of North America.
Ewers, "The Indian Trade of the Upper Missouri."
Encyclopedia of Chemical Technology, Kirk-Othner, 2d ed., vol. 20.
John Fayey, *The Flathead Indians* (University of Oklahoma Press, 1974).
R. P. Fisher, *The Odyssey of Tobacco.*
T. H. Goodspeed, "The Genus Nicotiana," *Chronica Botanica*, vol. 16.
R. K. Heimann, *Tobacco and Americans* (McGraw-Hill, 1960).
G. M. Herndon, *William Tatham and the Culture of Tobacco* (University of Miami Press, 1969).
F. W. Hodges, *Handbook of American Indians North of Mexico*, 2 vols. (Pageant Books, 1960).
G. K. Holmes, *Some Features of Tobacco History*, Annual Report of the American Historical Association, 1919, vol. 1.
Harold A. Innis, *The Fur Trade in Canada* (University of Toronto, 1970).
Diamond Jenness, *The Indians of Canada*, National Museum of Canada Bulletin 65, Anthropological Series 15, 1967.
Olga Weydemeyer Johnson, *Flathead and Kootenai* (A. H. Clark, 1969).
Olga Weydemeyer Johnson, *et al.*, *The Story of the Tobacco Plains Country* (Caxton Printers, 1950).
Baron de Lahontan, *New Voyages to North America* (A. C. McClurg and Company, 1905).
Marc Lescarbot, *The History of New France*, Champlain Society, vols. 1, 7, and 9 (Greenwood Press, 1968).

Liggett and Myers Tobacco Company. Personal communication from J. D. Rogers, Assistant to the Director of Research.

Ralph Linton, *Use of Tobacco among North American Indians*, Field Museum of Natural History, Leaflet 15, 1924.

J. Long, *Voyages and Travels of an Indian Interpreter and Trader* (A. H. Clark Co., 1904).

Robert H. Lowie, *Indians of the Plains* (Museum of Natural History, 1954).

R. J. Pool, *Flowers and Flowering Plants* (McGraw-Hill, 1929).

W. E. Safford, *Narcotic Plants and Stimulants of the Ancient Americans*, Report of the Smithsonian Institution, 1916.

Teit and Boas, *The Salishan Tribes of the Western Plateau*, 45th B.A.E. Annual Report (Shorey reprint, 1973).

Terrell, *The Western Morning*.

R. G. Thwaites, *Early Western Travels*, vol. 29 (AMS Press, 1966).

H. H. Turney-High, *Ethnography of the Kutenai*, Memoirs of the American Anthropological Assn., no. 56, 1941.

Catherine White, *David Thompson's Journals Relating to Montana and Adjacent Regions* (Montana State University Press, 1950).

Clark Wissler, *Indians of the United States*, rev. ed. (Doubleday and Company, 1966).

Chapter 4
The Ripple Effect of the Horse and Gun
(pages 31-41)

1. Rather than voluminous and detailed notes on the various points of this essay and having to alter the style to accommodate those details, I have chosen to leave the style as it is and make this commentary on my sources.

For general background on the Indians, the main families, the derivation of names, their pre-White distribution with their subsequent fragmentation, and their culture, many sources have been used. The principal works were: Frederick W. Hodge's *Handbook of American Indians*; Clark Wissler's *Indians of the United States*; Harold E. Driver's *Indians of North America*; Diamond Jenness's *The Indians of Canada*; Geographic Board of Canada's Report, *Handbook of Indians of Canada* (Ottawa, Canada, 1913, reprinted by Coles Publishing Company, 1971); John R. Swanton's *The Indian Tribes of North America*, Bulletin 145, Bureau of American Ethnology, Smithsonian Institution, 1952; James A. Teit and Franz Boas's *The Salishan Tribes of the Western Plateaus*, 45th Bureau of American Ethnology's Annual Report (facsimile reproduction by The Shorey Book Store, 1973); The American Museum of Natural History's composite publication of Robert H. Lowie's *Indians of the Plains* and Philip Drucker's

Indians of the Northwest Coast (Natural History Press, 1973); Alvin M. Josephy, Jr.'s *The Indian Heritage of America* (Alfred A. Knopf, 1968); and Michael S. Kennedy's *The Red Man's West* (Hastings House, 1965). One of the best presentations of Indian life, culture, and their conflict with Europeans is an encapsulated account by William T. Hagan. It is found in the History of American Civilization Series of the University of Chicago Press and is titled simply *American Indians*.

References to the effect of the gun upon the Indian's life are found scattered through practically all of the fur-trade literature. Seldom, however, is a remark made commenting on the introduction of a new, potent force, but by extrapolation of remarks or by the narration of events and then correlating several such musings, the working of the gun's effect can be understood. Two exceptions to the preceding sentence are noteworthy. One exception is David Thompson's account of a story related by Saukamappee, a Cree who was living with the Piegans, concerning a battle between the Piegans and Shoshoni (*David Thompson's Narrative*, ed. Richard Glover, the Champlain Society, 40: 240-243.). This account clearly describes the effect of the gun upon people to whom it was unknown. Louise Kellog's *French Regime in Wisconsin and the Northwest* (State Historical Society of Wisconsin, 1925) is the other exception. She devoted one chapter (pp. 84-100) to detailing the gun ripples that were created around the Great Lakes by the early acquisition of the gun by eastern Indians.

The vast majority of the fur-trade books merely mention that the Indians prized guns and traded for them at every opportunity, and give instances of their use against both Indians and whites.

Four of the more recent books, fortunately, delineate the use of the gun by an Indian against his neighbors of long standing as one of the prime agents altering the existing balance of power that had been in effect for years before the coming of the white man. The gun enhanced the gun-bearing Indian's status, and he used this status to increase his material benefits. The "gun" Indian could do this only until his neighbors acquired guns. Then he was constrained but the gun ripples in that area had been set in motion.

For straightforward, documented statements on the initial role of the gun in eastern Indian hands, see Ray's *Indians in the Fur Trade*, 13, 14, 19, 21, 23. Also, Jaenen's *Friend and Foe*, 134-138. Ray and Freeman's *Give Us Good Measure* touches on this matter. Wym. J. Denevan specifically recognizes this ripple effect in his *The Native Population of the American since 1492* (University of Wisconsin Press, 1976), 22n.

The question of the horse is solved easily. There are four books that delve not only into the details of the introduction of the horse onto this continent but also its expansion over vast areas. They cite all the necessary sources. Robert Denhardt's *Horse of the Americas* (University of Oklahoma Press, 1947) is primarily concerned with the development of the Quarter Horse, the cowhorse of the cattle industry which, justly, has become the most popular breed of horses in the United States today. In developing this story he gives comprehensive treatment to the early spread of the horse on the continent. Cunningham-Graham's *Horses of the Conquest* (University of Oklahoma Press, 1949) is devoted to the development of the various South American breeds and types of horses, but the background material on the Spanish introduction of the horse into the western hemisphere is extensive. Frank Gilbert Roe's *The Indian and the Horse* (University of Oklahoma Press, 1955) concerns itself with the role of the horse in Indian life. It deals with the Indian preoccupation with and desire for horses after they became available. The fourth book, Ewer's *The Horse in Blackfoot Indian Culture*, is, as the title indicates, a study of the horse in one Indian tribe. The first 32 pages of this book review how the horse got to the Blackfeet, who lived on the northern plains. Especially interesting are three pages in these cited pages giving the wealth in horses in various tribes in various years. Also, Figure 1 on page 11 shows the early horse diffusion on the Great Plains.

For detailed information on specific tribes and their use of the horse, the following magazine articles may be of value: John C. Ewer's "Intertribal Warfare as the Precursor of Indian-White Warfare on the Northern Great Plains," *Western Historical Quarterly* (Oct. 1975): 379-410; Lois L. Nelsen Schmidlin's "The Role of the Horse in the Life of the Comanche," *Journal of the West* (Jan. 1974): 47-65; and H. D. Smiley's "The Cherokee Side of the Quarter Horse," *The Quarter Horse Journal* (Dec. 1954): 18-20.

Chapter 5
The Sleep by the Frozen Sea
(pages 42-56)

1. E. E. Rich, *The History of the Hudson's Bay Company; 1670-1870* (Hudson's Bay Record Society, 1958), 1: 556-590.
2. Joseph Robson, *An Account of Six Years' Residence in Hudson's Bay* (Johnson Reprint Corp., 1965), 29.
3. Glyndur Williams, "The Dobbs Crisis," *Beaver Magazine* (Autumn, 1970). Doughty and Martin, *The Kelsey Papers* (Public Archives of Canada, 1929), xix. Rich, *Hudson's Bay Company*, 1: 297.
4. *Ibid.*, 1:119.
5. E. E. Rich, *Cumberland House Journals and Inland Journal, 1775-1782*, 1st series, 1775-1779 (Hudson's Bay Record Society, 1951), 28.

6. *Ibid.*, 67.

7. *Ibid.*, 87.

8. *Ibid.*, 109-110.

9. E. E. Rich, *Cumberland House Journals and Inland Journals*, 2d series, 1779-1783 (Hudson's Bay Record Society, 1952), 15: 80.

10. *Ibid.*, ii.

11. *Ibid.*, 97.

12. *Ibid.*, 46.

13. A. S. Morton, *A History of the Canadian West to 1870-1871* (Thomas Nelson and Sons, n.d. [1939?]), 302-303.

14. Allen W. Trelease, *Indian Affairs in Colonial New York* (Kennikat Press reprint, 1971), 219-226. Douglas E. Leach, *The Northern Colonial Frontier* (Holt, Rinehart, and Winston, 1966), 99. Thomas J. Condon, *New York Beginnings* (New York University Press, 1968), Chap. 2.

15. Thomas E. Norton, *The Fur Trade in Colonial New York* (University of Wisconsin Press, 1974), 49, 52.

16. Trelease, *Indian Affairs*, 210.

17. G. Lawson Murray, *Fur — A Study in English Mercantilism, 1700-1775* (University of Toronto Press, 1943).

18. Leach, *Northern Colonial Frontier,* 105-106. Norton, *Fur Trade in Colonial New York*, 48. W. J. Eccles, *Frontenac: The Courtier Governor* (McClelland and Stewart, 1959), 99. Allen W. Echert, *Wilderness Empire* (Little Brown, 1969), *passim.* Peter Kalm, *Travels into North America*, trans. J. R. Forster (Imprint Society, 1972), 331.

19. Kalm, *Travels*, 33, 104.

20. Francis X. Maloney, *The Fur Trade in New England* (Harvard University Press, 1931), 17-20.

21. Leach, *Northern Colonial Frontier*, 95, 96. Harry M. Ward, *Statism in Plymouth Colony* (Kennikat Press, 1973), 36-41. Douglas R. McManis, *Colonial New England* (Oxford University Press, 1975), 26, 29n.

22. Phillips, *The Fur Trade*, 1: 121-135.

23. *Ibid.*, 116. Maloney, *The Fur Trade in New England* (Archon Books, n.d.), 95-108.

24. Peter N. Carroll, *Puritanism and the Wilderness* (Columbia University Press, 1969), 143.

25. Leach, *Northern Colonial Frontier*, 94.

26. For a good discussion of intercolonial bickering, not only between Pennsylvania and Virginia over the trans-Alleghany fur traffic and between all the colonies over this lucrative income, see McIlwain's introduction to Wraxall's *Abridgment of Indian Affairs* (Harvard University Press, 1915).

27. Clarence E. Carter, *Great Britain and the Illinois Country* (Kennikat

Press, 1970).

28. Paul A. W. Wallace, *Conrad Weiser* (Russell and Russell, 1971), 42.

Chapter 6
The Rendezvous
(pages 57-71)

1. John Bradbury, *Travels in the Interior of America* (Readex Microprint, 1966), 84-94, 110. Thwaites, *Early Western Travels* (A. H. Clark Company, 1904), Brackenridge Journal, 6: 83. Walter B. Douglas, *Manuel Lisa*, ed. A. P. Nasatir (Argosy-Antiquarian Press, 1964), 62-63. Thomas James, *Three Years among the Mexicans and Indians* (Rio Grande Press, 1962), 28-29.

2. Confusion exists as to the actual number of men engaged in the enterprise. The newspaper advertisement seeking to engage employees specified 100 men. Yet the same newspaper's editorial comment concerning the departure of Henry's first contingent gives a figure of 180. Perhaps the latter figure is a typographical error. The same comment indicates that all the employees accompanied Henry, yet we know that 46 men were in Ashley's second group. I am inclined to believe that the complete party had about 100 employees with 54 going in Henry's group and 46 in Ashley's group. A party of 180 plus 46 would have been an unwieldy group to go that far up the river, establish a new location, and try to get a foothold. At this stage, the overhead would have eaten up any possible profit. Contrary to this rationalization is the mention by a member of Henry's group, in a letter to his brother, that there were 100 men in the first group and the fact that Ashley, when he went by the place the second boat had sunk, picked up the crew that had been sent with that ill-fated boat. So, what *was* the total complement?

3. Dale L. Morgan, *The West of William H. Ashley* (Old West Publishing Co., 1964), 6-7.

4. *Ibid.*, 11-12.

5. Donald McKay Frost, *Notes on General Ashley* (Barre, MA: Barre Gazette, 1960), 15, 16. Dale L. Morgan, *Jedediah Smith and the Opening of the West* (Bobbs-Merrill, 1953), 42.

6. *Ibid.*, 49, 50.

7. *Ibid.*, 50-77. Morgan, *William H. Ashley*, 25-40, 52-47. H. M. Chittenden, *A History of the American Fur Trade of the Far West* (Academic Reprints, 1954), 2: 588-600. Hafen and Ghent, *Broken Hand* (Old West Publishing Co., 1931), 26-28.

8. Morgan, *Jedediah Smith*, 80-94. Hafen and Ghent, *Broken Hand*, 21-36. Charles L. Camp, *James Clyman, Frontiersman* (Champoeg Press, 1960),

15-23. Harrison C. Dale, *Ashley-Smith Explorations and the Discovery of a Central Route to the Pacific, 1822-1829* (A. H. Clark Co., 1941), 82-91.

9. Morgan, *Jedediah Smith*, 154.

10. *Ibid.*, 162.

11. Morgan, *William H. Ashley*, 136-138.

12. Fred R. Gowans, *Rocky Mountain Rendezvous* (Brigham Young University, 1976), 32. This work is the main source of the remainder of this essay unless I have noted otherwise.

13. Phillips, *The Fur Trade*, 2: 424.

14. Dorothy O. Johansen, *Robert Newell's Memoranda* (Champoeg Press, 1949), 39.

15. F. A. Wislizenus, M.D., *A Journey to the Rocky Mountains in the Year 1839* (Missouri Historical Society, 1912), 88-89.

16 Innis, *The Fur Trade in Canada*, 139. Elaine A. Mitchell, *Fort Timiskaming and the Fur Trade* (University of Toronto Press, 1977), *passim.*

Chapter 7
A Reappraisal of the Blackfoot Hostility
to the American Trader
(pages 72-78)

1. R. G. Thwaites, *Original Journals of the Lewis and Clark Expedition* (Antiquarian Press, 1959), 2: 131. Donald Jackson, *Letters of the Lewis and Clark Expedition with Related Documents* (University of Illinois Press, 1962), 341.

2. Thwaites, *Lewis and Clark Journals*, 5: 219-225. For further remarks concerning this encounter, see Jackson, *Lewis and Clark Letters*, 342.

3. Chittenden, *American Fur Trade of the Far West*, 714.

4. Missouri Historical Society Bulletin (July 1954): 429-446. Terrell, *Western Morning*, 106. Ewers, *People and Pelts*, 1-6. Thwaites, *Lewis and Clark Journals*, 1: 190. Marcel Trudel, *The Beginnings of New France* (McClelland and Stewart, 1973), 166. Richard E. Oglesby, *Manuel Lisa and the Opening of the Missouri Fur Trade* (University of Oklahoma Press, 1963), 188-190.

5. Hunt, *The Wars of the Iroquois*, 35.

6. Bernard DeVoto, *The Course of Empire* (Houghton-Mifflin Co., 1952), 93. Similar remarks are common in literature. Trader after trader remarked upon this Indian attitude and deplored it as their business was thus hindered. Many writers dealing with various tribes and areas are specific about this Indian acumen. See also: E. E. Rich, *The Fur Trade and the Northwest to 1857* (McClelland and Stewart, 1967), 9, 14, 74.

Hyde, *The Life of George Bent* 31, 32. Hunt, *The Wars of the Iroquois*, 17, 35. Innis, *The Fur Trade in Canada*, 139, 150. Trudel, *New France*, 144. L. J. Burpee, *The Search for the Western Sea* (Macmillan Company of Canada, 1935), 2: 373-374. J. C. McGregor, *Peter Fidler: Canada's Forgotten Surveyor* (McClelland and Stewart, 1967), 78, 79. Oscar Lewis, *The Effects of White Contact upon Blackfoot Culture* (University of Washington Press, 1966), 18-20. Oglesby, *Maneul Lisa*, 186-187. Ida Amanda Johnson, *The Michigan Fur Trade* (Black Letter Press, 1971), 9. Driver, *Indians of North America*, 211-221.

7. L. J. Burpee, *Journal of a Journey Performed by Anthony Hendry* [sic] *To Explore the Country Inland and to Endeavor to Increase the Hudson's Bay Company's Trade*, Proceedings and Transactions of the Royal Society of Canada (3d series, 1907), 1: 38.

8. Victor G. Hopwood, *David Thompson: Travels to Western North America 1784-1812* (Macmillan of Canada, 1971), 216-222.

9. The Champlain Society, *David Thompson's Narrative*, 40:273. Ewers, *People and Pelts*, 4.

10. Hopwood, *David Thompson*, 247.

11. Peter Fidler to Hudson's Bay Company 10 July 1802, quoted in D. W. Moody and Barry Kaye, "The Act Ko Mok Ki Map," *The Beaver Magazine* of the Hudson's Bay Company (Spring 1977): 15.

12. The Canadian traders may have encouraged the Blackfeet in this animosity towards the Americans. Such would have been good business; retain all the Blackfoot trade for themselves. The Hudson's Bay Company and the North West Company employed this strategy against each other constantly, and there was no reason for them not to gang up on the Americans. If the Canadians did so act they were only abetting the Blackfoot inclination.

Chapter 8
The Jeremy Pinch Enigma
(pages 79-94)

1. *Oregon Historical Quarterly* (Dec. 1937): 391, 392.

2. *Ibid.*, 394.

3. *Ibid.*, 394.

4. *Ibid.* (June 1939), 191.

5. A. P. Nasatir, *Before Lewis and Clark* (Saint Louis Historical Documents Foundation, 1952), 2:461-462.

6. Donald Jackson, *The Journals of Zebulon Montgomery Pike* (University of Oklahoma Press, 1966), 1:256-259.

7. Coues, *New Light on . . . the Greater Northwest*, 1:274.

8. *Oregon Historical Quarterly* (June 1939): 159.

9. Claude E. Schaeffer, *LaBlanc and Le Gasse: Predecessors of David Thompson in the Columbian Plateau* (Browning, MT: Museum of the Plains Indians, 1966), 3, 6, 9.

10. White, *David Thompson's Journals*, xcvi.

11. A. S. Morton, *Journal of Duncan McGillivray* (Macmillan Company, 1929), 56.

12. The Champlain Society, *David Thompson's Narrative*, 40: 50.

13. N. L. Barlee, *Gold Creeks and Ghost Towns* (Canada West Magazine, 6th printing, 1964), 35-38.

14. F. W. Hollensteiner, A letter to the editor in *MONTANA: The Magazine of Western History* (Winter 1977), 74.

15. Douglas, *Manuel Lisa*, 59, 65.

16. Hafen, Hollen, and Rister, *Western America*, 3d ed. (Prentice-Hall, 1971), 155.

17. John W. Hakola, ed., *Frontier Omnibus* (Montana State University Press, 1962), 27.

18. Jackson, *Lewis and Clark Letters*, 437n, 483.

19. This man is not to be confused with the Robert McClellan who had been a partner of Ramsey Crooks on the Missouri River and joined Wilson Price Hunt's Overland Astorians on their way upriver in 1810.

20. Alvin M. Josephy, Jr., *The Nez Percé Indians and the Opening of the Northwest* (Yale University Press, 1965), 656, 662.

21. L. B. Masson, *Les Bourgeois de la Compagnie du Nord-Ouest* (Antiquarian Press, 1960), 2:41n.

22. The Champlain Society, *David Thompson's Narrative*, 40:302.

23. Hopwood, *David Thompson's Travels in Western North America: 1784-1812*, 286. J. F. McDermott, *Frenchmen and French Ways in the Mississippi Valley* (University of Illinois Press, 1969), 57, 58. Louis Phelps Kellogg, *The British Regime in Wisconsin and the Northwest* (Da Capo Press, 1971), 96, 121-129.

24. Personal communication from Alvin M. Josephy, Jr.

25. J. F. McDermott, *French Settlers and Settlements in the Illinois Country in the Eighteenth Century in The French, The Indians, and George Rogers Clark in the Illinois Country: Proceedings of the Indiana American Revolution Bicentennial Symposium* (Indianapolis: Indiana Historical Society, 1977).

26. *Ibid.*

27. *Ibid.*

28. Personal communication with Thane White, Dayton, Montana.

29. Merrill D. Beal and Merle W. Wells, *History of Idaho* (Lewis Historical Publishing Co., 1959), 1:94, 95.

30. *Ibid.*, 94.
31. Clarence E. Crater, *Territorial Papers of the United States*, 13:243.
32. Ross Cox, *The Columbia River*, ed. Edgar I. and Jane R. Stewart (University of Oklahoma Press, 1957), 191, 192. White, *David Thompson's Journals*, 106n. Johnson, *Flathead and Kootenay*, 171, 172.
33. George A. Fuller, *A History of the Pacific Northwest* (Alfred A. Knopf, 1966), 78. Mrs. Coralee Paull, private research in Missouri documentary sources.
34. Morgan, *Willaim H. Ashley*, xxxi, 9n. Morgan, *Jedediah Smith*, 123.
35. S. B. Braunberger and Thane White, *Howse's House: An Examination of the Historical and Archeological Evidence, The Washington Archeologist*, (Apr. and July 1964): 8, *passim*.
36. J. S. Myers, "Jacques Rapheal Finlay," *Washington Historical Quarterly*, (July 1919).

Chapter 9
On the Dalliance of David Thompson
(pages 95-104)

1. Coues, *New Light on . . . the Greater Northwest*, 2:608.
2. *Ibid.*, 2:650.
3. James K. Smith, *David Thompson, Fur Trader, Explorer, Geographer* (Oxford University Press, 1971), 84.
4. The Champlain Society, *David Thompson's Narrative*, 40:1-1xiv.
5. David Lavender, *The Fist in the Wilderness* (Doubleday and Company, 1964), 443, n8.
6. Innis, *The Fur Trade in Canada*, 201.
7. *Ibid.*, 203.
8. Rich, *Hudson's Bay Company*, 2:143.
9. White, *David Thompson's Journals*, 1vii.
10. From *The Fur Trade and the Northwest to 1857*, by E. E. Rich, used by permission of the Canadian publishers (Toronto: McClelland and Stewart, Ltd.).
11. Morton, *The History of the Canadian West to 1870-1871*, 468-469.
12. E. E. Rich, *Montreal and the Fur Trade* (McGill University, 1966), 93-94.
13. Morton, *The Canadian West*, 478.
14. *Ibid.*, 480.
15. J. B. Tyrrell, "Letter of Roseman and Perch," *Oregon Historical Quarterly*, 38 (Dec., 1937): 395.
16. In my opinion, he was trying to find the Columbia River, not dodge the Piegans. He was familiar enough with the area by that time to know that to

avoid the Piegans he would have to devise a new route based upon Kootenae House, not Salish House or Kullyspell House.

Chapter 10
Spy and Counterspy?
(pages 105-127)

1. Bernard DeVoto, *The Year of Decision* (Little Brown and Co., 1943), 21.
2. For detailed information on all the negotiations, various pressures and attitudes involved in the Oregon Question see the works of H. H. Bancroft, *The History of the Northwest Coast* (Arno Press reprint, n.d.), 28:319-413. Robert Greenhow, *The History of Oregon and California* (Sherwin and Freutel, 1970 reprint), 306-364, 375-403. Lavender, *The Fist in the Wilderness*, 430, n1. Dorothy O. Johansen, *The Empire of the Columbia*, 2d ed. (Harper and Row, 1967), 195-210. For a Canadian viewpoint, see Morton, *The Canadian West*, 506, 732-738, 742-749. And for a possible influence of the Oregon Question on Great Britain's people and politicians, see Charles Grenfell Nicolay, *The Oregon Territory* (Ye Galleon Press, 1967), *passim*.
3. Leroy R. Hafen, *The Mountain Man and the Fur Trade of the Far West* (Arthur H. Clark Co., 1968), 5:45-47.
4. C. G. Coutant, *History of Wyoming* (Argonaut Press reprint, 1966), 1:166n.
5. Washington Irving, *The Adventures of Captain Bonneville*, rev. ed. (G. P. Putnam, 1861), 427-428.
6. *Ibid.*, xv.
7. *Ibid.*, xvi.
8. *Ibid.*, 184.
9. Hafen, *The Mountain Man*, 5:48n.
10. *Ibid.*, 5:56, 23n.
11. *Ibid.*, 5:58.
12. *Ibid.*, 2:257, 26n, 259-260.
13. Rich, *The Hudson's Bay Company*, 2:684.
14. Johansen, *Empire*, 179, 199; Fuller, *History of the Pacific Northwest*, 50, 174, 185; Rich, *The Hudson's Bay Company*, 689.
15. Johansen, *Empire*, 199, 200.
16. Frederick Merk, *The Oregon Question* (Harvard University Press, 1967), 125; Bancroft, *History of the Northwest Coast*, 27:649, 668-684, 672, 672n; Johansen, *Empire*, 185, 199-200.
17. Rich, *The Hudson's Bay Company*, 2:727, 729, 732; John S. Galbraith, *The Hudson's Bay Company as an Imperial Factor* (University of California Press, 1957), 238-242; Morton, *The Canadian West to 1870-1871*, 749, 808.

18. Clyde Porter and Mae Reed, *Ruxton of the Rockies* (University of Oklahoma Press, 1950), 54. The summary of Ruxton's life used in this essay has been abstracted from this book. The interested reader is referred to that work for details.
19. *Ibid.*, xvii.
20. George F. Ruxton, *Adventures in Mexico and the Rocky Mountains* (London: John Murray, 1847), a2.
21. Hafen, *The Mountain Man*, 1:287, 1n.
22. Porter and Reed, *Ruxton*, 219.

Chapter 11
In Defense of the Indian
(pages 128-137)

1. Fr. Francis J. LaFitau, *Customs of the American Indians Compared with the Customs of Primitive Tribes*, trans. Fenton and Moore, The Champlain Society, 48 (1974):xliv-lix. Jaenen, *Friend and Foe*, 12-19; Josephy, Jr., *The Indian Heritage of America*, 5.
2. Francis Jennings, *The Invasion of America: Indians, Colonialism, and the Cant of Conquest* (University of North Carolina Press, 1975), *passim*.
3. *Tobacco Valley News*, Eureka, MT (24 June 1976).
4. Jacobs, *Dispossessing the American Indian*, xi-xii, 1-3.
5. For more detailed information on the woman's role, the duties of both men and women in Indian life and polygyny, see Walter O'Meara's *Daughters of the Country* (Harcourt Brace and World, 1968), 44-67. Also, John Upton and Donna M. Terrell, *Indian Women of the Western Morning* (Anchor Books, 1976), 23-90; Priscilla K. Buffalohead, "Farmers, Warriors, Traders: A Fresh Look at Ojibway Women," *Minnesota History* (Summer 1983): 236-244. (Minnesota Historical Society Quarterly.)
6. Jennings, *The Invasion of America*.

Chapter 12
Blue-Eyed Indians
(pages 138-150)

1. The basis of this essay comes from so many sources, usually interlocking, that I find it impractical to cite specifics for each and every statement. Such would necessarily overlap.

Readers interested in pursuing the details should first read Eugene R. Fingerhut's *Who First Discovered America?* (Regina Books, 1984). This small treatise has a wealth of information on the background of this essay.

The second book recommended, which treats of the subject in profuse detail, presenting both the diffusionist and independent development adherents is *Man Across the Sea*, by Riley, Kelly, Pennington, and Rands (University of Texas, 1971).

Then come the books that mention, in varying degrees, various viewpoints. Some of these are devoted to presenting a single interpretation, others incorporate several notations of certain incidents or writings, still others are ardent exponents of a belief or ridicule of a belief. These are:

Samuel Eliot Morrison, *The European Discovery of America: The Northern Voyages* (Oxford University Press, 1971).

David B. Quinn, *North America from Earliest Discovery to First Settlements* (Harper and Row, 1977).

Olson and Bourne, eds., *The Northmen, Columbus, and Cabot* (Barnes and Noble, 1967).

Harold Lamb, *New Found World* (Doubleday & Co., 1955).

Richard Hakluyt, *Divers Voyages Touching the Discovery of America* (Readex Microprint, 1966).

Thor Heyerdahl, *Early Man and the Ocean* (Doubleday & Co., 1979).

Alexander Von Wuthenau, *Unexpected Faces in Ancient America* (Crown Publishers, 1975).

Nigel Davies, *Voyagers to the New World* (William Morrow & Co., 1979).

Henriette Mertz, *Pale Ink* (Swallow Press, 1972).

Barry Fell, *Saga America* (Times Books, 1980).

Fell, *America, B. C.* (Quadrangle Press, 1976).

Cyrus H. Gordon, *Before Columbus* (Crown Publishers, 1971).

Samuel D. Marble, *Before Columbus* (A. S. Barnes & Co., 1980).

Tryggvi Oleson, *Early Voyages and Northern Approaches: 1000 to 1632* (McClelland and Stewart, 1968).

Carl O. Sauer, *Northern Mists* (University of California Press, 1968).

Richard Deacon, *Madoc and the Discovery of America* (George Braziller, 1966).

Jeffrey R. Redmond, *Viking Hoaxes in North America* (Carlton Press, 1979).

Theodore C. Blegen, *The Kensington Rune Stone* (Minnesota Historical Society, 1968).

Hjalmar R. Holand, *Explorations in America before Columbus* (Twayne Publishers, 1956).

Alfred W. Crosby, *The Columbian Exchange* (Greenwood Publishing Co., 1972).

Farley Mowat, *West Viking* (Little Brown & Co., 1965).

Chapter 13
Topography's Influence on Colonial Mores
(pages 151-159)

1. Walter Prescott Webb, *The Great Frontier* (University of Texas Press, 1964), 30.

Appendix A

1. The First Pinch Letter

(Extracted from the article by J. B. Tyrell in the December 1937 issue of the *Oregon Historical Quarterly*)

We the undersigned by the Power delegated to us by General Braithwaite Commander of all the new ceded Territo(r)ies northward of the Illinois do hereby make known and declare the Instructions we have received relating to Foreigners who may at present by [*sic*] carrying on a Traffic with the Indians within our Territories for Peltries &c, or who may in future carry on a Traffic with the said Indians — 1st. By a standing law of Congress, and now more especially to be enforced, no Traders under whatever denomination, whether Americans or Foreigners are permitted to sell or give Spiritous Liquors of any Kind to the Natives under any pretence whatever, under the Penalty of forfeiting all the property in their Possession, the half of which belongs to him that is the Informer, the other half to him that is authorized & shall receive the said Property: and for the second Offence forfeiture of Goods and imprisonment of Body.

2nd. No trader has a right to hoist a Flag of any kind whatever at his place of residence, whether Camp or House; any Offence of this kind will be considered as an Insult on the American Nation and punished accordingly. If it is found necessary for the sake of Peace &c to display a Flag, permission must be requested of the Commanding Officer of the nearest military Post, who, if he finds the request reasonable will permit the American Flag to be hoisted, but that of no other Nation.

3rd. No Indian Trader under any pretence has a right to give Flags, Medals or any other honorary Marks of Distinction to any Indian whether Chief or not. Whatever marks of Merit or Honor an Indian shall merit will be bestowed by the Commanding Officer, and by him alone. All other Persons are hereby prohibited from so doing, under pain of being fined for said offence or Offences against the Jurisdiction of America.

4th. As much Inconvenience and Confusion is found to arise from the Competition of Traders, who often lavish their Goods to the great hurt of their Creditors, it is hereby made known to all Indian Traders, native as well as foreign, that no one shall presume to sell beyond the price fixed by the Commanding Officer. For the first Offence, the offending Trader shall be severely reprimanded, and, for the Second, his Magazine of Goods shall be shut up and he, himself with his Servants prohibited from any further Commerce with the Natives: his Property shall be under the Seal of the Commanding Officer till the Season permits his Embarkation for the Place from whence he came.

5th. No trader or any of his Servants shall revenge an Injury, Affront, Misdemeanor &c that shall be done unto them by the Native Indians, otherwise than may concern his direct personal safety or property; but shall make his Complaint to the Commanding Officer, who shall punish the Offender according to Justice.

6th. As all Indian Traders in the American Territory enjoy the Protection of America and its Salutary Laws, Justice requires that they in return shall contribute towards the support of the Armed Force that protects them; all Indian Traders who are native Americans [and who would that be except an Indian? Question is the author's.] and come direct from the United States with their Merchandize &c, having paid the ordinary Duties at the Customs House, are free from any farther [*sic*] Duty on producing the Custom House Voucher; all Foreigners shall pay 10 P Cent on the Imports and 8 P Cent on the Exports, or 20 P Cent on the Goods imported; but inasmuch as the Subjects of Great Britain trading direct from Canada, on Account of the reciprocal Commerce and good Neighborhood between the Inhabitants of the said Province and the Citizens of America, have an Indulgence above others, the Commander in Chief, by the Powers vested in him, has thought proper to abate the Duty on all foreign Goods &c, to 12 p Ct., on the Imports direct from Canada; the Exports to be free, Merchandize coming from Canada that have paid the American duties, either at Detroit or Michillimacana [Michilimackinac?] on producing the Custom House Voucher are to pay no farther [*sic*] Duty. Every Indian Trader must deliver to the Commanding Officer an exact Account of his Exports and Imports.

7th. And whereas the great Distance between some parts of the new ceded Territores [*sic*] and Civilized Towns may prevent the foreign Traders from having it in their Power to pay at all Times their Duty on their Merchandize, Peltries &c in Money, the Commander in Chief has thought proper to permit the Duty to be paid in Kind, the Duty on the Imports in Goods, provided they be such as may be of Use to the Military Posts; the Exports to be paid in Furrs [*sic*] being every ninth Skin, according to the Book of Custom House rates.

8th. Indian Traders whether native, or foreign are requested to furnish themselves with the Laws of Congress relating to Commerce in general and the buy [*sic*] laws of the upper Provinces, relating to the Indian Trade, in particular as, thereby they will probably save themselves and the commanding Officer much Trouble.

9th. By Information received at the Monden [Mandan] Village on the Mississourie [*sic*] we were given to understand that, some of the Subjects of Great Britain are about to carry on a trade and traffic with the western Indians we have therefore given a Copy of the above Instructions, Rules, and Regulations to be observed in the Indian Traffic to the principal Chief of each of the Indian tribes the most likely to see these foreign Traders that, the said Traders may not pretend Ignorance that they are within the Jurisdiction of Congress and consequently obliged to obey all its Laws & Regulations &c. It is expected of the Indian Traders or Traders who may see these our Instructions &c, that, they will take a copy, leaving the Original in the Hands of the Indian Chief.

10th. The new ceded Territories to the American States northward and westward of the Illinois, comprehend the Mississourie [*sic*] Red River and all the Lands westward to the Coast of California and the Columbia River with all its Branches; of which we have now taken Possession and on which we are now settled down to the Pacific Ocean; extending northward to about 50 Degrees north Latitude, according to the Boundaries settled at the Treaty of Peace between the United States and the Court of Great Britain, although it is by no means allowed here nor does any of our Expressions bear the Sense that, Great Britian [*sic*] has any special right to any of the Lands on the Pacific Ocean or to the Commerce of any of the rivers that flow into the said Ocean, all of which we shall comprehend as within our said Territories until some further Explanation takes place on this head between the United States of America and the Court of St. James.

Signed

Fort Lewis,	James Roseman Lieutenant
Yellow River,	Zachary Perch Captain &
Columbia	Commanding Officer
10th July. 1807	

2. The Second Pinch Letter

(Extracted from the article by T. C. Elliott in the June 1939 issue of the *Oregon Historical Quarterly*)

Poltito Palton Lake
Sept 29th 1807

To the British Mercht, Trafficking with the Cabanaws [Kutenais]
Sir,

I have been informed by a chief of the Poltito palton that the regulations intrusted to him for the instruction of such British Merchants as may traffic with the Indians under the Jurisdiction of Congress have been delivered to you, and of course an answer was expected whether you chose to abide by such Regulations as are or may be promulgated for the good order of Society and Civilization of the Indians. Your silence[,] Sir[,] I am to construe into a a tacit disrespect, and thereby am apt to think you do not acknowledge the authority of Congress over these Countries, which are certainly the property of the United States both by discovery and Cession. If such is your ideas you must learn[,] Sir[,] that we have more powerful means of persuasion in our hands than we have hitherto used, we shall with regret apply force, but where necessary it will be done with vigor, so as fully to enforce the Decrees of Congress, and support the Honor and Rights of the United States — and if my private opinion be of any weight, you nor any British Merchant will be suffered to traffic with our Indian Allies.

As soon as our Military Posts are fortified, strong Patroles will be sent out to survey the Country and where necessary and eligible American Merchants will be placed who will second the philanthropic views of Congress in the Civilization of the Natives. You will see[,] Sir[,] the necessity of submitting and with a good grace, — you may evade our useful Regulations for a year but the time is certainly at hand when the authority of Congress will be as fully established over these Countries as over New York or Washington.

The Pilchenees with thier [*sic*] blood-thirsty allies made an inroad into the territories of the Polito palton, our friends and wounded one of our brave Soldiers.

We expect[,] Sir[,] you will no longer supply those Marauders with Arms and Ammunition, and also signify this our desire to the other British Merchants at the same time we hope whenever we may find it necessary to chastise these scoundrels you will assist us with men and as far as your abilities will permit.

Signed
Jeremy Pinch Lieutenant

(This letter was replied to by Thompson. The following quotation is, presumably, the way it appears in the Edmonton House Journal that is preserved in the Hudson's Bay Company's archives. It is quoted here verbatim as it is in the T. C. Elliott article.)

3. Letter from D. T. dated Dec. 26, 1807
To Lieut. Jeremy Pinch

Sir,

Two days ago I received your polite Favour of the 29th Sept and must confess myself neither authorized nor competent to give a direct answer to the Question proposed, nor am I politician enough to settle the Boundaries of our respective Countries. If prior discovery forms any right to a Country, Lieut. Broughton of the British Navy many years ago explored the Columbia for 120 miles from the sea and was the first that made known its Geography.

The high Duties you require will be submitted to the consideration of all the Partners of the N.W. Compy. — and if complied with, they will pay custom for the Merchandise that may be sent here, at Michlimacance [Michilimackinac?], as is usual for all other Merchandise intended for the Indians in the American Territories, and the Custom House Certificates will be produced when required.

I am etc.

(signed) D. T.

(Note of copyist)

The copy for [from] which the foregoing letters have been transcribed is in the handwriting of Mr. D. Thompson who adds the following note.

It seems this officer was on a party of Discovery when he wrote the above. His Politito [sic] paltons are the Greenwood Indians, — his Pilchenees the Fall Indians, I suppose, as it was they wounded the soldier — not one of these petty officers but what has as much arrogance as Buonaparte at the head of his Invincibles.

Appendix B

The Lieutenant Pike to Hugh McGillis Letter

(From *The Journals of Zebulon Montgomery Pike: With Letters and Related Documents*, vol. 1: 256-258, by Zebulon Montgomery Pike, edited and annotated by Donald Jackson (University of Oklahoma Press, 1966).

N. W. Establishment, on Lake Leech, February 1806.

Sir,

As a proprietor of the N.W. Company, and director of the Zond [Fond] du Lac department, I conceive it my. duty as an officer of the United States, (in whose territory you are) to address you solely on the subject of the many houses under your instructions. As a member of the greatest commercial nation in the world, and a company long renowned for their extent of connections and greatness of views you cannot be ignorant of the rigor of the laws of the duties of imports of a foreign power.

Mr. Jay's treaty, it is true, gave the right of trade with the savages to British subjects in the United States territories, but by no means exempted them from paying the duties, obtaining licenses, and subscribing unto all the rules and restrictions of our laws. I find your establishments at every suitable place along the whole extent of the south side of Lake Superior to its head, from thence to the source of the Mississippi, and down Red River, and even extending to the centre of our newly acquired territory of Louisiana in which it will probably yet become a question between the two governments, if our treaties will authorize the British subjects to enter into the Indian trade on the same footing, as in the other parts of our frontiers; this not having been an integral part of the United States, at the time of the said treaty. Our traders to the south, on the Lower Mississippi, complain to our government, with justice, that the members of the N.W. company, encircle them on the frontiers of our N.W. territory, and trade with the savages upon superior terms, to what they can afford, who pay the duties of their goods imported from Europe, and subscribe to the regulations prescribed by law.

These representations have at length attracted the attention of our government to the object in question, and with the intention to do themselves as well as citizens justice, they the last year took some steps to ascertain the facts and make provision against the growing evil. With this, some geographical, and also local objects in view was I dispatched with discretionary orders, with a party of troops to the source of the Mississippi. I have found, sir, your commerce and establishments, extending beyond our most exaggerated ideas, and in addition to the injury done our revenue, by the evasion of the duties, other acts which are more particularly injurious to the *honor* and *dignity* of our government. The transactions alluded to, are the presenting *medals* of his Britannic majesty, and *flags* of the said government, to the chiefs and warriors resident in the territory of the United States. If political subjects are strictly prohibited to our traders, what would be the ideas of the executive to see foreigners making chiefs, and distributing flags, the standard of a European power. The savages being accustomed to look on that standard, which has been the only one prevailing for years, as that which alone has authority in the country, it would not be in the least astonishing to see them revolt from the United States, limited subjection which is claimed over them by the American government, and thereby be the cause of their receiving a chastisement: although necessary, yet unfortunate as they have been led astray by the policy of the traders of your country.

I must likewise observe, sir, that your establishments, if properly known, would be looked on with an eye of dissatisfaction by our government, for another reason, *viz.* there being so many furnished posts in case of a rupture between the two powers, the English government would not fail to make use of those as places of deposit of arms, ammunition, &c. to be distributed to the savages who joined their arms; to the great annoyance of our territory, and the loss of the lives of many of our citizens. Your flags, sir, when hoisted in inclosed works, are in direct contradiction of the laws of nations, and their practice in like cases, which only admits of foreign flags being expanded on board of vessels, and at the residence of Ambassadors, or consuls. I am not ignorant of the necessity of your being in such a position as to protect you from the sallies of the drunken savages, or the more deliberate plans of the intended plunderer; and under those considerations, have I considered you stockades.

You, and the company of which you are a member, must be conscious from the foregoing statement that strict justice would demand, and I assure you that the law directs, under similar circumstances, a total confiscation of your property, personal imprisonment and fines. But having discretionary instructions and no reason to think the above conduct was dictated through ill will or disrespect to our government, and conceiving it in some degree departing from the character of an officer, to embrace the first opportunity of executing those laws, I am willing to sacrifice my prospect of private advantage, conscious that the government look not to interest, but its *dignity* in the transaction, I have therefore to request of you, assurances on the following heads, which setting aside the chicanery of law, as a gentleman, you will strictly adhere to *viz.* =

That you will make representations of your agents, at your headquarters, on Lake Superior, of the quantity of goods wanted the ensuing spring, for your establishments in the territory of the United States, in time sufficient, or as early as possible, for them to enter them at the C.H. [Custom House] of Michilimackinac, and obtain a clearance and licence [*sic*] to trade in due form.

2nd. That you will give immediate instruction to all your posts in said territory, under your direction, at no time and on no pretence whatever to hoist, or suffer to be hoisted, the English Flag. If you conceive a flag necessary you may make use of that of the United States, which is the only one which can be admitted.

3rd. That you will on no further occassion, [*sic*] present a flag or medal to an Indian: hold councils with them on political subjects, or others foreign from that of trade: but on being applied to on those heads, refer them to the American agents, informing them that they are the only persons authorized to hold councils of a political nature with them.

There are many other subjects, such as the distribution of liquor, &c. which would be too lengthy to be treated of in detail. But the company will do well to furnish themselves with our laws, regulating the commerce with the savages, and regulate themselves in our territories accordingly. I embrace this opportunity, to acknowledge myself and my command under singular obligations to yourselves and agents, for the assistance which you have rendered us, and the polite treatment with which I have been honored. With sentiments of high respect, for the establishment and yourself, I am, sir, Your obedient servant.

Z. M. Pike

Hugh McGillis, Esq.
Proprietor and agent of the N.W. company, established at Fond du Lac

Appendix C

Instruction to Captain Bonneville from the Major General Commanding the Army of the United States.

Headquarters of the Army
Washington, August 3, 1831.

Sir:

The leave of absence which you have asked, for the purpose of enabling you to carry into execution your design of exploring the country to the Rocky Mountains and beyond, with the view of ascertaining the nature and character of the several tribes of Indians inhabiting those regions; the trade which might profitably be carried on with them; the quality of the soil, the productions, the minerals, the natural history, the climate, the geography and topography, as well as geology, of the various parts of the country within the limits of the territories belonging to the United States, between our frontier and the Pacific — has been duly considered and submitted to the War Department for approval, and has been sanctioned. You are, therefore, authorized to be absent from the army until October, 1833. It is understood that the government is to be at no expense in reference to your proposed expedition, it having originated with yourself; and all that you required was the permission from the proper authority to undertake the enterprise. You will, naturally, in preparing yourself for the expedition, provide suitable instruments, and especially the best maps of the interior to be found.

It is desirable, besides what is enumerated as the object of your enterprise, that you note particularly the number of warriors that may be in each tribe or nation that you may meet with; their alliances with other tribes, and their relative position as to the state of peace or war, and whether their friendly or warlike dispositions towards each other are recent or of long standing. You will gratify us by describing their manner of making war; of the mode of subsisting themselves during a state of war, and a state of peace; their arms, and the effect of them; whether they act on foot or on horseback; detailing the discipline and maneuvers of the war parties; the power of their horses, size, and general description; in short, every information that you may conceive would be useful to the government.

You will avail yourself of every opportunity of informing us of your position and progress, and, at the expiration of your leave of absence, will join your proper station.

> I have the honor to be Sir,
> Your ob't servant
> Alexander Macomb
> Major General, Commanding the Army.

Capt. B. L. E. Bonneville,
7th Reg't of Infantry, New York

(reprinted from C. G. Coutant, *History of Wyoming* (New York: Argonaut Press reprint, 1966), 1:166n)

Index

Compiled by Terry G. Colbert